ON SNAKEBITE

'Devastating . . . It explains why the world's most sophisticated armed forces are being defeated by the world's least sophisticated'
Simon Jenkins, Books of the Year 2009, *The Times Literary Supplement*

'One of the most courageous and important pieces of reporting of the Afghanistan campaign' General Sir Richard Dannatt

'G[...] he story with [imme]diacy, drama and sometimes anger. A [...]ripping and moving narrative' *Soldier* Magazine

'A [...] piece of reportage' *New Statesman*

'[...] *News of the World*

'Pe[...]ive and thou[...] manages to get across the chaos and th[...] those under fire at the sharp end of [...] events it recounts' *Glasgow Herald*

'Th[...] of the Helmand book generation . . . combines th[...] of interview, observation and reportage as M[...] in [...] to stunning effect . . . Farce, betrayal, intr[...] and b[...] they are all here, examined with a deliberate and [...] [g]rippi[ng] for its detail . . . ignore it at your peril' [...] orrespondent of *The Times*

'Highly recommended' John A. Nagl, Lieutenant Colonel (retired), author of *Learning to Eat Soup with a Knife*

'The [siege of ...] s the story of coalition combat, courage, and the political undertones that colour a combatant's every move. It is also a story of those who paid the ultimate price for their comrades, their units, and their countries . . . A useful and significant book'
Lester W. Grau, *Military Review* (USA)

'Of the recent first-hand accounts of Helmand, Stephen Grey's book is the best. It is gripping and insightful in equal measure . . . a powerful and poignant account of a critical phase in the British campaign'
Theo Farrell, Professor of War Studies, King's College, London

'The most astonishing piece of reportage . . . After reading his account of the British operation in 2007 to capture the northern Helmand town of Musa Qala, you are both in awe of the courage of the men on the ground and enraged by the shillyshallying of the politicians who sent them there' Stephen Robinson, *Sunday Times*

ABOUT THE AUTHOR

Stephen Grey is a London-based writer and broadcaster, specializing in national security issues. He is best known for his extensive frontline reports from the conflicts in Iraq and Afghanistan and his world exclusive revelations on the CIA's secret rendition program. A former foreign correspondent for the *Sunday Times* in south Asia and in Europe, he went on to be editor of the paper's investigations unit, the Insight team, and has continued to contribute to that newspaper, as well as to *The New York Times*, *Guardian*, *The Times*, *Independent*, *New Statesman* and *Newsweek*. He has reported for Channel 4's *Dispatches*, BBC *Newsnight*, BBC Radio Four and the World Service. His book on the CIA rendition program, *Ghost Plane*, was published in 2006. He has been nominated for, and won, several major press awards.

www.stephengrey.com

Operation Snakebite

STEPHEN GREY

PENGUIN BOOKS

PENGUIN BOOKS

Published by the Penguin Group
Penguin Books Ltd, 80 Strand, London WC2R ORL, England
Penguin Group (USA), Inc., 375 Hudson Street, New York, New York 10014, USA
Penguin Group (Canada), 90 Eglinton Avenue East, Suite 700, Toronto, Ontario, Canada M4P 2Y3
(a division of Pearson Penguin Canada Inc.)
Penguin Ireland, 25 St Stephen's Green, Dublin 2, Ireland
(a division of Penguin Books Ltd)
Penguin Group (Australia), 250 Camberwell Road, Camberwell, Victoria 3124, Australia
(a division of Pearson Australia Group Pty Ltd)
Penguin Books India Pvt Ltd, 11 Community Centre, Panchsheel Park, New Delhi – 110 017, India
Penguin Group (NZ), 67 Apollo Drive, Rosedale, North Shore 0632, New Zealand
(a division of Pearson New Zealand Ltd)
Penguin Books (South Africa) (Pty) Ltd, 24 Sturdee Avenue, Rosebank, Johannesburg 2196, South Africa

Penguin Books Ltd, Registered Offices: 80 Strand, London WC2R ORL, England

www.penguin.com

First published by Viking 2009
Published with a new epilogue in Penguin Books 2010

1

Copyright © Stephen Grey, 2009, 2010
Maps copyright © Ian Moores, 2009

The moral right of the author has been asserted

Printed in Great Britain by Clays Ltd, St Ives plc

A CIP catalogue record for this book is available from the British Library

ISBN: 978-0-141-03830-8

www.greenpenguin.co.uk

Penguin Books is committed to a sustainable future
for our business, our readers and our planet.
The book in your hands is made from paper
certified by the Forest Stewardship Council.

'Both the American and the British forces guaranteed to me they knew what they were doing, and I made the mistake of listening to them. And when they came in, the Taliban came.'

Hamid Karzai, president of Afghanistan

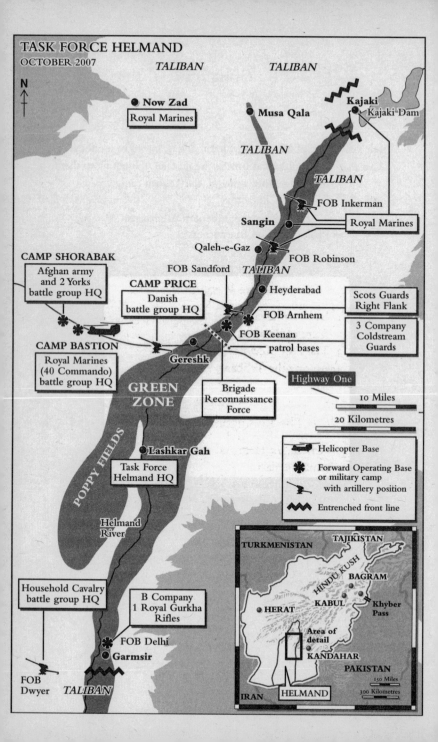

Contents

PART 4
The Plan

PART 5
The Battle

PART 6
The Aftermath

List of Maps

List of Illustrations

* Reproduced with the permission of the Controller of Her Majesty's Stationery Office

Author's Note

War is organized chaos. It involves men and women who have to make decisions about the lives of others under conditions of great stress. What follows is neither an official nor a comprehensive or definitive account of the war in Afghanistan. It is an attempt to look in detail at one small snapshot of a modern counter-insurgency action through the eyes and ears of a few key individuals, both in command and on the front line. It seeks to try to understand what it meant for those involved, to provide an insight into the decisive factors at work and so to allow readers to form their own pro-visional judgement on the events taking place and some lessons that might be learned. The consequences of much that happened are still to play out, and I have not sought to draw any hard conclusions. My only hope is that all of us – myself, readers and decision-makers – may be better informed about the reality of a twenty-first-century war.

Conversations reported here or thoughts attributed to indi-viduals are based on the recollections of one or other of the parties involved, of those briefed on conversations shortly after they took place, or of those with access to the records of conversations. Some parties will remember what happened differently, and some of what they said at certain moments may not reflect their complete view or, unless stated, their settled view in hindsight. The intention is not to convey the exact words or attribute responsibility to any person but rather to give an impression of what it felt like to be part of these intense and momentous times.

Any political views expressed by individuals represent their per-sonal impressions. None should be taken to represent the official view of the UK's Ministry of Defence, the United States army, the Afghan government or any of the other agencies mentioned.

I am happy to correct any errors in future editions of the book.

Principal Characters

Afghan

Hamid Karzai is the president of the Islamic Republic of Afghanistan and has ruled the country since 2001.

Asadullah Wafa is the governor of Helmand.

Mullah Muhammad Omar is the supreme leader of the rebel Taliban movement and is in hiding with a $10 million bounty on his head.

Mullah Abdul Salaam, of the Alizai tribe (Pirzai subtribe), is described by intelligence as a Taliban commander in the Musa Qala district of Helmand.

Mullah Sadiq is the Taliban commander for the Kajaki front line and lives with his family in the town of Sangin.

British

Brigadier Andrew Mackay is a one-star general commanding both the multi-national Task Force Helmand and, as Commander of British Forces (COMBRITFOR), all British service personnel in Afghanistan.

Sir Sherard Cowper-Coles is a career diplomat who is the British ambassador to Afghanistan.

Major Jason Alexis ('Jake') Little commands an infantry unit

– B Company, 2nd Battalion, the Yorkshire Regiment – deployed to mentor the Afghan National Army.

Sergeant Lee 'Jonno' Johnson is a platoon sergeant with B Company.

Major Tony Phillips commands the Brigade Reconnaissance Force.

Major Chris Bell commands the mechanized Right Flank company of the 1st Battalion, Scots Guards. They are deployed in Warrior armoured fighting vehicles.

Irish

Michael Semple is a deputy European Union representative to Afghanistan.

American

General Dan K. McNeill is commander of the International Security Assistance Force of NATO in Afghanistan and is known as COMISAF.

Lieutenant Colonel Brian Mennes is the commander of Task Force 1 Fury, an Afghanistan-wide reserve strike force formed from the 1st Battalion, the 508th Parachute Infantry Regiment, 82nd Airborne division.

Prologue: The Eyewitness

'Only thing I can tell you that might actually do you some good is to go back to your room and practise hitting the floor for a while.'

Dana Stone, war photographer, Saigon, to a rookie reporter.[1]

In the blur of combat, there is so much you see so clearly and there is so much that lies hidden so that there is little chance of understanding what is happening around you. Then you move on, and more events consume you. There is no time for real reflection – even if in the busiest, most frantically crazy moment of your life there is sometimes an intensity of thought or a brief vision of some far-off place that suddenly distracts you, often with no relevance at all to the moment. Then afterwards, the mantra of the army is 'crack on'. Put feelings to one side, for now.

Only later, much later, does the fog lift and the pieces fall into place. Everything starts to make sense. In your head you construct a picture of what really happened – partly from your own memories and partly from the tales of others who were there. Now, you have a picture that stays with you. Even so, it is only one reality. A nagging doubt may plague you by day or in your dreams. *Was it really like that?*

On 6 December 2007, I was in the desert of Afghanistan, lying under the stars. Of all the places in the world, I would have been in no other. Nowhere could have seemed more serene. That night was cold, moonless and dark, and I doubted that I would sleep. I wasn't sure that I wanted to. Under my back was hard earth. The wind cut through my down sleeping bag and thin bivvy bag. I drew the strings at the top of my bag tight so I could only stare skyward through a narrow slit. Every so often I wondered if I should dig out another layer of clothes to wear. But I couldn't face the cold of the night to get up and find them. So I just lay there, shivering gently.

Just looking to the timeless heavens, I could forget for a moment why I was here. I could imagine how many countless others – whether shepherds or soldiers – were at this moment doing as I was and staring at the same Milky Way. But all these dreamlike thoughts were only to escape. If I peered closely, I could see the stars did not only twinkle. Some were also moving. The slow track of aeroplanes or satellites. And if I listened I could hear the rumble of truck engines and Afghan music and laughter inside their heated cabs. There were snores too and the crackle and whispers of the radio operators on duty.

These were the noises of a *leaguer*, a term for the temporary camp of a besieging army. We had arrived in a 12-mile-long convoy, tracked everywhere by the Taliban.

I was alone that night only in my thoughts. Tomorrow's dawn light would sketch out on the desert plain an encampment of men preparing for war. I was among thousands of men there that night who were one prong in the biggest manoeuvre by the British army in Afghanistan since the days of the long-gone Empire. Its purpose was to support an attack on a town called Musa Qala, a town now infamous as a rebel stronghold.

That night, like generations of men before me, I wondered how, if it really came to it, I would react to extreme danger. As a reporter for twenty years, I had been on this edge before, staring at the sky and surrounded by the snores of men who would wake up and be prepared to kill. But always the tension had faded away. I had been arrested at gunpoint, seen bombs and mortars explode, seen the burning homes of ethnic cleansing and charred remains of the victims of massacres. I had met bad men all over the world, had friends who had been kidnapped and held hostage and had felt very afraid. Sometimes, though, I felt like a mere observer in some surreal scene which had no impact on me or posed no threat to me. What would I do if I came under direct fire myself?

Like the soldiers, I did have a serious mission: I wanted to understand this war, to report on what we were doing in this foreign land and to see if we could ever win or do any good. But, if I'm being honest, it wasn't the only thing. I felt a thrill that I'd be an eyewitness to something important, and something real. I might also find out something about myself.

I found my war in Afghanistan the next day in a place called Deh Zohr e Sofla, which translates as 'Lower Noon Village'.

We were walking across an open field. Beyond us were the mud walls of the compounds that marked the outer edge of the village. The point section of the lead platoon was already close. Through all the hours of waiting that morning, and in the heat of the midday sun, the tension of the night before had disappeared. As we strolled along, my mood was almost light-hearted.

I was attached that day to British soldiers of B Company of the 2nd Battalion, the Yorkshire Regiment. I was following the company commander, Major Jake Little, and his group of radio operators. Their aerials were flapping above their rucksacks. In two columns ahead were his soldiers and the two Afghan army units they were supposed to be mentoring. On our flanks were the trucks with heavy machine guns on their roofs. They belonged to an 'A-Team' of US special force Green Berets, an elite unit.

The interpreter, a small man dressed in green fatigues, turned to me.

'We'll be the big target here . . . you look like an interpreter. They know the officers are always near by. That's where they fire.'

I looked down to the left and right, at the shallow depression at the side of the track. I reflected on which way I would jump if a battle suddenly started. Not much cover to choose. 'If it kicks off, I'll be in that ditch,' I joked to Jake.

'I'll be joining you there,' he replied.

We walked forward in waves. One column moved while the other kneeled, ready to provide supporting gunfire. I realized how unfit I was and how useless my clothing was. With a belt bag digging into my stomach and the weight of the armour plates

3

inside my padded flak jacket, I found it hard to kneel comfortably.

Then the firing began. A volley of bullets screaming in our direction. A cracking sound as they came near. We dived right into the shallow ditch. Again, my clothes didn't seem to fit. My jeans were slipping, and I needed a belt. The firing was now intense. I concentrated on keeping my head down. I didn't know who was firing or where it came from.

Jake and his group got up to run, and I followed in a stumble. We ran left across the track towards the shelter of one of the American trucks, a 4 x 4 Humvee. It was then the gunfire came closest. I remember a 'zing zing' and then – in a memory that exists only in slow motion – I saw the bullets strike the earth around my feet, kicking up little bursts of dust. But we made it to the vehicle, and I crouched behind the wheels, catching my breath.

'If the enemy could shoot straight you would have been dead,' someone told me later.

I remember just a feeling of confusion (or 'flapping' as the soldiers would put it) – not quite sure what I should be doing, which way I should be running, and a wish that I had spent the last few weeks in a gym and could run like the wind. The motto of Jake's B Company was 'Fortune favours the fittest'. My fortunes were fading fast. And I remember thinking of my wife, Rebecca, and one-year-old daughter, Sophie, and wondering how fair I was being to them in this crazy, precarious scene.

Jake had told me to follow him. At one point he got up from behind the vehicle. I stood up too, thinking we were about to move. But then he opened fire with his rifle. Stupid me. I got back down.

It was some time in the middle of this, I forget when, that I turned my head and looked behind me. I realized now that, bound up in my own dramas, I had missed something big. A white Toyota saloon car was now overturned, upside down and sideways on the track, and I could make out a gush of blood down the driver's door. Even closer along the road was a small open-backed lorry. I had seen it before with women and children crowded in the back, whom I had taken to be refugees. There was a crowd of people standing in front of the cab and two bundles of cloth on the road in front: bodies, I presumed. Some British soldiers were approaching and being shouted at in English. 'Go away, Go away!'

Captain Dan, the US special forces commander, had now joined us, looking impassive. 'Who fired at them?' I asked him.

'I'm not sure. I'm trying to work it all out,' he said.

For now, no one seemed to know. I finally remembered the video camera in my pocket and began to film.

Our shelter, the Humvee truck, now had to move, and so we ran across to the ditch to the right, going a little forward. The firing appeared to be dying down. Jake was giving orders. A team was sent forward to the front compound wall. I heard the shout of 'Grenade' and watched something thrown over the wall. Afghan soldiers rushed into the compound, and there was firing. A little later, the body of a man was brought out and dumped in the road.

The soldiers advanced into the village, and there was sporadic fighting. We finally reached the relative safety of the front compound wall. I sat down and rested. I felt I had had my story. I had seen my bit of war. Now I just wanted to sit down and smoke, and to stay safe. I began thinking of my family again and wondering if the Taliban might try to flank us.

Gradually, what had happened was beginning to make sense. The Americans, I was now told, were the soldiers who had opened fire on the cars. When the firing began, the civilian cars had tried to drive away. But the Americans thought they were suicide bombers and had engaged them.

A British medic, Corporal Philip French, came forward to join us. His face expressed shock. He had tried to save the driver of one of the cars, but hadn't succeeded. The man had died in his arms.

I had met 'Frenchy' before, in the Iraq war. He was the medic at the scene of what became known as the Battle of Danny Boy near the town of al Amarah, when British troops had charged a trench line with bayonets. French had told me of a wounded prisoner he fought to save on that battlefield. He too had died in his care, his lungs flapping around.

Now French was pretty angry. He told me there were also children injured in the gunfire. For some reason, a few of the children were in the boot of the car. The lid had popped open after the car was hit. There were also women injured. But none would let the soldiers approach and treat them.

Captain Dan came over to speak to me again. He still wasn't sure what had happened, but he was outraged with the Taliban.

'It shows you what we are up against. The Taliban were in control of the village, and they sent these vehicles forward, knowing they were going into an ambush, knowing they would be shot at.'

Dan thought it was pretty weird that the children had been locked in the boot. He supposed it was some Taliban tactic to get them killed and give the coalition a bad name. But I wondered instead whether the father of these kids simply thought they would be safer in the boot.

The locals wanted to take the wounded to hospital. But it was four or five hours' drive away. The soldiers wanted to call a helicopter. They tried to make the locals wait. It got tense. A promised helicopter didn't arrive. Eventually, the locals just drove off with the wounded.

All this time the battle in the village was continuing behind me. A US fighter jet screeched down to strafe Taliban positions with a cannon that fired with a deep-throated gargle. Rocket-propelled grenades (RPGs) were fired. A Taliban prisoner, a young Pakistani boy, was marched forward in plastic handcuffs. He was taken away to the rear. Heavy machine guns of the Afghan army opened up from the hill behind. The Americans and British feared fratricide and told them to stop firing – or they would be shot at themselves.

As the light began to fade, the battle drew near to a close. The Taliban were firing now from a greater distance, from further down the hill. The Americans were opening up with their .50 calibre (pronounced 'fifty cal') heavy weapons over a wall. Finally, there was word that a high-altitude B-1B bomber was coming in to strike. There was a countdown and shouts of 'Yeeee ha!' as the blast threw up a mushroom cloud from down in the valley.

Jake now called the retreat. We had done enough for one day, and we trudged back up the track in the orange glow of the sunset. The body of the Taliban fighter was left behind for his comrades to collect; so too were the bodies of the two civilians left by the shot-up truck.

At the top of the track was our camp, surrounded on three sides by a hill.

'Were you afraid, then?' asked Corporal David 'Percy' Percival as we ate our rations.

'I was petrified.'

'I was afraid too,' he said. Seventeen years in the army and he had never seen anything like it.

Others told me a similar story. When I eventually slept that night, after filing my story to the newspaper and climbing back into my shallow trench, I no longer felt alone in my thoughts.

Our attack had been a diversion, a *feint* as they call it. For all its ferocity, it was just one of many that day. The aim was to deceive the Taliban into believing that our main attack would come from the south and south-west, the same direction from which the Soviets had attacked this town, twenty-four years before. As we had withdrawn, the real attack had come in from the north. Hundreds of American paratroopers were dropped by helicopter.

The plan called for the Americans to surround and beat the Taliban on the outskirts of the town. If all went well, their enemy would realize it was outgunned and overwhelmed and then flee. We would then enter and secure the town with the Afghan army. The operation would be announced to the world as an Afghan success. The Americans told us the aim was not just a tactical win but an Information Operations win – an 'IO victory'.

What had happened in the village could have been a public relations disaster. It almost was. Except that, at the time, rather lost in my own personal drama, I hadn't done a great job in collecting the facts. I was to report that two civilians were killed in the fight. But, reporting on the front line in a fast-paced environment, I didn't really have the chance to get at the full story. The truth, I later discovered, was that many more innocent people were killed, including two children. As the operation unfolded my under-estimate of the numbers of civilians killed seemed to become the official word. Right up to Kabul and up the command chain the word was given out: just two civilians died in the operation to recapture Musa Qala.

Does a leaf fall in the forest if no one is there to see it?

Do civilians die in a war if no journalist is there to witness it?

I didn't then, and I still don't now, blame the soldiers for those deaths I witnessed. If a car comes hurtling towards you in Afghanistan, there is a high chance it *is* a suicide bomber, as others have found to their cost. 'If that was a suicide bomber there would have been fifteen of us dead on the ground,' one soldier told me that night.

I had arrived in Afghanistan a week earlier as an outsider and a sceptic. My last trip to the country had been ten years earlier when, over three successive trips, I had reported for the *Sunday Times* on life under the then Taliban government. I wrote a feature about the treatment of educated women in Kabul, about teachers and graduates driven to prostitution and suicide. Radio Sharia, the Taliban radio station, declared me an enemy.

But in the years since I had been equally critical of the way we had responded to the Taliban and to the terrorist threat that grew from guerrilla training camps which the Taliban sheltered. As the 'war on terror' erupted after 9/11, I reported from Iraq on the misdirected conflict that seemed to be stoking up hatred against the West. I reported too on the CIA's programme of extraordinary rendition – another aspect of this new war in which the tactics employed seemed as likely to increase the threat of terrorism as abate it.

The war in Afghanistan was portrayed as another front in this global war on terror. The Taliban were described as proxies for Al Qaeda. From my own experience, however, I knew the Taliban themselves had few global ambitions, regardless of the rogues to whom they gave hospitality. I was aware too of the historical

8

context: that the Helmand River basin, where British troops had now returned, was the scene of one of the British Empire's greatest military disasters, the Battle of Maiwand, in which more than 1,700 troops of the British army and their camp followers were slain. Some Afghans regarded our return as a vengeance for Maiwand. British and NATO presence on Afghan soil might help suppress terrorist bases, but it might also recruit new volunteers back in the West to the cause of *jihadi* terrorism.

As we waited at Kandahar Airport for permission to reach the front line, Nick Cornish, the *Sunday Times* photographer who was travelling with me, had summed up another concern.

'I don't understand,' he said. 'The mission in Afghanistan is to prevent the country being used for training bases for terrorists. Surely in this war, the *whole country* is now one big training base for them?'

Corporal Gregory Roberts, known as 'Cagey' for his remarkable resemblance to the actor Nicholas Cage, was the driver of our Vector, a standard-issue lightly armoured six-wheeled mini truck. Cagey was a wizard with vehicles. A day after the fight in the village, he was trying to fix up an Afghan ammunition truck that had broken down in a small gully that led up from the valley floor where we had spent the night.

We were standing behind the Vector, concerned that the steel tow rope being used was going to snap. Cagey was standing pretty close, and, though it was hardly my business, I said to him then: 'It's not worth anyone dying to save this truck.' A trite remark.

The explosion when it came is hard to remember. All I see now is a thick fog of dust and a shout from Neil 'Brum' Warrington, our Royal Marine minder and saviour, of 'Mortars!' We jumped in the back of the Vector and slammed the door shut. The dust came raining down through the hatch. But, as the cloud settled, Brum put his head outside and realized what had really happened: a mine strike.

'Those poor fuckers!' he said, reaching for his weapon.

I stepped outside, and it was clear things were serious. A British

Vector had blown up. I stayed alongside Captain Nick Mantell, Jake Little's fresh-faced no. 2. He had been standing beside the Vector when it hit the mine, and his face was now streaked with blood. I watched as he called through the nine-liner, a standardized casualty report. 'One casualty T1,' said Nick on the radio, a code-word for a casualty requiring immediate evacuation. 'Both legs gone,' added Nick. Clearly he might be dead.

A little later we moved away from the scene and away from our own vehicle, which was the command wagon. We were told that one of B Company's most beloved men had died, a man whom Jake had known for years. Being there at this moment of tragedy presented us with a dilemma. We had been with B Company for only three days. We asked Jake if we should move across to another unit, but he asked us to stay. He had spoken to the lads. And though they hardly knew us, the feeling was it was better we stayed. Maybe that death might get more than the usual few paragraphs in a newspaper.

Throughout the day it was impossible to move the soldier's body. There was no helicopter available to bring an explosives disposal team to clear the potential minefield. In the evening, B Company decided to do the job themselves. Even so, there was still no helicopter to bring back the soldier's body. So we spent the night outside on the hilltop while the body lay in our 'wagon', and I wrote my news report that night from the inside of my sleeping bag, shielding the laptop's bright lights so it did not give away our position.

Before they went to sleep or stood sentry, Jake gathered his men in whispers on the hilltop. He was struggling, he said, to find the right words. 'I'm shit at this,' he confessed to the men. He spoke of how their comrade died doing what he loved. 'He would have been proud of what each and every one of you did, both today in this incident, and yesterday in the village,' he said. 'We have to move on but not forget.'

During the night that followed the skyline was lit not only by shooting stars but also by the sparks of tracer fire, of flares spinning up and then floating down, and the deep thunder and flashes of heavy ordnance. As the rain began to fall and the temperature dropped towards zero, there was a steady drone of planes and helicopters circling above.

Three days later, when the men were preparing for the final advance into Musa Qala, they paused for reflection again. There was a feeling there would be more dead by nightfall. In the orange light of the morning, by the belching black smoke of burning stoves, the men gathered by a soldier from Fiji, Private Lawrence Fong, who led a prayer in his own language. The men said 'Amen'. Jake shook hands with every man of his company and urged them to put fear to one side. Some looked excited and eager, others looked worn and apprehensive. As we drove forward to the drop-off point, there were legs that were shaking like scissors.

When it was all over and the town had been taken, the commanders arrived with TV cameras. American gun trucks were frantically hidden and then the brigadiers, one Afghan and one British, arrived to celebrate the Afghan army victory. Someone called the president. The national flag was raised on a precarious scaffold, and the soldiers cheered.

The legend began from there that the Afghans had done the 'heavy lifting' to take the town, proof of the emerging strength, it was said by commanders, of the Afghan National Army (ANA). All poppycock, of course. But it served as useful propaganda for the British, to help strengthen Afghan confidence.

After days with little sleep and so much drama, it all felt like an anticlimax.

'Another battle for another pile of rubble in a far-off place whose name the world will soon forget,' I said with a weary smile to a special forces gunner.

'Roger that!' he replied.

But should it be forgotten?

In these few days, I had seen a snapshot of the front line of this war. I had glimpsed the intense pressure under which these soldiers operated and seen the horror both they and ordinary Afghans had to cope with. But I was a reporter, and all this had just whetted my appetite.

After being with soldiers who coped with death, I wanted to know ever more urgently what they really thought of this war. Was their sacrifice really worth it? Were we close to winning this war, or at least just making some progress? As I posed more questions and tried to gain more access to the military, I discovered I was pushing at an open door. The same questions that I was asking were being asked at the same time by the soldiers themselves, and by their commanders too.

When I returned to England I heard the critics deride the war. In the following months, many more soldiers died. The public began to ask: why are we in Afghanistan at all?

Just after Christmas there was an intriguing development. Two envoys – one from the European Union mission and another from the United Nations – were expelled from Afghanistan for unauthorized contacts with the Taliban. The expulsion was made, it was said, after they had undertaken a trip to Musa Qala. There were rumours the officials were working with the British. Another story, in the *Daily Telegraph*, had mentioned contacts by Britain's Secret Intelligence Service with leaders of the Taliban who were fighting the British.

What were the secret dimensions of this war, I wondered. And how did what happened in the shadows affect the lives and progress of the soldiers who fought on the ground?

I set out then to report this story from many points of view – from soldier to general, from diplomat to president. It seemed to me that only by getting behind the scenes could anyone pretend to understand what was happening. And it seemed far better to understand one battle in its complexity than span a great history and learn nothing new.

I soon discovered the real story of the Battle of Musa Qala, and the events leading up to it, had all the dimensions of a thriller – courage, love and betrayal, intrigues at the palace in Kabul, tension between friends, assassination and intelligence blunders, and occasionally high farce.

But it also seemed to sum up the whole Afghan war.

What became clear as I began speaking to soldiers and diplomats was that the Musa Qala battle occurred when the Afghan war was at a crossroads, at a point where all involved were beginning to see that quelling the Taliban revolt was going to need more than a military solution.

Hundreds, perhaps thousands, of people called 'the enemy' have been killed since the war began. Hundreds of the innocent – ordinary Afghan villagers caught in the fighting – have been slain too. They have been the victims of both 'enemy' atrocities and of NATO bombs. Whole towns and villages have been laid waste, and others are almost ghost towns, from where the population has fled in terror. The new Afghan war was launched in the name of combating terrorism and defeating the allies of Osama bin Laden and Al Qaeda. But soldiers know their 'enemy' included many ordinary men and boys from the villages who were inspired to defeat the foreigner. 'In the early days we probably wound up – maybe still are – killing lots of farmers,' the head of the army, General Sir Richard Dannatt, told me.

The new Afghan war is being fought also in the name of the new 'democratic' Afghan government. But soldiers know this government is corrupt and often reviled by the local population. Crops of illegal opium poppies are grown on government lands. Soldiers have met an Afghan army hooked on hashish and a police force addicted to heroin. Many police set up checkpoints not to provide security but to rob the traveller and control the movement of drugs.

After the Afghan flag had been raised in Musa Qala, I met the British brigadier who commanded all British forces. Sitting outside an abandoned shop, Andrew Mackay candidly revealed his own concerns about the war and his own strategy for beginning to win against the odds. Later, he sent me a copy of his latest thinking, which spoke of avoiding battles and killing. After days of bombardment and fighting, this struck me as rather odd. The centre of Musa Qala had escaped any destruction, but I had yet to see anything of the softer side of this conflict.

Mackay was not alone in his views, though. They were shared by the British ambassador, Sir Sherard Cowper-Coles, and by others. All wanted to stop the *needless* killing. But Mackay's new strategy of gearing military operations to winning the support of the Afghan public was easier said than done, as I had seen in Musa Qala.

What follows in this book, then, is not a theoretical or an academic story but a glimpse at how wars are really fought, and how men like Mackay and Cowper-Coles might often share the same opinions but – under the pressure of their commands and in the heat and passion of the moment – might regard each other with suspicion and sometimes clash openly.

The story begins in the autumn of 2007 after a summer of bloody and destructive fighting along the Helmand River. As Mackay arrives with a new brigade of British soldiers, he preaches a message of caution. But, as the weeks pass, the Taliban resume their attacks, and British and allied casualties mount up. Suddenly, as the result of a discreet dialogue with some Taliban leaders, President Karzai wants the military to push north to support a promised 'tribal uprising' against the enemy stronghold of Musa Qala. This becomes the biggest operation that the British have conducted in Afghanistan for over a century.

And all for a little dusty town.

PART I

The Rebellion

'"You know, you never beat us on the battlefield."
  – US army Colonel Harry G. Summers, Jr

"That may be so, but it is also irrelevant."'
  – Colonel Tu, his former North Vietnamese counterpart[2]

1. Desert of Death

About 120 million years ago, a small tectonic plate was driven out of the Indian Ocean and crashed up into the Asiatic landmass. As the plate was compressed, it began to crumple up in front, throwing up to the north the hostile terrain of the central mountains of Afghanistan. More recently, a mere forty million years back, the Indian tectonic plate came smashing in behind, throwing up another range of mountains to the west and south, a wilderness of almost impassable peaks and troughs in what is now western Pakistan and Baluchistan. In between these mountain ranges was left a vast inland basin and a single river that drained all its rainfall: the Helmand River.

The climate in this land-locked basin has fluctuated over the millennia. In some eras the snow that fell on the mountains of Afghanistan was plentiful, and the melt waters that flowed down into the Helmand basin cut deep valleys through the mountain rock, and left layer upon layer of sand and gravel in the land beneath. In arid times – as in the modern day – the snow and rainfall became pitiful, and only the tall canyons in the plateaus to the north preserved the memory of the once plentiful water. Rivers still trickled through them, but most became seasonal: dry-river courses, known to the British as *wadis* and to Afghans as *nalas* or *mandahs*, that occasionally burst into life when sudden mountain storms sent torrents of water tumbling down them, sometimes with no warning. The desert came to be called the Dasht-e-Margo, the Desert of Death.

The Helmand River itself, though, continued flowing through the desert, whatever the season, the only permanent desert water-course between the Indus River in Pakistan to the east and the Tigris-Euphrates in Iraq to the west. Unlike those two other great rivers, the Helmand's waters were trapped between two ranges of mountains and did not reach the sea. After flowing southwards for hundreds of miles, the river snaked round to the south-west and settled and evaporated, as it still does today, in great shallow lakes in the desert.

For humans who settled in the basin, the constant waters of the Helmand became the source of life. Agriculture, fed by irrigation, sprang up along its banks. Some of the wadis that fed into the Helmand became sparsely settled too, exploiting the alluvial soils. At the mountains' edge, the ancients began building underground tunnels, or *karezes*, to tap into the aquifers and underground rivers that still flowed freely beneath the dry surface sands. Access to these water flows and the scarce land into which they fed became the key to power and survival in this desert. And so it also became the source of conflict and war between the tribes that came to occupy these lands.

For wider humanity, the river had a greater strategic importance. As a gap between two hostile mountain ranges, the Helmand basin became – as it has remained for centuries – a great land corridor between East and West, a route for traders between Persia and India. The taxing, robbing or protecting of trade became the other great source of income for local dwellers in this land. It was also a route of conquest: for invaders from Alexander the Great in 329 BC to the hordes of Genghis Khan in 1226, to Tamerlane (or Timur the Lame) in 1383, to the Soviet army in 1979.[3]

Along this strategic route there were few natural barriers to hold back an invading army except the waters of the Helmand itself. Forts sprang up along the River Helmand's banks. The Sultan Mahmood of Ghazni built the city of Bost in the tenth century,[4] close to the present capital of Helmand province, Lashkar Gah. It was later destroyed by Genghis Khan. Later still, the capital of what became the modern Afghan Empire was established to the east of the Helmand in a place called Kandahar, just north of the Bolan pass through to what was then India. The Helmand valley became, as it is today, both the gateway to and a line of defence for this great city.

But, though protected by forts against advancing armies, the

Helmand River itself was never much of a barrier. There were too many easy places to ford. In 1880, during the second Afghan war, the British discovered this to their cost. A British force advanced to Gereshk, the town that controlled the bridge on the great trunk road from Herat, on the Persian border, to Kandahar. Their enemy was a pretender to the Afghan throne, Ayub Khan, who advanced with his army from Herat. Rather than confront the British at Gereshk, he swung up and crossed the river at Heyderabad further north. Outflanked, the British made a hasty retreat and finally came to battle on 27 July at Maiwand, on the road back to Kandahar. It proved to be one of Britain's greatest military defeats of the Victorian era.

The Helmand the British found in the nineteenth century had much in common with what the British soldiers and their allies found in the dawn of the twenty-first. The people of Helmand were the Pashto-speaking tribes and subtribes, the same ethnic group who formed the majority of Afghanistan and who had overthrown the Persians and ruled the country since 1747. After centuries of dispute, the Pashtun people (or *Pathans* as they were known in British India) had settled a system of intricate land ownership and water rights that was rarely disturbed and was strictly divided up between tribes, each of whom was generally ruled locally by a pre-eminent chief, known as a *khan*.

By the end of the twentieth century new outside influences were beginning to be felt – arising from both the central Afghan government, now based in Kabul, and from foreigners. Once part of a greater Kandahar region, the lower part of the Helmand River basin had now become its own province, a region stretching from where the Helmand River left the high mountains to the north-east, to Pakistan and the Baluchi mountains to the south, and the empty desert of Nimroz province to the south-west, where the river flowed out to dry in salt pans on the Iranian border. From one corner of the province to another was 302 miles, a little less than the distance between London and Edinburgh.

Between 1946 and 1959, American contractors constructed a new canal system to channel the Helmand waters.[5] A vast acreage of newly irrigated land came into being along the river to the west of Lashkar Gah, a city that was now reborn and rebuilt along a series of square gridlines that was more akin to the American mid-west than the Orient. Crucially for the future, much of the new land was government-owned rather than tribally owned.

Then came the Soviet invasion on 27 December 1979. The war changed Afghanistan radically. It was not so much what the Soviets did themselves but how the foreign-backed war against the Soviets changed society. As the armed struggle gathered strength, powerful and ambitious new warlords challenged and displaced the old tribal khans. With them gone, some of the truces and understandings between local tribes that had kept relative peace in this land for centuries were shattered. And as society began to alter in war, Helmand suddenly discovered a new source of wealth and notoriety.

The first word of this change came in a report from the Helmand town of Musa Qala by a *New York Times* reporter named Arthur Bonner, who in 1986 had just completed a 1,000-mile journey across southern Afghanistan. He described the scene:

Fields of purple, red and white poppy flowers, contrasting brilliantly with the dull gray of the surrounding deserts, stretched toward the horizon. In one field, where the petals had fallen to the ground, a line of farmers scraped a brownish-black gum from pale green pods about the size of golf balls.[6]

Bonner claimed to have spoken to dozens of rebel commanders who asserted that the opium poppy was now being planted with a vengeance, apparently as a deliberate act of war. The most powerful commander in Helmand, reported Bonner, was Nassim Akhund-zada, whose Alizai tribe was scattered over the mountainous north of the province. His home and major landholdings were in Musa Qala. And it was in that town that Bonner found his elderly brother, Muhammad Rasul Akhundzada, who described himself as an Islamic teacher and had 'a thick gray-and-black beard and large, watery eyes'. In the shade of an ancient tree beside the poppy fields, Muhammad Rasul explained his teachings to the farmers. The article read:

'We must grow and sell opium to fight our holy war against the Russian nonbelievers,' Mr Rasul said. Comments like his were heard from dozens of rebels during the journey. Islam does not forbid the harvest, Mr Rasul asserted. 'Islamic law bans the taking of opium, but there is no prohibition against growing it,' he said.

In the years that followed the Akhundzada family grew in power, and poppy cultivation spread far and wide. Within two decades, Helmand province would produce more illegal drugs, according to the United Nations, than any country in the world.[7]

When the Soviet army and its Communist puppet regime in Kabul were driven out of power at the end of the 1980s, it was Nassim Akhundzada who became the first governor of Helmand under the Mujahidin who took over. But the civil war continued, and his clan was driven from power in the mid-1990s by a new group of Islamic students who called themselves the Taliban (literally 'the students' in Arabic). Nassim Akhundzada and his brother were both assassinated.

Though the Taliban was popular across much of the country for driving out the warlords and restoring security, the movement's weakness was its close ties with some of the most violent anti-western groups in the world. After Osama bin Laden used a base in Afghanistan to train and prepare for the terrorist attacks of 11 September 2001, the United States invaded the country and toppled the Taliban with the help of its enemies.

Backed by other world powers, the US persuaded the United Nations to help gather a *loya jirga*, a traditional gathering of tribal elders, to endorse its chosen new ruler, Hamid Karzai, a Pashtun tribal elder, as the new president of Afghanistan. The decision was later ratified with national elections.

The toppling of the Taliban also brought the return of the Akhundzada clan to Helmand. Muhammad Rasul's son, Sher Muhammad Akhundzada, was now head of the family and became the new governor. He had befriended Karzai in exile in Pakistan. Karzai's government, for Helmand and much of Afghanistan, meant the return of the warlords.

And the civil war was not over. Osama bin Laden had survived the US invasion, and so had Mullah Muhammad Omar, the reclusive Taliban supreme leader. From a hide-out just over the border in Pakistan, the latter started rebuilding his forces.

In the summer of 2006, the British army returned to the banks of the Helmand after a gap of 126 years. Although the British had been in the north of the country since 2001, this was the first major combat mission. The aim was to bolster the Afghan government and provide security for economic development as part of a multi-nation deployment organized by NATO, known as the International Security Assistance Force (ISAF).

Soon, like the Soviets before them, the NATO troops were attacked wherever they went. Fighting was intense, probably as intense as anything seen here during the Soviet occupation. Within a year, the British force had swollen from a planned deployment of 3,300 men and women to nearly 7,000 – more troops than the Red Army had ever deployed to the province.

As it had for centuries, power in Helmand rested on three pillars: land, water and the trade routes. With the annual poppy crop of Helmand now estimated by the UN to be worth half a billion dollars a year to farmers,[8] each of these was more valuable than ever. Control of scarce land and water meant control of the poppy crop, and control of the roads meant control over the smuggling of it. The Afghan government under President Karzai claimed that Taliban rebels were intimately involved with the poppy trade and taxed its revenues to fund their guerrilla war. But British and American intelligence also knew a more uncomfortable truth: that Afghan authorities in Helmand were as involved in the poppy trade as the Taliban.

Of all the scarce land in the Helmand basin, the most fertile and best irrigated was the land reclaimed from the desert with the help of American tax dollars in the 1950s. Most of it was government-owned and most of it lay in the central strip of Helmand near Lashkar Gah. The best of Helmand's poppy crop was in the zone claimed to be under the control of the government backed by Britain and America.

To the public, the war in Helmand was described as a battle for political power – a fledgling democracy fighting an Islamic radical movement, the Taliban, who were linked to terrorists. In reality, the war was more than anything about drugs. Drugs were turning tribe against tribe and family against family. It was shattering the old agreements that divided up the land and water. One tribe might choose the government to support its claim on the opium trade; another might choose the Taliban; and others might play off one side against the other.

Before they arrived, the British had tried to intervene decisively against the drugs mafia. They had persuaded President Karzai to sack Sher Muhammad Akhundzada as governor after a raid by US drug enforcement agents and Afghan police on Akhundzada's compound found 9 metric tonnes of opium, the largest US seizure in the country since 2002. The governor said it was stored contraband awaiting destruction, but few believed him.[9]

Yet when they arrived the British declared a policy of noninterference with opium cultivation. Bases were built right next to poppy fields. The army declared destroying these crops would simply lead the population to support the Taliban. While Akhundzada might have been replaced as governor on paper by a more pro-British technocrat, Muhammad Daoud, the sacked governor remained as close as ever to President Karzai. And then there were doubts about the Karzai family's connections to others in the drugs trade, not least his own brother in Kandahar, Ahmed Wali Karzai, who was frequently named in intelligence reports as being involved in the heroin business, although he denied any involvement.[10]

There were some who began to wonder, darkly, if Britain's military were being drawn into what was essentially a drug turf war.

In the autumn of 2007 – nearly eighteen months after the first deployment in Helmand – a fresh set of British servicemen arrived to take over. Out of a deployment of 7,800 men and women, some 6,000 were destined for Helmand, to take charge of a multinational NATO brigade known as Task Force Helmand. Also under British command were Danish, Czech and Estonian forces, making up a total strength in the province of just over 7,000 people.

The troops arriving came to a battleground that was mostly the fertile irrigated land that stretched along the Helmand River as well as in its main tributary wadis. This was where the province's population of just under one million people lived. The British called it the 'green zone'.

In broad terms, the Afghan government and NATO troops now controlled the main towns, where about one in twenty people normally lived. The Taliban generally controlled the populated countryside. No one controlled the open desert, through which both sides could move with ease but where there was little shelter for the Taliban to hide from NATO air power. It made little sense, then, for the Taliban to fight their battles here.

At the point where the Helmand River entered Helmand province was the large Kajaki lake and dam.[11] The hydroelectric plant was supposed to supply electricity from here across southern Afghanistan, but only one of its three turbines worked at full capacity: one had failed completely and another was due to be shut down for maintenance. With the villages around deserted due to the fighting, a British outpost was in place to guard the dam and protect a team of US-funded contractors who were hoping to repair the plant. The Taliban lay behind clear front lines to the north and south of the dam.

From Kajaki, the river flowed in a broadly south-westerly direction through a wide Taliban-controlled canyon to the town of Sangin, a market town on the south bank of the river with a population of around 14,000 that had been heavily fought-over but had returned to British control in the spring of 2007. From Sangin, the river continued to the south-west through a wider green valley and meandered 20 miles to Gereshk, a town with a population of 60,000, the second-biggest urban centre in the province. The strategic Herat–Kandahar highway that bridged the

Helmand at Gereshk had been rebuilt in recent years and was now called the national Highway One. Like Russian troops before them, NATO relied on this road to transport its essential supplies. But it was also an essential artery of normal commerce for the country. Along Highway One in the desert to the west of Gereshk lay Camp Bastion, the largest British military base built anywhere since the Second World War.

Next on the river from Gereshk, just above the confluence with the Arghandhab River and at the point where the valley flattened out to snake across sandy desert, lay Lashkar Gah, the American-built provincial capital with a population of 70,000 swelled by refugees from the war. The town housed the headquarters of Task Force Helmand and civilian advisers known as the Provincial Reconstruction Team (PRT).

Thirty-five miles south of here lay Garmsir, the most southern town held by British forces. It was almost deserted due to the fighting and close to a fixed First World War-like front line, complete with trenches and a no man's land. The main market bazaar had now moved south into territory controlled by the Taliban, who also ran a field hospital there. The main roads from the Pakistan border, 110 miles further south, converged at Garmsir. It was the gateway to Helmand.

South of Garmsir was an area the British called the Fish Hook, where the river turned to the west and flowed across into neighbouring Nimroz province. All of this was enemy territory, challenged only by raids from US and British special forces and reconnaissance troops.

Apart from the towns along the Helmand River, there were two further towns of importance to the battle. Both of them lay in the rocky desert plateau in the north. Now Zad was an oasis in the desert north-west of Sangin. It was now a 'Marie Celeste' town deserted due to the fighting. Finally, there was the town of Musa Qala. With a population of 30,000 it lay due north of Sangin, halfway up the wide Musa Qala wadi, down which a river flowed in flood. It was the biggest centre of opium production in the world.

For the last six months, all the major towns of Helmand had been in government hands and either had a NATO garrison or were peaceful. All except one: the Taliban stronghold of Musa Qala.

2. Band of Brothers

'How vain the power that defies
The bonnie English Rose.'

Green Howards regimental march

Queen Street, Blackpool, Lancashire, 9 September

B Company of the 2nd Battalion of the Yorkshire Regiment (Green Howards) was formed up and ready for action. The officer commanding (OC) approached and reviewed his men, the same soldiers that I would meet three months later on the battlefield.

'Permission to have a go, sir?' said Corporal Carl Peterson, a section commander.

The men standing before the OC certainly had a skinful of courage. They were men in the peak of fitness, and they had the drills and skills, the discipline and plenty of experience too for a fight like this. But it was also true that tonight they were not in uniform and had no weapons. And it was dark, by the seaside, and they were in Blackpool, Lancashire. Not Afghanistan.

'I don't think so, lads,' said the OC. 'Not tonight.'

Major Jason Alexis Little, aged thirty-six, had a twinkle in his eyes as he looked down the line of men. He was looking at people who were family. He had known some of these men for nearly sixteen years. He had grown up with them. He knew all their strengths and weaknesses. They knew his too. They all addressed him formally as sir or Major Little or the OC. But for the seniors amongst them, in their minds at least he was simply 'Jake', and he was one of them. He had been in and out of B Company for years.

Like so many other officers that you found in Helmand, Jake was very much the army brat. His father, Peter Little, had served thirty years in the army, mostly with the Gurkhas, and had retired

27

as a brigadier. Jake spent most of his early life in Hong Kong before boarding at a prep school and then Tonbridge School in Kent. After studying history at Newcastle University, he followed his dad and his elder brother Paddy to train at Sandhurst as an army officer. It wasn't family pressure that led him to the military, he would say, but just the grim thought of other options, like sitting in an office. He did also feel a plain pride in the army. That certainly was inherited.

Jake's first job in the regiment had been in B Company as a second lieutenant or subaltern in charge of a platoon. Promoted to captain, he became the second-in-command. Then he returned as the OC in the summer of 2006, taking over from his brother Paddy.

Many thought being company commander was the best job in the army, at least among the officers. As a major this was the last rank of command where you fought your war with the soldiers and where leadership still meant getting close to the thickest of action. Step one rank up to lieutenant colonel and you might just get charge of a battalion, something like a position of being God. But it was also a more remote position: both from the men and from the action.

Against a guerrilla army like the Taliban it was small units that counted. Helmand was very much a company commander's war. Higher-up ranks might set missions, but it was people like Jake who really worked out the tactics and directed the battle. And then it was often down to his sergeants and young officers (most fresh out of training) to actually run the fight.

The company was due out to Helmand in four days' time with a mission from 52 Brigade to act as mentors for the Afghan National Army. The task was known as an OMLT, pronounced 'omelette' and standing for Operational Mentoring and Liaison Team. It was not just about training but about fighting with and often leading the Afghan soldier, the type of work that in other conflicts had been done by elite special forces. This one company would be mentoring an entire ANA battalion, what the Afghans called a *kandak*, of 400 men. And what they were doing would be at the heart of the conflict. Everyone knew any sensible exit strategy from the Helmand war involved getting the Afghan army up to strength.

The full complement of Jake's B Company was 120 men. But the OMLT role demanded a smaller team, a bit heavier in officers and senior ranks. So two of his platoons had been hived off to other jobs. That left behind thirty-five in his team – and these were the men out tonight.

Of all in the 2 Yorks, it was father-of-three Sergeant Lee 'Jonno' Johnson, thirty-three, whom Jake probably knew best. Jonno was something of a legend in the regiment, described by its commanding officer, Simon Downey, as 'one of life's little gems'. His reputation had not always been won for the best of reasons.

Jonno was the reason they were all standing out here in the street outside the Walkabout. The bouncers had just evicted him for being drunk, not to mention for wearing flip-flops. Jake had gone out to remonstrate. If Jonno was a little drunk, as most were that night, then he was a happy drunk and no cause for worry. The rest of the company had followed Jake out, and that was why they were lined up for action.

The trouble for Jonno, as he grew up, was that he became plagued by a certain legend. As a boxer for the regiment and a judo champion for the army, his nicknames varied from 'Judo Johnson' to 'Mad Dog Johnson'. Everyone who wanted to prove himself in every bar wanted to take Jonno on. And it invariably ended up in big trouble.

Jonno had moved up ranks and been busted down again more times than anyone could ever remember. But his offences – generally for fighting – had never taken him on the expected route to a spell in Colchester, the army military jail. And the reason was that every one of his commanding officers had intervened on his behalf. It had taken Jonno a long time, he would say himself, to realize why – to realize he was a good soldier, a man that others looked up to, a born leader. Now, for the first time, things were going right. For the first time he had come to realize his own potential and had mended his ways. And everyone in the regiment was proud of what Jonno had become.

Jonno had been in Jake's platoon when Jake had joined B Company. And though they were poles apart in many ways, everyone around them remembered them as very close, often drinking together into the small hours. Dealing with a young green subaltern, Jonno had seen himself as Jake's protector. If they were in a club and someone started to pick a fight with Jake and the officers, for example, Jonno would suddenly appear from nowhere, steaming to the rescue.

Time, of course, had moved them on a long path since then. Jake had risen up the ranks and was no longer quite the party animal and night owl. He had been married now for six years and had two young children. And Jonno too had become a different man, a classic 'poacher turned gamekeeper', as his friends would say.

Like Jake, Jonno had a brother in the Green Howards, in his case a younger brother, four years his junior. Lance-Corporal Don Johnson was in C Company. Both would be going out on the tour, and Jonno would worry incessantly about how 'our kid' was doing.

There were others who had been there when Jake first joined. Nearly all had a connection with North Yorkshire, the historic recruiting ground of this regiment which until a year back was simply called the Green Howards, a name dating back to 1688. Now it was just one battalion in a new and super-sized Yorkshire Regiment. Still, the tradition of the Green Howards was important. Jake's soldiers talked of people they admired in the regiment as having 'green blood'.

At forty-one, Corporal Dave McCarrick was the oldest man in the company and was one of those who had been there when Jake had first joined B Company. Plagued by injuries, including a dodgy knee, McCarrick had never got the chance to do the courses to step him up to the rank of sergeant. But he would be acting sergeant in the coming tour and, after lobbying to be on the front line, he would also be Jake's gunner – manning the machine gun on the back of the OC's wagon. Like Jonno, McCarrick was from Stockton, on Teesside, and a Middlesbrough Football Club fan, and they had known each other long before the army.

Then there was Jimmy Lynas, thirty-four, probably Jonno's best friend, from Thornaby-on-Tees, not far from Stockton. He had also been in B Company all his career and, like Jonno, had had his ups and downs. But – also like Jonno – he had just finally been promoted to sergeant.

All of these men – Jake included – had some close old friends from the Green Howards who were not there that night. They were part of other companies. But they would all soon be out together in OMLT teams in Helmand. All would play a crucial part in the events that followed.

It was Jonno who had organized that night, spending hours sourcing venues and striking deals with landlords around Blackpool. They had begun in the Eagle & Child, a pub in the village of Weeton, halfway between Blackpool and Preston and just by the 2 Yorks' new home. The regiment had moved up to the barracks some two months ago from their previous home in Chepstow, Gwent.

Jonno had overestimated the wine requirement, and at dinner early in the evening the company was faced with a veritable wine lake to consume, which they did with gusto. They moved on in hired mini-buses, singing Middlesbrough FC songs, a few bouts of 'There's only one Jake Little!', and the first verse of the Green Howards regimental song, 'The Bonnie English Rose'.

> Old England's emblem is the Rose
> There is no other flower
> Hath half the graces that adorn
> This beauty of the bower
> And England's daughters are as fair
> As any bud that blows . . .

By the time they reached Blackpool, a few were the worse for wear – particularly Jonno and Jimmy Lynas and Andy Breach, a lieutenant who was to get the rank of acting captain on the tour. A tall twenty-six-year-old, Breach had been trained as an accountant but ditched that career to join the army. He had been in about three years by now and would act as a senior platoon commander for Jake.

One man who was stone-cold sober that night was Jake's second in command, Captain Nick Mantell. Nicknamed 'the Boy' for his youthful looks, Mantell was the son of a legendary Green Howard and former SAS officer and, like Breach, had been in the army for three years. They had been in training together, in fact, although Mantell got promoted faster because he was a graduate. That night Mantell was getting grief as he was unable to drink because he had an early flight to catch.

The men trawled through a few bars. At one rather empty club, Lynas jumped up and performed a pole dance. Between water holes they lined up to get a photo taken. The first passer-by could not work the camera.

'That civvie is broke. Get me another one!' ordered Jake.

That was before they settled at the Walkabout, where the little discussion with the bouncers occurred.

Although the behaviour was 'slightly undesirable', as Jake put it, it did show how well bonded the team already was. This was very much their final blowout before departure.

Jake ordered the company to disperse and to reform at a night-club. 'That's how we were. The lads were ready for a fight, but Jake ruled us all. We were gelled as a unit,' recalled Lynas. And the evening ended peacefully.

It had been a jovial night, concentrated mainly on getting the beers in. For the next six months, any alcohol, they knew, would be strictly forbidden. And then, as they were soldiers in a dangerous profession, there was always that extra feeling in the back of their minds. They knew what Afghanistan was like. They knew that perhaps this might be the last drink and their last real word with someone who might not return.

'Quite a few of the lads were slightly apprehensive,' remembered Jake later, 'but all seemed to be excited about the tour. I think I spoke to everybody that night over countless beers, and my over-riding memory was how happy they all were. We had a strong and close team, and that bred confidence amongst them. You know the training had been so intense that we all just wanted to get on with it.'

Jake woke up the next morning on Blackpool beach.

3. The Fort of Moses

*Headquarters, International Security and
Assistance Force (ISAF), Kabul, late September*

The phone rang on the desk of Dan McNeill, the commander of the International Security Assistance Force of NATO in Afghanistan. 'The president is on the line,' said his assistant.

President Hamid Karzai was like that. Never reluctant to pick up the phone himself but sometimes hard to reach when you wanted him. No one seemed to know his mobile number, and there wasn't a switchboard at the palace. For days you might speak to him constantly, and then for a while he would just disappear.

The president's tones were hushed, as if he were trying to be conspiratorial. A Taliban commander from the sensitive Helmand town of Musa Qala was ready for betrayal. He had come to see Karzai in the quiet of the night and told him, 'I want to come over to your side.' Karzai was playing all mysterious. 'I can't tell you his name for now,' he said. But he was clearly excited. This could be a turning point, just what both men had been waiting for. The Taliban commander had left Kabul, but he would be coming back.

Ever since the British had retreated from Musa Qala a year back, the town had been a source of controversy. They had made a 'truce' with the town's elders for them to keep the town peaceful. Most Americans thought it was a thinly disguised deal with the Taliban. On 2 February, two days before McNeill had taken command in Kabul, the Taliban had rolled back into the town. McNeill got his spokesman to promise his forces would return.

'We will take it back but in a manner and timing of our choosing,' said Mark Laity, a NATO press officer. 'It's not a question of if, but when.'

McNeill had wanted to act immediately. He suggested to Karzai that a mission be organized to recapture the place. He had enough forces. Karzai had said 'not yet'. Everything about Musa Qala spelled trouble, and Karzai was unwilling to gamble his credibility on a new venture there. He wanted to go on working with the elders. With hindsight, McNeill wondered if it had been a mistake to ask him. Perhaps McNeill should have just gone ahead. But once he had popped the question, and the president had declined, it meant he had become stuck. It would have been a gross affront to go ahead now without Karzai's explicit backing.

Now, McNeill gently put the question again. Was now the time to take some action? To start planning for the town's recapture? But Karzai said no. 'Don't do anything for now.' By McNeill's tally – and he was keeping a note – that was the fifth time that Karzai had turned him down on Musa Qala.

In the big military scheme of things, a town like Musa Qala hardly seemed important. And yet it was. The war was not just about adding up the number of towns you held or the strength of the enemy. It was about winning the psychological advantage. The name Musa Qala translated literally meant the 'Fort of Moses', and it was becoming as important as the name sounded.

Musa Qala was like a sore wound that was festering. Leaving the Taliban there meant a constant reminder of the fault-lines that lay embedded between Britain and America. It gave the impression of NATO impotence, was a symbol of Taliban alternative government and also gave the Taliban a secure base inside the country from where they could stage operations across the south. And it had a central role in the opium trade. For McNeill, a lot came down to opium. Follow the money. He could not understand why the Brits did not quite get it. It wasn't an accident that Helmand was both the world's capital of heroin production and the most volatile region of the country.

Mention an operation to take back Musa Qala to the Brits, McNeill knew, and they would start to get all nervous. They had been so damn keen on their agreement with the tribes that had covered their withdrawal from the town the previous October. They had tried so hard to sell its virtues: in such a defensive way

35

that it seemed pretty obvious they hardly believed their own words. When the agreement was made – by the then governor of Helmand, Daoud, and indirectly by the British under the then commander, Brigadier Ed Butler – it was portrayed as a deal with the elders of the town. But every indication the Americans had was that it was really an agreement with the Taliban itself. And it was negotiated from a position of weakness.[12]

Over the winter, the British had claimed the agreement was working, and that the Taliban were staying out of the town. A million dollars' worth of reconstruction projects were earmarked to support the agreement. And a new police force – that the locals approved of – was due to get trained.

McNeill had been briefed on the deal at the British Embassy in Washington. Then on his way out to Afghanistan he had got a request to stop by in London and was briefed again to say what a good deal it was. But McNeill was sceptical. As far as he was concerned the Taliban and their allies, the drugs bosses, had moved back in within days. When he got to Kabul, Karzai had told him bluntly that the deal was a failure and claimed he'd had nothing to do with it.

McNeill was now getting word of something new going on down in Helmand with the Brits, something that was causing tension between them and President Karzai. After Karzai's phone call, he asked an intelligence officer if he knew who the Taliban leader from Musa Qala was that Karzai was talking about. He found some way to avoid the question. Intel people were good at that.

4. Among the Taliban

Gereshk district centre, 6 October

To the Guards officer the civilian official looked like a native. He spoke the language. He wore a turban, the long cotton pyjamas and a woollen waistcoat. And he had a wild, scraggly beard. His hair was ginger, but then Afghans came in many shapes and sizes. Perhaps this was an Uzbek from the north of the country, perhaps the lost child of a Russian soldier.

Captain Rob Sugden had not been in Afghanistan long when he first saw this strange figure. As a member of the Coldstream Guards – the battalion that was broken up during this deployment and sent in different directions – Sugden had been put in charge of working with the police force in the town of Gereshk.

Aged twenty-seven and the son of a half-Kenyan father who had served in the army, Sugden was a high-flyer. He had joined after an Oxford University geography degree. He had been an officer now for just over three years and had come to Afghanistan after a spell of guarding Buckingham Palace. Nothing in his background could have prepared him for Helmand.

Sugden was present today at a strange meeting. On one side were a couple of colonels, the Afghan chief of police, some British officials and then this strange 'Uzbek'. Sugden was informed that he was in fact Irish. And that his name was Michael Semple.

The party of people had come down to meet two tribal leaders, Mullah Qassim and Mullah Bashir. The meeting was important because, until a few weeks back, they and their men were Taliban. Now they were known simply as 'the Group'.

Sugden got a fill-in from his commanders. 'We were told they were indeed ex-Taliban and this was the beginnings of a reconciliation programme,' he remembered. But the details were scarce.

Semple struck Sugden as very laid-back and 'not fazed by rank or anything like that'. Obviously, he had spent a lot of 'time with generals or presidents . . . he was very at ease, a very kind of calm guy. He didn't so much lead the proceedings, but it was quite obvious that he was central to them. And they kind of came in the whirlwind, stayed about two-and-a-half hours, and then they all disappeared again.'

Sugden was told to do some monitoring of the Group, 'check in with them occasionally' and see they did not get into any major dramas. He was told that Mullah Qassim would be mainly dealing with his contacts in Kabul, principally Michael Semple and one of Semple's Afghan contacts. 'He seemed to be the voice of this reconciliation from the ex-Taliban side,' said Sugden.

Mullah Qassim, it transpired later, had just two business cards in his wallet: Michael Semple's and that of Sir Sherard Cowper-Coles, the British ambassador.

Talking to the Taliban was a sensitive issue. In private, almost everyone thought that it needed to happen urgently. But, in public, they were wary. The politicians called it 'reconciliation' and stressed it was 'not negotiation'. If the Taliban wanted to come forward and talk about laying down their weapons, then great.

The British were the most keen on discreet contacts. Talking with the enemy was how the British did business in countering rebel forces. They had done it in Malaya with the Communist guerrillas; they had done it in Oman with the Dhofar tribesmen who backed the Communists; and they had done it with the IRA in Northern Ireland. The doctrine was simple: 'Divide your enemy. Engage with those who can be reconciled. Kill or capture those who cannot.'

In Afghanistan, the British knew, there was an honourable tradition of switching sides. A tribe might be your brutal enemy one day and then be your ally the next. When the Taliban had swept to power in Kabul in September 1996, it was not only through fighting. One warlord after another had decided to join their cause. Likewise, when the Northern Alliance toppled the

Taliban in 2001, it came about when key strongmen across the country, enticed by CIA dollars, decided to switch sides again.

Ever since they had come to Helmand, the British had been engaged quietly in a discreet programme of contacts with the Taliban. What lay behind that was an early assessment that the 'enemy' fighting NATO soldiers consisted not just of hardened ideologues but ordinary tribal Afghans who, if they might not accept the presence of foreign troops, might ultimately come to accept the Afghan government.

When a truce was struck with the elders of Musa Qala in 2006 to enable British forces to withdraw, commanders privately knew they were talking, among others, to local Taliban commanders. But, apart from covering a necessary pull-out, their hope was to use these talks to help separate out these 'tribal Taliban' from the more extremist elements based in Pakistan who opposed the deal.

As General Sir David Richards, the NATO commander at the time of the truce, told me: 'This was a real local initiative and, yes, some of them were Taliban, some of them weren't. It all depends on your definition of Taliban.'

Brought up in Dublin and Belfast and with an Irish passport, Michael Semple had moved to the region some twenty-two years earlier after he met his future Pakistani wife at Sussex University and they settled in her country. He first came to Afghanistan in 1989 – just after the Soviets had left – and began working for the British charity Oxfam.

Over the years, Semple became fluent in the languages, both the Pashtu language of the south and the Persian dialect, Dari, used in the western provinces and in big cities like Kabul. He began very early on to adopt local dress. It was practical; it put people at ease; and most seemed to regard it as a mark of respect.

By the time the Taliban were evicted from Kabul at the end of 2001, there were few foreigners left who had such deep knowledge of the troubled country that Afghanistan had become, or such a fat contacts book. By then, he was working as a political officer for the United Nations, along with his close friend the Northern

Irishman Mervyn Patterson, who, like Semple, had now been working in the country for years.

One former British diplomat and author Rory Stewart, who knew Afghanistan well, would describe Semple and Patterson as 'two of the best political officers in the country . . . There is no shortage in Kabul of charmers with flattering analyses and tickets home. But there are few such genuine and constant friends of Afghanistan.'

When one Irish ambassador met Karzai to present his credentials, the president told him: 'Michael knows every Afghan.' At the time, it seemed like a compliment to Semple. But, for the president, someone with such deep knowledge was also someone to fear.

It was a message taken by Semple's son, Eireamhan, down a crackly phone line in November 2001 that had begun it all. A Taliban leader named Abdul Hakim Munib asked the boy to take down his satellite phone number. By now Kabul had fallen into the hands of the Northern Alliance and the Americans. The Taliban had become fugitives. When Semple got back to him, Munib said, 'Whatever the UN is doing, I want to be part of it.'

The Americans were on the hunt for Osama bin Laden and they regarded his Taliban allies as equally complicit in the attack of 11 September. But Semple, in his role as a United Nations official, was able to work around the edges – helping those Taliban who wanted to declare early and publicly that they backed the new government. He helped bring them into the *loya jirga*, the gathering of tribal leaders that had endorsed Karzai as president.

Munib ended up as a provincial governor. Another one who phoned up was an old Mujahidin fighter named Salam Rocketi (awarded that name for his skill in the use of rocket-propelled grenades). Rocketi had become the Taliban's eastern corps commander. But Semple helped him survive the vetting process for parliamentary elections, and he was elected. There were others he could not save, who wanted to join the new government but were denounced as terrorists and who ended up in Guantanamo Bay, he said.

From the very beginning, Semple saw a tragedy unfolding. There had been those in the Taliban who were hardcore Islamists, people who fight foreign forces. But there were others who had joined for different reasons, for example because they welcomed the security that the Taliban had brought, or just for career reasons.

Now, with the 'war on terror' declared, every Talib was being branded a terrorist. US special forces hared round the country looking to catch them 'dead or alive'. Some managed to slip back peacefully to their homes. But they lived in fear of denunciation by jealous rivals. So some fled across the border into Pakistan – and back into the patronage of the Taliban's old leadership.

'What you had was a shift to predatory mode,' Semple said, 'where the warlords and those with connections to Karzai came back and started grabbing land and booty. They were seizing weapons, cars and stored opium. And sometimes they were tricking Americans into going after so-called terrorists. It forced people over to Quetta – to where the Taliban leadership had stayed on.'

Two years after 9/11, the old Taliban leadership started to get new sources of money. They were physically closer now to Al Qaeda and tapped into the same Gulf Arabs who were prepared to fund the terror network. And the actions of the foreigners and the warlords Karzai had installed started to encourage the idea of a war against the foreigners. The Taliban had started to recrystallize.

Now employed by the European Union, Semple was tasked to assist an official reconciliation programme – reaching through his old contact books and helping steer people out of the insurgency. For his partner he recruited General Naquib Stanikzai, who had quit as head of the Taliban's air force on the day after the US bombed all his planes. Stanikzai was a nationalist who had served under one regime after another. He had the virtue that almost everyone on both sides knew him.

Nearly 5,000 people were 'reconciled' through the official channels, and in a few cases it did some good. President Karzai claimed the reconciliation was vital. He used to get emotional on the subject, once appearing tearfully on television and offering to go round and knock on the door of Mullah Omar and another top rebel commander to urge them to end their violence. 'If I find their address, there is no need for them to come to me, I'll personally go there and get in touch with them,' he said.

But Semple became convinced that Karzai's public rhetoric and the whole official programme was bogus. 'I realized the official show was seriously underperforming; no one in government really gave a damn.' Few of those 'turned' were anything significant. Those who were important were treated abysmally, and worst of all the security guarantees were 'totally meaningless'. Semple and his team had given assurances to people who changed sides but 'before you knew it they had been targeted by corrupt, wicked officials and locked up'.

Semple also thought it was pointless targeting individuals. Whole tribes, villages and families were involved in the rebellion, and they needed to be dealt with collectively. He began to think of the western-funded official programme as simply another way of handing out money to the cronies of those in power.

It was clear to him that the talks with the Taliban had to be bolder and distant from the official channels. There had to be another path opened. But he knew this too would need government approval. Only with the backing of Afghan security agencies could the 'package deals' be guaranteed to protect a group's security and livelihood after they changed sides.

Of all the ten provinces he was working in, Semple found most interest in Helmand, particularly from the British there. He would reckon he got in touch with all but three or four of the province's rebel networks. 'I was able to work deep into the insurgency, face to face, heart to heart, with a large proportion of insurgents in Helmand.'

That summer, Taliban leaders and elders in six villages up the river from Gereshk were contacted. At least six Taliban leaders were reconciled, with 150 fighters. Among them were Mullah Qassim and Mullah Bashir, the Taliban that the Coldstream Guards now had under their wing. On the ground the initiative was backed by the British. But Semple made sure he got Afghan backing, both from the Interior Ministry and from the governor of Helmand.

In the end he had probably spoken to more than 200 Taliban commanders. 'I think I probably got to meet more commanders than Mullah Omar himself,' he told me with a smile, referring to the reclusive Taliban supreme leader.

After they met the leadership of the ex-Taliban Group down in Gereshk with Semple, Captain Sugden and his sergeant-major, Michael Murphy, helped them set themselves up as a militia running a checkpoint in the green zone. They used to ask them about life in the Taliban and why they had joined. The answer to them was obvious, recalled Sugden, and not 'particularly deep'.

'Helmand was an utter Taliban stronghold. So, if you were a young man, you looked at this tidal wave of Taliban force that was sweeping through Helmand. Everyone else had joined the Taliban, why would you not? It was just the thing to do.'

After the Soviets had left, they said, there had just been total chaos. The Taliban had brought a religious and calming influence. 'They used a lot of force, but they were seen as a good thing. And of course they are all Muslim so they were glad to have a Muslim entity taking control.'

They only got disillusioned when they saw some of the Taliban's more brutal side – like the corporal punishment, the death penalties that they'd dole out for various minor transgressions like whistling or dancing or humming a tune. By then they were trapped and could not pull out. For Sugden, all this underlined 'how important it was to extend the olive branch to those kinds of people'.

Sugden and Murphy got to like the Group more than anyone they had dealt with. Compared to the Afghan police, whom they described as the 'dregs of society', these men were polite, enthusiastic, punctual and did whatever they promised. Were these men a sign of how NATO's enemies could become their allies? The British could only hope.

PART 2

The Population Is the Prize

'You know, some brigadiers and battalion commanders aren't going to like what I'm going to tell them.
They won't be able to use battalions or companies in sweeping movements any more. They'll have to reconcile themselves to war being fought by junior commanders down to lance-corporals.'

Lieutenant General Sir Harold Briggs, director of operations, Malaya Emergency, 1950.[13]

5. Arriving in Helmand

On board an RAF Hercules,
Kabul to Kandahar, 7 October

Brigadier Andrew Mackay was finally heading for Helmand. At his side was his military assistant, Captain Euan Goodman. They were clutching a pile of briefing notes.

The next day he would reach his new headquarters in Lashkar Gah and two days later he would assume command of the multi-national brigade of more than 7,000 soldiers in Helmand as well as all the British servicemen and servicewomen deployed across Afghanistan.

Mackay believed in the mission but was not someone who approached it with blinkered eyes. It was an irony that the more you cared about the Afghan war, the more critical your voice became. Those who hardly cared rarely bothered to dissent.

Up in Kabul these last two days, the brief on the politics of Afghanistan had not been encouraging. One senior western diplomat told him bluntly that President Karzai was 'not the president we want or need'. Karzai was isolated and increasingly erratic. He could not manage governance. He was surrounded, many said, by corrupt and venal ministers.

The advice the brigadier was getting was widespread in military and diplomatic circles. One senior British military officer spelled out to me what was now an accepted view: 'I think there are issues right at the top of the government in Afghanistan from Karzai downwards. There are question marks over whether even his own family is closely involved in the drugs trade. My understanding is that is probably the case.' Even some of Karzai's own advisers told me the same story. One senior Afghan diplomat said, 'Every time there is a corrupt minister identified, the western governments force Karzai to sack him. But each time this corrupt man is reappointed to another post. You can forgive the president for this once or twice. But, after a while, you have to ask yourself: why is this man protecting these people?'

For Mackay, these briefings made for depressing reading. How was the British army supposed to support the Afghan government and extend its reach of power in Helmand unless the president took decisive steps to purge the warlords whose actions helped to encourage the Taliban?

Back in London, the atmosphere had been no more positive.

Perhaps it was a matter of timing. The build-up to his deployment came when the British government had seemed in virtual meltdown. This was when a major mortgage lender, Northern Rock, had collapsed and had had to be bailed out; when Gordon Brown had threatened a general election and then changed his mind; and when Brown was accused of playing politics over the army when he visited Iraq during the Tory conference. This was a time when one could find officials in Whitehall describing a prime minister who was dithering and inaccessible, did not understand what the military was up to and was hardly interested anyway because Afghanistan was not going to win or lose votes.

Mackay himself, as he toured the offices of civilian and military experts and leaders before he left for Afghanistan, had been struck by what he found to be a succession of relentlessly downbeat assessments. He questioned whether, at least in London, there really was the *will* to succeed. There seemed to be plenty of advice – but a paucity of anyone with solutions.

Meeting one general, Mackay told him how struck he was by the negative views he was hearing. 'Have we actually got the will to succeed here?' he asked. The general replied that Britain had three options – to stay in Helmand and provide the resources to succeed; to muddle through; or to get out. The general said, 'You can guarantee that it will be the second option that we pursue:

constant muddling through, making it up as we go along, being reactive, not proactive.'

For Mackay, it had been a long journey to take up command in Helmand. At fifty, he was one of the oldest commanders of an operational brigade in living memory. Born in Elgin, Scotland, and educated in Edinburgh, he was the son of an army musician. He himself took an unusual path to the military, becoming an officer after a three-year career serving as a policeman in Hong Kong, including running a drugs squad.

After returning to get his army commission, Mackay had seen combat in Northern Ireland as a junior officer and returned there again as a company commander. Getting a degree from the Open University, he rose through the ranks and finally took command of his own regiment, the King's Own Scottish Borderers. But he was disappointed that it was not deployed on operations during his time.

Deployed in his career to senior staff posts in Bosnia, Kosovo and Iraq, Mackay had established his reputation not in running combat operations but in thinking through what happened afterwards, what the army called 'stabilization'. A critic of what he described as the incompetence and dysfunction of what happened after the 2003 invasion of Iraq, Mackay had turned his 52 Brigade, which he took over in December 2004, into specialists in addressing the obvious shortcomings – namely the total lack of planning for how to establish a stable government and the rule of law after Saddam's army was defeated. He proposed to have a small but deployable headquarters that could plug that gap. Headquartered at Edinburgh Castle, 52 Brigade was what the army called a 'Type B' brigade. In command of several regiments when they were back at their bases and with a small role in running the annual Edinburgh Tattoo, it was not earmarked for any operational duties. Mackay started with barely seven full-time staff officers working for him that were in any way deployable on a mission. Then in late summer 2006, as the Afghanistan venture escalated and the Iraq war de-escalated only slowly, the army ran out of 'Type A' brigades. Mackay got a call to say his brigade was earmarked to be promoted to the first division and he was to lead its deployment to Helmand for the 'winter tour' beginning October 2007. His operational brigade staff would swell from seven to 150.

But gaining the command would also win him some enemies. Some in the army spoke of him and the brigade with undisguised scorn. Was the brigade that helped to run the Edinburgh Tattoo really suitable to run an actual war? Were his men simply B-list players? Did they actually know how to lead and fight?

Over the previous year, Mackay had felt like a student: getting to grips with Afghanistan, with thinking on counter-insurgency, and with the principles of management of a large organization.

He decided he should aspire to run his brigade in Helmand along the lines dictated by General Templar, who ran the Malaya campaign:[14]

1. Get the priorities right.
2. Get the instructions right.
3. Get the organization right.
4. Get the right people in the organization.
5. Get the right spirit into the people.
6. Leave them to get on with it.

One of the most striking things Mackay found was the lack of clear direction from above. There was more a sense that 'we were making it up as we go along.'

Ever since the disasters of the First World War, western armies had adopted an important doctrine called 'Mission Command'. A commander set out his intentions and his basic objective. And then a subordinate was left to work out how to accomplish that mission in detail. It was the opposite of micro-management. It brought flexibility and speed and brought out the best in people. But a strategy for counter-insurgency, thought Mackay, had to be developed over the long term. It wasn't something that could simply be thought anew every six months when a new brigadier came along. His formal orders from British headquarters turned out to be simply a cut-and-paste version of those to the previous commander. They were 'riddled with errors'. He had been surprised to find they got the name of the British task force wrong in several places. Mackay put that down to careless staff work. But in some ways it might appear symptomatic.

It was true that the chain of command was confused. Effectively, he would have four bosses. First and foremost, British forces in Afghanistan were subordinate to NATO, and Mackay was in a chain of command headed by the American four-star general Dan McNeill. Secondly, as COMBRITFOR, the commander of all British forces in Afghanistan, Mackay would also be reporting in the British hierarchy, in the first instance to Lieutenant General Nick Houghton, the Commander of Joint Operations, at the UK's Permanent Joint Headquarters. Thirdly, since the British mission was to support the government of Afghanistan, Mackay had to do, or at least take account of, what the Afghans wanted: in particular the Afghan president, Hamid Karzai, and his governor in Helmand. His last boss was the British ambassador in Kabul. Sir Sherard Cowper-Coles was officially in charge of all Her Majesty's interests in the country and thus had a right to be consulted about military matters on behalf of the British government. Britain's policy was of 'civilian lead' – the military acting in support of civilian objectives like reconstruction. So Mackay also had to take advice from a Provincial Reconstruction Team in Lashkar Gah that reported to Cowper-Coles.

The chain of command, then, was about as clear and neat as twigs in a bird's nest. The real problem with this mess was that, when things went wrong, everyone could blame everyone else. No one truly felt as if they were in charge. Or had the authority to take real risks. Or show moral courage. It was a set-up for muddle-headed thinking.

Compared to the few hundred paratroopers who had begun the deployment to Helmand a year and a half before, Mackay now had a formidable force under his command. As he took charge, the part of Helmand where government troops ventured would be divided into three – with the north zone around Sangin, Now Zad and Kajaki run by 40 Commando of the Royal Marines, the centre around Gereshk run by a Danish battalion, and the south around Garmsir under the Household Cavalry Regiment. The 2 Yorks battle group, including Major Jake Little's company, would work in parallel across the province with the Afghan army.

Most problematic for Mackay was not his fighting soldiers but the lack of aviation. Helicopters had made a critical difference to winning the insurgencies of Malaya, Oman and Northern Ireland. The helicopter most adapted for the heat and dust of Afghanistan was the heavy-lift Chinook, with its signature twin rotors. But Mackay would have just seven at his disposal, of which he could expect – on a good day – to have only four that were serviceable: two for emergencies and two for regular transport.

Sitting on the plane, Mackay put the politics and logistics out of his mind for a second. He had some more immediate issues to think through.

The last few months had been difficult ones for the Helmand Task Force. Twenty-eight soldiers had been killed in the previous six months, as well as two Danes allegedly killed by a British Javelin missile. And additionally from among his own troops from 52 Brigade, most of whom were arriving ahead of him in Helmand, there had already been two deaths – that of Corporal Ivano Violino, an engineer, killed on 17 September, and Major Alexis Roberts, a company commander with the Gurkhas, killed by a roadside bomb on 4 October.

All wars carry the risk of casualties and tragedy. So does normal army training, which had its regular share of fatal accidents. But Mackay got the sense from Whitehall that public support was shallow for this war. Any attempt to devise a long-term strategy to win the war would be pointless if the costs – human and financial – could not be sustained.

In the previous few weeks, an offensive by the departing brigade had not only swept through the green zone along the Helmand

River, it had also established a series of new patrol bases that extended the area of the province under government control. Mackay was going to have to decide whether those lines should be maintained, how they could be consolidated, and whether his forces should try to push further.

And then there was the question that had faced every British commander since they got here: what should be done about Musa Qala?

6. Mullah Salaam

Presidential palace, Kabul, late October

Sherard Cowper-Coles opened his black canvas briefcase and pulled out a map of Afghanistan that was folded inside. It was an RAF 'Escaper's Map' printed on fake silk: the sort of thing used by downed pilots to navigate out of enemy territory. His was specially made and, printed in the languages of Central Asia, it said: 'I am British and I do not speak your language. I will not harm you!'

They were in Karzai's outer study in the palace. It was an elegant room – ordered but not opulent. The sofas and chairs were dark-stained wood, and, despite the secret nature of the talks, the windows were left open. Shrieks from peacocks outside would interrupt proceedings.

It was the usual crowd. In the centre were the key players: the president, General McNeill, Cowper-Coles and the US ambassador, Bill Wood. In the outer orbit were the key advisers – including Karzai's chief of staff, national security adviser and head of intelligence.

The meeting was to debate a war. But no one seemed to have a map.

Karzai wanted to talk about Musa Qala. He said he had been on the phone with a certain Mullah Salaam, a Taliban commander. Salaam was from the Pirzai subtribe of the Alizai: the tribe that dominated northern Helmand.

'I've been speaking to him on the phone. He says the people in Musa Qala are fed up with the Taliban. He was saying, "If you give me some weapons and help we can take Musa Qala. There's no need for military forces."

'He is at home in his compound now,' continued Karzai. Salaam was apparently already in conflict with other Taliban leaders. And they were threatening to attack his home.

The men who ran the Afghanistan pictured on Cowper-Coles's map clustered round and tried to locate the spot where Salaam was holed up. It was a village called Shah Kariz, which lay between Musa Qala and Kajaki.

'We've got to find a way of helping him,' said the president.

Cowper-Coles was cautious in his response, and for good reason. The one thing he knew was that Britain *did not need* another hasty and ill-planned military adventure in Helmand. That would undermine everything he was trying to do.

The ambassador had been in his post in Kabul now since May, after a hurried transfer from Riyadh, Saudi Arabia. The idea behind his appointment was to beef up Britain's diplomatic presence, reflecting its now £1.6 billion-a-year commitment to Afghanistan. His position was now made the second-most senior ambassadorship to any country in the world.

What he came to discover was that British politicians were being misled. Endless reports from both the military and the diplomats had poured forth a stream of stories of progress. Yet the facts on the ground were at odds with these reports. The ambassador came to see that the country as a whole was slipping ever deeper into rebellion. Back in the spring, three permanent secretaries from the Foreign Office, the Ministry of Defence and the Department for International Development had toured the theatre. Their report, said UK officials, began: 'Overall, we are optimistic.' How exactly had they reached this conclusion? others wondered.

Cowper-Coles believed firmly his job was to send back the unvarnished truth. 'I thought that one of the things that had bedevilled our engagement in Iraq was the failure to offer ministers honest advice,' he told me when I met him later. He added: 'You know, a lot of people had been rather naive about what could be done here in Afghanistan. There was still sort of a hangover of misplaced optimism.'

A month after he arrived, Gordon Brown took over from Tony Blair as prime minister, opening the door for a fresh view of what

Britain was doing in the country. There were some in Brown's new government who were said by Whitehall sources to regard the whole Helmand venture as a huge strategic blunder. The new Foreign Secretary, David Miliband, was 'very insistent with me then that he wanted honest advice and he got it,' recalled Cowper-Coles.

Soon afterwards, the ambassador's telegrams were getting a reputation in Whitehall. There were murmurs from the military about their 'undue negativity'.

In Helmand, the ambassador saw a military campaign that was beating the Taliban tactically. But he was said to think the army's policy of constant rotation of commanders was a poor idea, and that the campaign had also still to address the root cause of the conflict. The Taliban were strong because the Afghan government was weak. And the people of Helmand had not decided who to support.

Of the chiefs of the different government departments in Helmand, only four out of eight could even read or write. One Karzai adviser was said to have told the ambassador there were only 200 capable officials across the whole Afghan government. The current Helmand governor, Asadullah Wafa, was ruling the province by mobile phone with virtually no staff. It was almost medieval.

Between Cowper-Coles in Kabul and Adam Thomson, the senior official for the region in London, the elements of a 'strategy refresh' were now coming together. Cowper-Coles told me: 'We faced a persistent insurgency that I was convinced wasn't going to be dealt with by military force alone. We had a serious counter-narcotics problem. We concluded early on that success here was going to take a very long time.'

The campaign in Helmand, they believed, needed civilian leadership. The emphasis should be on building up the Afghans. Above all the accent should be on the long term. The population would not be won over by shiny new bridges or brand new schools or wells. The Soviets had tried that. What counted for Afghans was to know who was going to be in charge in five years' time. Then they would step off the fence and back a winner.

In his telegrams back to London, according to other sources, much of what Cowper-Coles began advocating involved a better understanding of the tribal politics of Afghanistan. He began to argue for creating a sort of home guard in the villages to be called Community Defence Volunteers, and for a greater emphasis on reconciliation, with some real outreach to the Taliban, at least to those who could perhaps be turned.

The arrival of Mullah Salaam, then, was exactly the kind of opportunity the ambassador wanted. And if Mullah Salaam could be turned, how many more Taliban leaders were out there waiting to be reconciled?

Yet something held him back. The one thing the ambassador did not want was for Salaam's phone calls to become an excuse for another operation in Musa Qala that ended in embarrassment for Britain, or worse, a bloodbath. Seven British servicemen had died defending Musa Qala in vain last year.

'I had a gun with me, a pistol in the pocket. I freed myself with it,' said Mullah Salaam, describing his daring escape after being kidnapped by the Taliban. 'They came and arrested me. The people helped me, and they released me. I made my stand against them.'

He was talking by phone to the Pashto-speaking source handler from British military intelligence at the brigade headquarters.

'What's your situation now?' said the handler.

'They have come back. They are surrounding my home. I need some weapons,' he said.

The handler said he would see what he could do. He could not promise anything.

Military intelligence had been in touch with Salaam for a few days now. They had even sent an agent up to his compound deep within Taliban territory to deliver a satellite phone to him. But he was still a mystery to them.

Their files included reports of a meeting in June between Salaam and an Afghan who worked on Taliban contacts with the European Union diplomat, Michael Semple. Salaam had claimed he was no longer an active fighter but kept a group of twenty bodyguards for protection. Swearing he had no plans to fight the Afghan government, his main concern was how to get hold of more weapons to protect himself. Semple's adviser could not help with that. In the weeks that followed Semple's team kept in touch with him – 'softening him up' for his switch of allegiance.

Two months later, Salaam began appearing on the diagrams that indicated Taliban leaders that could potentially be targeted for 'kill or capture' operations. And then, in the last days of Ramadan (which ended on 12 October), returning from a trip to Pakistan, Salaam had gone up to Kabul and slipped into the presidential palace.

There was little other detail. Salaam was said to have once been a Taliban governor in Uruzghan province next door to Helmand. He was also said to have fought in the 1990s with the Taliban army – helping in the bloody battle to take the northern city of Mazar e Sharif.

Salaam would also claim he had been present in the *shura* a year back when the British had negotiated handing Musa Qala back to its elders. He said he had watched the agreement collapse in the following months after NATO started bombing. But, like many local Taliban leaders, he said, he had been offended by the subsequent arrival in Musa Qala of the most extreme of jihadists. 'Outsiders came in,' he told me later. 'They were making jackets for explosives, suicide vests. And they were putting heroin factories everywhere.'

'We have got to look for the tipping point,' said Mackay when he was briefed on the latest phone call. His staff could see he was enthused by Salaam's approach. 'If there's going to be a tribal uprising, there will be a point where it becomes a reality, and it will happen quite quickly.'

For the Brigadier, the very core of a successful counter-insurgency campaign should be the identification of the reasons why an enemy was fighting – and then addressing what grievances could reasonably be dealt with.

The more he learned of the Helmand Taliban, the more convinced he was that so many of them were on completely the wrong side. The bulk of the fighters, he thought, were not terrorists or jihadists or ideologues. They were ordinary tribesmen who were embittered with their government – and desperate for security.

Salaam could be a golden opportunity, a man who could help turn those tribes. If it worked, he offered the opportunity of retaking the town of Musa Qala without a fight. But working out how to help him was another matter. The best Mackay could do was send Apache helicopters and fighter jets to swoop around his compound two days running in a 'show of force' to scare off the Taliban threatening Salaam.

Salaam clearly needed more help, but, as Mackay reported back to London, President Karzai's ideas of exploiting the Salaam factor to drive the Taliban from Musa Qala seemed vague and floundering. After all, Salaam's compound at Shah Kariz was deep behind enemy lines. And if Salaam was already calling up the military for help, he was hardly going to have the strength to take a Taliban stronghold with his own fighters, whatever Karzai might suggest.

For now, barely a fortnight after taking command, and with the tempo of fighting picking up again elsewhere in Helmand, Mackay's brigade already had plenty to deal with without an escapade into new territory. There had been far too many of them, he thought. But they should keep their eyes out for that tipping point.

At the palace in Kabul, Cowper-Coles met President Karzai. The president was convinced Mullah Salaam was the real thing: a Taliban and tribal leader with some genuine influence. The British confessed they knew almost nothing about him.

From now the Salaam operation was to be handled direct from Kabul, with the assistance of the British. This was not running a secret agent. Salaam was not a secret source. Now he had a satellite phone, Salaam started to talk to everyone. He talked to his British contacts. He called Michael Semple's team. He talked to contacts at Afghan intelligence and Afghan officials of every variety. But, most of all, this man from a small town who no one really seemed to know stayed in direct and personal touch with the president of Afghanistan himself.

7. Corrupt Measures

*Forward Operating Base Keenan, in the green zone
north-east of Gereshk*

It was a visit to a base in the green zone that finally clinched Brigadier Mackay's opinion there had been too much killing: too many pointless 'clearances' of Taliban territory and too much emphasis on counting the enemy dead. For the last six days, Forward Operating Base Keenan had been run by the eighty-strong 3 Company of the Coldstream Guards, part of Mackay's 52 Brigade. The place had been captured during the previous brigade's push north from Gereshk. The new arrivals thought they would be there for four to six weeks, and then rotate out through Camp Bastion. Mackay told them they would spend six months there.

'You're going to be staying here. You need to get to know your ground, to know your enemy and you've got to get to know your population.'

The Guardsmen took a look at the bare interior of the base. The previous unit here, A Company of the 2 Mercians, had been living out of their bergens (rucksacks) and day sacks, and with nothing else there except some walls made of Hesco Bastion, the mud-filled wire baskets that had become the instant defensive ramparts on British and American bases across Iraq and Afghanistan. They looked shocked. One turned round: 'But, sir, there is no population!'

They had all fled; they were living in the desert. 'And sure enough, when you put your head over the wall, there was no population,' Mackay recalled. Looking out of the *sangars*, what the soldiers called their watchtowers, Mackay could see the ruins of a local school. The Taliban had used it as a firing position and so it had been pounded by the Mercians and then pounded again these last few days. Across the province, the destruction was not hard to see.

Mackay's brigade was taking over Helmand after a summer of intense violence. Brigadier John Lorimer, his predecessor, had taken the fight into the countryside between the towns along the Helmand River. Putting together large-sized manoeuvre forces, flanked by armour, he attacked the Taliban in their strongholds. But Lorimer did not have the forces to hold every compound or village he captured. The Taliban would creep back in afterwards. He described his operations to journalists as 'mowing the lawn'.

Lorimer's last operation, code-named 'Palk Wahel', had involved a sweep through the green zone between Gereshk and Sangin. It had proved costly – and controversial. In the month of September, seven British soldiers lost their lives, and another was killed the following month as he returned from the same operation.

Within a week of Mackay taking command, the Taliban had shown they were far from cowed. On 15 October, a Danish company commander, Major Anders Storrud, was injured by mortar fire just north of Gereshk and died of his wounds. The same day, the Royal Marines base at FOB Inkerman on the outskirts of Sangin came under full-scale attack.

Four days later, the Mercians were on the helipad at Keenan – ready to fly off – when mortars started landing, and rockets started pounding the base and the checkpoints around. For the Mercians, it was just routine. They did not need an officer or a senior to tell the private soldiers what to do.

Lieutenant Daniel McMahon, a young officer with 3 Company, found the handover daunting. 'There were us junior officers turning up with no operational experience at all. And there were all these strong, tanned guys talking as if it was the most normal thing in the world to have fire fights, to have rocket-propelled grenades going around, and mortars landing.'

The departing soldiers had established this base and others deep into what had been Taliban-controlled countryside. But, Mackay now asked himself, to what purpose unless these places were held over the long term, and by soldiers who got to know the people? The company here – with all its tremendous fighting strength – could, if he chose, be used to push further north and to extend the boundaries of the British-controlled zone. Mackay had seen the way that soldiers like the Mercians had bounced around from one area to another. They had defeated the Taliban every time. But there was a bitter lesson learned from conflicts like the Vietnam war – that a battlefield victory might contribute little or nothing to a strategic success. There were already signs that, over the ground where the previous brigade had won their battles, the Taliban were coming back. Hundreds of the 'enemy' had been killed, but that did not seem to make the least difference. In fact, in a Pashtun culture of revenge, killing one man might recruit two others to avenge his death.

Every war was different, every terrain different, and every enemy had different tactics. But this was not an excuse for throwing out the rule book and ignoring all the hard lessons, those learned over decades about how to fight and defeat guerrilla armies.

At the heart of a winning strategy, thought Mackay, was the population. Yes, the insurgents had to be fought and defeated. But the population had to be brought to your side. When your enemy was like the Taliban and wore no uniform and blended seamlessly with the locals, only those locals could be your eyes and ears. They needed to see that you were on their side.

When it arrived in Helmand, the British army proposed to implement what they called the 'ink-spot theory', a doctrine used in the Malaya campaign to defeat a Communist revolt. It preached a cautious approach of concentrating effort on creating safe zones free of guerrilla influence from which the 'ink' of security and development would spread out gradually across the people and the terrain. People needed to see the benefits of stable government. Only then could they be allies in the war. The way the US army explained this doctrine, the idea was to clear, hold, then build. Drive the enemy from an area. Keep them away. And then start to build something positive for the population, win them over and turn their hearts against the enemy. But for the last year, as the British ranged across Helmand, Afghans had seen plenty of 'clear', precious little 'hold', and almost no 'build'.

The war had often been fought instead – despite the best of intentions – as a war against a conventional army, where the simple act of killing the enemy might somehow secure you victory. The trouble for NATO troops in Helmand and across Afghanistan was that there was rarely the number of troops required to hold an area for very long. 'We're not really doing counter-insurgency operations yet,' said one senior British general. 'We just haven't got enough people.'

Without actions to win over the population, endless operations to disrupt the enemy or to defend beleaguered government-held towns, as soldiers from the Parachute Regiment had done when they first arrived in Helmand, could be counter-productive. And that raised an uncomfortable question: had blood been shed in vain?

The sight of the destruction the war had brought, despite all the sacrifice, caused real anger among some of those freshly arrived soldiers. One young officer who visited the town of Sangin with Mackay's brigade spoke from the heart as he described his raw frustration to find that – almost six months after the town had been captured back from the Taliban – almost nothing noticeable had been done to clear the rubble of destruction, and no serious plans were in place for redevelopment, for giving something back to the people. It was not what they believed Britain was in Afghanistan for.

'All those stories that came out about the Paras and later are basically embarrassing. They aren't war!' he exclaimed. 'I mean, you were talking blokes put in unfair positions with thirty to forty men on a parapet dropping JDAMs [satellite-guided bombs] all around them night and day for weeks on end.' The effect on the local population and the towns had been disastrous, he felt. And then sweeps through the green zone over the last summer had been conducted on far too great a scale, with no real focus. 'There was no need for those blokes to die,' he confided. 'We have gone backwards. We have created rubble, and a load of blokes died clearing green zones, which is utterly pointless.'

There were other viewpoints. Many argued that in all wars it took time to find the right strategy and right tactics. All death was a tragedy and, in the preliminary stages of a long war, it was far too early to tell if someone's sacrifice had achieved something meaningful. Others said the previous brigades had fought necessary 'break-in battles', which established a psychological advantage by demonstrating to the population that the Taliban would lose every battle with the British.

Mackay diplomatically avoided discussion on the rights and wrongs of how the war had been fought until now. But, as he told his staff when he returned from his visit to FOB Keenan, he was determined to push strategy in a new direction.

 Three miles to the north-east up the Helmand River from FOB Keenan, another company of soldiers had also just arrived into the thick of fighting. Commanded by a thirty-five-year-old Oxford graduate, Major Chris Bell, the Right Flank company of the 1st Battalion, Scots Guards were mounted in Warrior armoured fighting vehicles, a new arrival to the Afghan battlefield. They were relieving 3 Company of the Grenadier Guards, who had just established a new base called FOB Arnhem.

'When we got there, it was in a pretty bad way,' recalled Bell. Mortars and rockets were coming in, he said, and 3 Company's flag was peppered with shrapnel holes. Its soldiers cheered when they saw the armour on the horizon.

The new base was on the edge of Heyderabad, a village halfway between Sangin and Gereshk with a reputation as the 'heart of darkness' – a Taliban stronghold where the stares of the farmers would send a chill through your bones and where a fight was guaranteed. As Bell was discovering, it was a place that illustrated well the dilemmas of this war. It seemed to have been 'cleared' of Taliban more often than anywhere.

Special forces also attacked the village regularly. To the north of Heyderabad and south of Sangin was FOB Robinson, the home of Task Force 32, the American special force Green Berets that operated outside NATO command. They regularly struck the village: moving through and provoking a fight. But afterwards they returned to base. The special forces operated in small numbers. They might organize a *shura* after the fighting, hand out some aid or dispense a bit of medical care and try to spread good feeling. But they weren't there to hold ground.

In the weeks that followed his arrival, Bell saw evidence that 'attrition' – the business of killing the enemy – was important. But the key thing was what came afterwards. Just as at FOB Keenan, when his soldiers arrived at Arnhem, they saw a landscape denuded of its population. 'To avoid the fighting, the locals would live in the desert,' he remembered. 'And they would walk into the green zone soon after morning prayers, do some work and then leave well before dusk to avoid the frequent fighting that took place at that time of day. They got it down to quite an art.'

As they pushed into the green zone from FOB Arnhem, the Scots Guards were confronted by a hardline Taliban commander who called himself Mullah Basheer (not to be confused with the Mullah Bashir who defected). For the Afghan army working with them the battle against Basheer became quite personal.

The Afghans had a two-way radio, and their sergeant-major spent hours trading insults with the Taliban leader, whom the Afghans called 'Basheer motherfucker'. Basheer would say, 'You sold out, you're a slave of Bush, the only thing that matters to you is the dollar, the devil's money.' The ANA sergeant-major would reply, 'You're paid in goat shit. I have money, I have schools, my children have a future.' The British cracked themselves up laughing as they listened.

Basheer finally met his end when the Afghans heard him detail his own position on his radio. 'I'm pinned down by mortar fire,' he said. And 'I'm by a tree.' There only was one tree in the area. The tree and Basheer were destroyed with a 500-pound bomb.

Basheer's death made a difference. Such Taliban leaders would intimate local people. After his death, the Scots Guards began to gain some ground. The attacks lessened off, and the people started to return. Bell pushed troops out of the base, which was on the edge of the desert, into a 'patrol base' that was in the green zone itself and among the people. It was dangerous work. 'They were very exposed, and our main effort as a company was to be ready to assist them and to keep them supplied,' said Captain Matthew Jamieson, Bell's second-in-command. The platoon was ambushed again and again as they patrolled around – often from multiple directions. And the Taliban crept up and laid mines and bombs in the fields around. One struck home, seriously injuring two men, including one lance-corporal who was hit in the eyes.

But the platoon and the company began to do small things for people like handing out blankets. They got their response. People started helping. Some began flashing lights when a Taliban patrol came close and pointing out the paths they used. Bell began to plan ambushes.

Ironically, it was 30 October, the day that Brigadier Mackay set out his new strategy for Helmand – an 'operational design' that called for a new emphasis away from short-lived 'clearances' – that Bell got his orders to move his Warrior company out of Arnhem and venture forth towards Musa Qala. He never got to do his ambushes, and the work of building up friendships with the population and of 'pacifying' Heyderabad had barely got going.

In the note circulated to all commanders, Mackay wrote: 'Unless we retain, gain and win the consent of the population within Helmand we lose the campaign. The population is the prize.' Too much emphasis placed on *attrition* of the enemy – killing them, in other words, with what the army euphemistically called 'kinetic' operations, or fighting – put consent-winning at risk and 'in reality the non-kinetic activities barely get off the ground'. Worst of all was to judge success by body counts, the routine practice of counting up the enemy dead. 'Body counts are a particularly corrupt measurement of success,' he said. They might show the effectiveness of some battle tactic but they were not a sign of success. 'Attrition of the enemy is not the object but his defeat is. This ensures that our military effort is concentrated on the "prize" – the population – and the purpose behind our presence in Helmand – pacification of the enemy and security.' You could be fighting and winning so many battles at such a speed that you could be fooled into thinking you were succeeding but 'every unnecessary bullet or bomb heightens insecurity and deters development'.

At FOB Arnhem, Bell figured they had already got this lesson. That morning at dawn, as he looked out from the base across the green zone, he could see a stirring. Smoke from cooking pots began to rise from the adobe compounds, and then their creaky metal doors began to open, and turbaned farmers began their daily trudge to their fields, some accompanied by young children with wheelbarrows to clear up rocks or herding out flocks of goats with wooden sticks. As his company prepared to leave this base, he could see the 'daily commute' from those desert mud huts was over, at least for now. The population had returned, and that was his own way of measuring their results 'rather than by killing'.

After all the early battles, it was clear the pattern of life had altered and that 'we had managed to change the whole dynamic of the area from a daily commute to avoid the fighting to people living in the green zone and reoccupying their old compounds . . .' But he knew the change might only be temporary. Bell was anxious about their departure. The soldiers replacing his were a smaller force without the heavy firepower of his Warriors. He worried the Taliban would infiltrate back.

8. The War Cabinet

Karzai's study, the presidential palace,
Kabul, 1 November

The intelligence chief was emphatic. 'This is a chance to break their backbone ... to break the tribal resistance in northern Helmand,' said Amrullah Saleh, head of the NDS, Afghanistan's secret police and intelligence service. This was the first meeting of the War Cabinet – a new body to run the war, and Musa Qala and the defection of the Taliban's Mullah Abdul Salaam was their first subject.

'This guy is not what you think, Mr President,' said Dan McNeill, the NATO commander, who was on the sofa opposite Karzai. He tried to lower expectations. 'Listen, he has got fifty-five fighters, tops, and it's probably all he ever had. He's a lightweight.'

But Karzai was firm. He was getting angry that nothing was being done. 'General, I want you to protect Mullah Salaam.'

McNeill said that Task Force Helmand already had a plan ready to deploy a company of Scots Guards soldiers (Chris Bell's armoured Warriors) up towards Salaam's home. The whole idea stuck in McNeill's craw. His preference was to have nothing to do with Salaam. If Salaam was a Taliban fighter worth having on your side, why did he need NATO's protection? But he knew this man was becoming Karzai's obsession and he knew his mission, after all, was to support the Afghan government. 'Let's put them in his compound for ten days and see what Salaam does and how many fighters he can recruit,' he said.

Cowper-Coles continued his cautious approach. He suggested a less direct intervention: keeping the Warriors nearby but not actually in his village. Karzai agreed but added: 'We have to support anyone who has turned on the Taliban. We must help Salaam *without question* in *any circumstances*!'

The president himself had just spoken to Salaam as well as to the former Helmand governor, Sher Muhammad Akhundzada. What he saw unfolding was a grand alliance of the Alizai tribe against the Taliban. Akhundzada might have imprisoned Salaam and tortured him when he was governor, but the two had now spoken and had been reconciled. Akhundzada had paid him some money.

'Salaam has told me that the two main Taliban commanders from the Alizai will work with me,' the president said. Musa Qala might be returned to government hands without the intervention of any NATO troops, thought Karzai. But, for now, Salaam needed to be kept alive.

'We're not talking here of a major military operation to take Musa Qala,' said the British ambassador. 'The idea instead is to let the population of Musa Qala come to us,' he added, in what later became something of a slogan. Karzai nodded.

McNeill left the meeting unconvinced. He wondered how diplomats like Cowper-Coles and their advisers – both UK and US – could be swept along with Karzai's rather impulsive thinking and apparently swallow this talk of a tribal solution. Perhaps they were just, well, being *diplomatic* – playing along with the palace politics. In McNeill's view, Musa Qala was in the grip of drug barons and extremists. Only force was going to drive them out.

PART 3

The Taliban Strikes Back

'*Di jin, wo tui*	Enemy advances, we withdraw
Di jiu, wo roa	Enemy rests, we harass
Di pi, wo da	Enemy tires, we attack
Di tui, wo jui	Enemy withdraws, we pursue'

Mao Tse Tung on guerrilla warfare[15]

Operation Snakebite

At 05.00 on 2 November, a day after the War Cabinet in Kabul, a large column of British troops set off from Camp Bastion to ride to the rescue of the man the soldiers would soon call 'Mullah Salami'.

At the head of more than fifty vehicles with 250 men and women on board, was Chris Bell's Warrior company. They would be the strike force, along with another eighteen armoured Mastiff vehicles from the King's Royal Hussars (the KRH). The latter's job was to protect a logistics convoy, bringing the food, fuel and ammunition to keep the hungry armoured vehicles and their crews going. There were also mortars, assault engineers, a combat troop of Royal Marine commandos and a troop of three 105 mm light guns from the Royal Artillery. Most involved would not be leaving the desert for weeks. As he surveyed the size of the force, Bell muttered: 'This guy Salami. He better be worth it. He better deliver.'

Just after first light on 3 November, a force of Royal Marine commandos crossed the Helmand River from their base in Sangin and temporarily secured the southern tip of the hostile Musa Qala wadi, allowing the convoy to cross over and reach the desert plateau around Salaam's home in Shah Kariz.

As he moved through, Bell noted the size of operation to get his force into position – requiring the greater part of 40 Commando's combat strength. If it took such combat power to get them in, it might take the same to get them out. 'Having the door in and out in an unknown area controlled by somebody else is never the most comfortable feeling,' he said later.

The mission had a name now: Operation Mar Changak, or, as the British translated it, 'Operation Snakebite'. Bell's orders were to reassure Salaam 'through a visible presence around his village but do not go in'.

The second part of his orders hinted at a future, bigger operation. He *was also to perform a 'feint', a military ruse. He was told to: 'FEINT and DECEIVE the Taliban by feinting at their Musa Qala defences – but do not be decisively engaged.'*

Mackay recalled he wanted the Taliban to get a message in capitals: 'We Are Coming To Get You.'

9. The Patrol to Khevalabad

It was quiet, far too quiet. The village was empty: not a sign of life up here. Not even a scrap of paper. Not an abandoned toy, nor a rag of clothing, only a broken wooden bucket. They felt the breeze on their sweat-covered foreheads – and it was the chill breath of ghosts.

Second Lieutenant Colin Lunn, the platoon commander, tried to peer through the darkness with his night-vision monocle. Through it he saw green circles of light from the soldiers' infra-red torches dancing on the pitch-black walls.

More whispers. The scrunch on gravel as a boot slipped. Heavy breathing. A bark from a distant dog. Then Lunn quietly exhaled: 'OK, go.'

BANG. The sound of a crashing door burst the silence. Echoing: once, twice. Then nothing. Nothing at all.

A crackle on the radio. 'All clear, boss,' came the thick Yorkshire voice of Sergeant Lee 'Jonno' Johnson.

While the armoured column of the Scots Guards and the Mastiffs passed into the desert by Musa Qala, the Taliban were showing their strength across Helmand. It was as if a hornet's nest had been stirred. The Royal Marines at Kajaki, supported by the Afghan troops mentored by Lunn and Jonno, were about to find out what good fighters the Taliban could be.

Cloaked by the dark, Charlie Company of 40 Commando had left just after 03.00 from the Kajaki FOB and crossed a bridge over the Helmand River. They turned left through the village of

Tangye. Two years back it had been a bustling bazaar, but now it was just an empty street.

Formed up into two rifle 'troops' (the marine equivalent of a platoon) plus a headquarters and sniper unit, the patrol headed due west and then turned up a dry riverbed they called the 'M1 wadi' after Britain's main north–south motorway. They pushed up it and then turned left into a smaller wadi they called the Chinah bypass. Between the 'bypass' and the larger riverbed lay a piece of land shaped like an upright cigar. At the bottom was the village of Chinah. And in the middle of the cigar, about three-quarters of a mile from its base, was the village of Khevalabad, the target for their patrol and the estimated position of the FLET – the forward line of enemy troops.

Moving up the Chinah bypass just after 04.00, the Afghan army team led by Lunn and Jonno were the first to peel away to the right to start clearing into Chinah village. Detached from Jake Little's B Company to mentor the Afghans at Kajaki, their job today was to cover the rear as the marines pushed onwards. At 04.50 – twenty minutes before first light – the marines turned right out of the bypass and made their first break into Khevalabad.

Like Lunn and Jonno, all the marines found as they moved from compound to compound under a brightening sky was an eerie, empty village. The only Taliban fighter they saw was in a village about a mile to the north-east. Major Duncan Manning, Charlie Company's officer commanding, ordered the snipers to fire a warning shot. The man went into a firing posture. Manning ordered lethal force. A precision shot from a sniper rifle echoed across the hillside.

Half an hour later and it seemed to be all over. Manning ordered photographs taken for future reference, and at 07.05 he ordered a withdrawal. One of the corporals, Jon Kersey, would remember thinking, 'Bloody hell, they are not going to fight us. Where are they?'

Lunn's and Jonno's soldiers had pushed north after finishing their clearance of Chinah village. They were now in compounds just south of a little rise they called Pyramid Hill, just south of Khevalabad.

Over the radio, they heard the marines calling the FOB and asking them to get the breakfast going. They were going to be back in early.

That was when it started. The tck-tck-tck-tck of incoming rounds. Manning sent a flash radio message at 07.10 to the FOB: 'Contact . . . gunfire . . . wait out!'

At first, as Jonno and Lunn listened, it was sporadic. A burst of gunfire from villages ahead to the north. Then silence. Then they saw a burst from the west, aimed at the marines. And then it came straight at them, piercing the air with the crack of incoming.

As he heard the bullets, Jonno's face creased into a grin. He couldn't help it. The buzz came naturally: a rush of adrenalin.

'This is it . . . Finally!' thought Jonno. Wasn't it funny? Seventeen years in the army. The men looked up to him. He had a reputation. But he still had to admit that he had never been in action.

The previous night, he and Lunn had stayed up putting the world to rights – with a bit of cursing of their marine brethren. They had been up for two weeks now in Kajaki, the supposed mother of all of Helmand's front lines. Almost no action. And in what there was of it – a couple of minor skirmishes – the marines were hogging the sharp end all for themselves. The 2 Yorks and their Afghan soldiers were only there, it seemed, to act as rearguards or to screen the flanks. Not that Jonno and Lunn had really blamed the marines. Here they were with fifteen Afghan soldiers and nine of their own pitched alongside some of the supposedly fittest and most highly trained soldiers in the whole British *military* (you didn't call the Royal Marines 'the army' unless you really wanted a scrap). Somehow, Jonno and Lunn had agreed, they needed to prove themselves. And this was their moment.

Jonno moved up to talk to Lunn, his platoon commander. They stood by a wall.

'Boss, are you all right?' he asked. A pause. Then: 'This is FUCKING brilliant!'

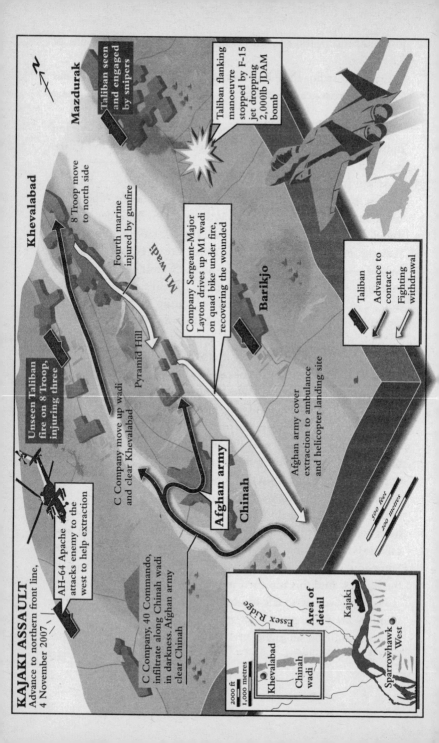

KAJAKI ASSAULT
Advance to northern front line,
4 November 2007

Mazdurak

Taliban seen and engaged by snipers

Taliban flanking manoeuvre stopped by F-15 jet dropping 2,000lb JDAM bomb

Khevalabad

8 Troop move to north side

Fourth marine injured by gunfire

M1 wadi

Company Sergeant-Major Layton drives up M1 wadi on quad bike under fire, recovering the wounded

Unseen Taliban fire on 8 Troop, injuring three

C Company move up wadi and clear Khevalabad

Pyramid Hill

Barikjo

Afghan army

Chinah

Afghan army cover extraction to ambulance and helicopter landing site

AH-64 Apache attacks enemy to the west to help extraction

C Company, 40 Commando, infiltrate along Chinah wadi in darkness. Afghan army clear Chinah

	Taliban
↘	Advance to contact
⇗	Fighting withdrawal

300 feet
200 metres

Area of detail

Essex Ridge

Kajaki

Khevalabad

Chinah wadi

Sparrowhawk
West

2000 ft
1,000 metres

Jonno was beaming with excitement. The two men updated each other and then shook hands and prepared to move off. Just as they did, a volley of bullets splashed into the wall beside them. The pair dived away.

'WHOAAH!' they shouted in unison.

They had just broken a rule that said a platoon commander and his sergeant should not get caught together in the open. 'Learning time,' thought Lunn.

Up in Khevalabad, the marines had 'gone firm' – lying or crouching in firing positions. Many were up on the roofs to cover a wide arc of fire. Most of the enemy bullets were coming from the north, although Lunn's ANA had just reported spotting a small group of Taliban coming up on their southern flank – right between the Afghans and the marines. The report, recalled Manning, 'came as such a shock that the position had to be repeated several times to confirm it.'

Manning deployed his 7 Troop down to investigate. By now, he was already calling in mortars. An F-15 strike fighter had arrived to assist. Over their radio network, the Taliban had announced: 'Get ready for the big thing!' There was suspense.

At 08.04 a burst of gunfire then hit 8 Troop from their rear-left, a position, recalled Manning, 'that we were not expecting'. It caught one section on a roof exposed. Three marines – Lance-Corporal Matt Kingston, and Marines Anthony Deakin and Nick Clarke – heard the bullets strike around them and they rolled desperately off the mud roof and on to the ground beneath.

Two of them at first thought they had just broken their ankles. In fact, Kingston had. But when they looked down, they saw blood spurting out. All three had been caught in the same burst of Taliban machine gun and were hit in their feet or ankles.

The first-aiders and medics got to work. Pete Leahy, the 8 Troop sergeant, stood still for a tiny moment, looking at the scene – boots coming off, dressings on, tourniquets being wrapped round. For many young lads, he knew, this was their first taste of real danger. But they all seemed to go into auto-pilot. 'Fucking hell! When it rains it pours!' he thought, and then got back on the radio and calmly reported he had taken three casualties. The network went silent.

The three injured were carried south first on top of plastic ponchos, with a man holding a handle on each corner. When that proved too difficult, they strapped them on to the portable ladders they carried with them. For Corporal Kersey it was to be the 'hardest thing I have ever had to do in my time in the Corps'. The weight was phenomenal.

The taking of casualties transforms a battle, particularly when the victims are wounded not dead. For every man down, the marines needed at least four men to carry them on a stretcher, with a fifth to carry their heavy kit. So three men injured needed fifteen men to get them to safety. Said Kersey: 'The lads were already carrying some seventy to eighty pounds, maybe a hundred pounds of kit, plus their weapons . . . So we had four lads who had to carry each of them casualties and you had to carry their weapons, their kit, put it on your back, on top of your kit and run as well. I have never done anything so physical in my entire life.'

They went at first through the compounds of Khevalabad, while the other troops and the fire support positions kept up the covering fire. The F-15 dropped a 2,000-pound bomb to the north-east across the M1 wadi, where it looked as though the Taliban were trying to flank them.

By now, Camp Bastion was reporting 'wheels up' of a rescue helicopter. Ominously, though, the Taliban radio network announced: 'We are waiting for the helicopter.'

Then it got worse. Leahy and his troop had reached an alleyway that was open to fire from the side. The men crouched by a wall and then dashed across one by one. At 08.35, as the last stretcher group ran across, Corporal Paul 'Tricky' Trickett, one of the bearers, screamed with pain. He had been shot through the leg – his injuries now more serious than anyone's. Marine Gordon 'Sulley' Sullivan, the oldest marine in Charlie, ran back and dragged him into cover.

Charlie Company was four men down.

At that moment, it seemed as if all their enemy zeroed on the alleyway. 'We were properly pinned down,' recalled Captain Sim Jemmett, the 'boss' of 7 Troop, although he said they needed to pause anyway to treat Trickett.

Kersey and others were lying in the dirt and watching the bullets come over their heads and ricochet around the walls. He was just thinking, 'Oh my God!' Afterwards he saw men with cuts on their legs where bullets had shaved them. He saw another section try to reach high ground and watched the dirt kick up around them. Above the din, he was trying to shout, 'Get back down here!' He began thinking of an Ali G film when the comedian stood by a wall with thousands of bullets being fired at him and remained miraculously untouched.

Duncan Manning, the OC, had further bad news. The Taliban was firing not only from the north, west and south-west, but from the south-*east* too. They had been creeping through villages on the far side of the M1 wadi, first one to the north-east and then another on their south-east flank. This was bad. The Taliban had now moved between the patrol and one of its fire support groups on a ridge behind. Engaging them from there would have risked a 'blue on blue', fratricide. Only a minor adjustment of a machine-gun barrel aimed at the hostile villages in front could have seen rounds flying across the M1 wadi to hit the marine positions in Khevalabad.

Charlie Company was almost surrounded. 'Our extraction route was cut off,' recalled Leahy. The two wadis on either side – the M1 and the Chinah Bypass, by which they had arrived – were both horribly exposed to raking gunfire. The only safe direction was due south towards the ANA and 2 Yorks. But even the path south to them meant crossing open ground in view of the enemy. There was, as Charlie's operations log drily recorded, a 'considerable coordination issue'. Beside that, they were also running out of mortar ammunition.

Manning decided to keep his marines moving, dropping a 'shake and bake' mixture of white smoke and high explosive to stir up the dust and give them cover. They managed to find an irrigation ditch just short of the M1 which they could move along. But it took them forty minutes to move just 400 yards.

Kersey got the feeling that every escape route they tried was blocked. 'Right, we are not getting out of this place,' he thought for a moment. 'Where are we going to go?' Their enemy was at 300 degrees around them. They were snuffed in a pocket. 'I think there were twenty-seven different enemy firing points that day,' he recalled.

Jonno realized the Afghan soldiers were nearly out of bullets. He announced, 'I'm going for a resupply.' He charged over the open fields to the edge of Chinah village, alone and under fire the whole way. The marines' company sergeant-major, Dave Layton, met him on his quad bike with the ammo stocks. Jonno came back breathless with chains of bullets wrapped around his neck and boxes in his hand. He looked shocked. 'Never again!' he grinned shyly.

The two marine troops were popping red and green smoke and phosphorous grenades to help mark their positions as they pulled back south. The fire support group could fire at anything beyond them. But they too were running out of ammo – down to their last 100 rounds of .50 cal.

At 09.30, one hour after Trickett was hit, they finally linked up with the ANA in a compound by the edge of the M1 wadi.

Just then, Layton, the sergeant-major, decided to act. Waiting further south, he was hearing on the radio that the rescue Chinook – now circling over the Kajaki dam – was shortly going to run out of fuel. Jumping into his six-wheeled quad bike, he bounced up the side of the M1 wadi, chased by bullets, and reached the ANA compound.

It took him two runs, carrying two casualties each time. As he moved, the 2 Yorks soldiers positioned the ANA to fire a deafening volley of covering fire. It was 09.54 when the chopper took off from a landing site at the base of the M1 wadi – nearly two hours from when the men were first shot.

The rest of Charlie fought their way back with an Apache helicopter now hitting the Taliban to the west. An F-15 jet strafed an attempt by the Taliban to creep up on the fire support team on the nearby ridge.

At the end of it all, Jemmett reflected that after being almost completely surrounded it 'should have been complete carnage'. Only the coordination they had achieved in the chaos, and the fact everyone kept their nerve, had kept them all alive. More than 19,000 bullets had been fired that day, including 10,170 from light machine guns, 123 sniper rounds, 3,075 bullets from the .50 heavy machine guns. There had also been three Javelin missiles fired.

That night Lunn wrote in his diary: 'So be careful what you wish for!'

10. Daft Orders

Delaram town, Nimroz province, 6 November

Under a deep blue sky, Major Jake Little was standing by the river bridge and inspecting the new sandbagged defences that Lieutenant Simon Farley and his platoon were putting into place with the Afghan army. There was an air of panic in the town behind them. The district governor had fled. The police had locked themselves into their central station. Few children ventured on the streets, and those that did cast a wary and dispirited eye.

To the north, across a table-flat desert of sand that stretched to the edge of the mountains, Little and Farley began to notice what looked like the gathering clouds of a dust storm. To the military eye, it meant one thing only: the approach of a large convoy of vehicles.

Up there into those dark peaks and canyons was Taliban country and the town of Golestan. It had just fallen to the enemy. Delaram, where Jake and his B Company, 2 Yorks, had arrived yesterday, was expected to fall next.

The commander of the convoy – an American special force reservist – came to tell his sorry tale in Jake's makeshift head-quarters, the bullet-marked compound of the absent governor. Setting off three days earlier to reconnoitre a route up the mountain gorge into Golestan, the convoy had been clinically and savagely ambushed. Nineteen Afghan soldiers were dead, some of them captured then executed by the Taliban.

B Company, which now had to pick up the pieces, had been in Helmand months now. Arriving on 15 September, they had been attached as mentors to the 400-strong 2nd *kandak* of an Afghan army brigade based in Helmand. They spent the first few weeks in training at Camp Shorobak, the ANA base by Camp Bastion, while a few of Jake's men like Sergeant Lee Johnson had been detached and sent up to the Kajaki dam to mentor the ANA up there.

They had learned some lessons. For the first few weeks it was Ramadan, and the Afghans refused to work more than two hours a day. They also resisted the training. 'That *kandak* was never keen to learn,' recalled Jake, 'mainly because of the Afghan nature of thinking they knew it all already. They felt it was slightly demeaning for them to be trained again.' But, over time, they had built relationships and got a sense of individuals.

Then the typically abrupt order had come from President Karzai. The ANA were told to grab their weapons as soon as possible and head out west from Helmand and straight to Delaram in next-door Nimroz province. If the Taliban captured the town it would be dire news. It controlled a bridge on Highway One – the main strategic ring road from Herat on the Iranian border through Helmand and on to Kandahar.

Then, when they got there, the orders changed again. Now Karzai wanted to move his army 35 miles north to take Golestan back from the Taliban. 'It was all very short notice, both times,' remembered Jake. 'Both times it was sort of we're going in four hours. Both times, we managed to stall them by saying, essentially, if you go now you'll be without us, and therefore you won't have cover. You won't have any helicopters for casualty evacuation. So wait until we're ready!'

While Karzai might have ordered an Afghan attack, it was Jake who had to lead the mission. Jake's ANA *kandak* commander, Colonel Rahimi, was already in an excitable state in Delaram, particularly when the Taliban began probing the town's defences and lobbing mortars. 'Every time they heard an explosion they sent for me to tell them what to do. It was a little pathetic,' said Jake. He had to calm Rahimi down by stationing him up a hill to 'survey his troops' and leaving the running of the *kandak* to B Company's teams. When the order came to move north, Rahimi was happy to send his men forward under Jake's command, but he refused point blank to go himself. That did make life a bit easier for B Company. But it was not a great omen.

In the end, Jake led a sixty-vehicle convoy north composed of the survivors of the local ANA force, about half of his ANA *kandak* and an A-Team of the US Green Berets. The US reservists stayed behind this time.

Intelligence said there were 400 to 1,000 Taliban around Golestan. This was exaggerated 'Afghan numbers', said Jake. But he was clear the enemy force was substantial, and they had mined the approaches from a mile away.

The direct approach to Delaram went up a steep-sided canyon. But, to avoid mines and ambush, Jake decided to cut a trail through the mountains in the ultimate of cross-country driving. 'It was the most beautiful terrain I think I have ever seen,' he said, 'utterly devoid of people, apart from the odd nomad, and utterly barren.'

By avoiding the enemy's defences, Jake and his force shocked them into simply abandoning the town: melting away sensibly to avoid a stand-up fight.

Looking back on it, Jake would regard the trip to Delaram and Golestan as one of the highlights of the tour. He and his sergeant-major, Daniel Benson, got to know their men and the Afghans better; it was beautiful country; everything went to plan and there were no casualties from his troops or from among his Afghans.

But it was also Jake's first taste of the gulf between tactics that worked and a broader strategy in Afghanistan that seemed to make little sense.

'The frustrating thing was we spent a week there in Golestan. We stabilized it, patrolled around and talked to the locals. We held *shura*s. Everything went very well. They wanted the government to stay there and told us of their intimidation by the Taliban, who had murdered several of the town's elders. They welcomed the ANA and ISAF troops. And then we left.'

After building up the hopes of the people of Golestan, a promise by the Italian military to take over security came to nothing. When B Company pulled out, the town was simply abandoned, and within four days was back in Taliban hands.

'So it was a clearance without a hold,' said Jake. 'And therefore in many ways a waste of time, other than it probably relieved the pressure on Delaram, which did not fall to the Taliban. It was very successful in the sense that we avoided fighting. It is a success when you don't have to flatten a place. So that's good.' But, though he was no expert on Afghan politics, this did strike him personally as at least one example of 'people not always being able to control President Karzai and therefore Karzai being able to just throw out pretty daft orders, which he is not backing up with resources to do the follow-up afterwards.'

At NATO headquarters, General McNeill was getting sick of such escapades. And they happened month after month after month. There was a routine to how it worked. Something like telephone terrorism. First the chief of staff of the Afghan army would call. 'We need to act!' he would say. Then the defence minister. 'We can't let the Taliban take this town,' he would be told. Then the interior minister: 'It would be a sign of weakness to let them move in!' Finally, the call would come from the man who had orchestrated all these appeals, President Karzai. 'General, we have to do something!'

It would all build up like a national crisis. A NATO and Afghan force would then be scrambled. When they arrived in the latest dust-ridden town in the back of beyond, they might find the police force packing up and getting ready to flee. But – nine times out of ten – it was down to politics, like these local cops had not got paid, or some drug dispute. Someone had then called the palace and brought in NATO to solve a local power struggle. Where was the long-term thinking? Where was the strategy?

Some diplomats in Kabul would put it more strongly. How could American and British lives be risked in an 'Afghan-led' campaign when the Afghan president was so out of touch? And why – some asked – did NATO commanders agree, time and again, to follow the whims of Karzai?

The British had done the same in 2006. When Karzai and the Helmand governor had asked them to push their thin forces across northern Helmand, they had agreed too readily, it was argued. The result had been the death of too many soldiers and a destruction that finally led to the Musa Qala truce.

11. Killer with a Conscience

'Every time I shoot at a soldier, I am not sure if it is right or wrong,' said the Taliban commander. He was using the old word *angleez*, English, for his enemy.

'Why?' said the journalist.

'Well, it is not the soldiers who are the occupiers. I think about their families. It is their leaders, the politicians and generals, that I would like in the sights of my gun,' he said.

Mullah Sadiq, the commander talking on the mobile phone, had a thing about politicians. He used to joke about putting Mullah Omar and Osama bin Laden in a boxing ring with Tony Blair, George Bush and John Howard, then the Australian prime minister.

'Lock them in the ring. Let them fight to the death. Whoever wins the match can win this war,' he said.

'That sounds a bit unfair. It's two against three!'

'That does not matter. Whoever will survive will survive!'

Sadiq was from Sangin and still kept his family at home there, but he was now the chief commander on the Kajaki frontline, in daily battle with the Royal Marines and one of those they used to see in the distance, talking on a mobile phone or a radio. Today, he was talking to Qais Azimy, a senior journalist with Al Jazeera's English channel. They had been in touch for many months after they met by accident at an emergency hospital in Lashkah Gah.

Wrapped in a white dressing gown, Sadiq, a lanky man with a toothy grin, had told how NATO had already announced his death in a press release. He had been driving through the desert when his pick-up was cornered by an Apache helicopter that opened fire. His three bodyguards saved him by leaping over and protecting him. All of them died, 'martyred' as Sadiq would put it. With a serious leg wound, Sadiq had to crawl alone to the nearest village to get someone to call for an ambulance.

A few days after the interview, Sadiq had called Qais and invited him up to Sangin. At the time, the British had claimed to occupy Sangin, but in reality they were besieged in their base. Armed Taliban fighters walked openly through the market place.

'These are George Bush's kites,' said Sadiq, pointing up at the aeroplanes that circled by. Qais was getting nervous. The Taliban were clearly unfazed, sitting with Sadiq's family in an open court-yard and eating rice and spinach, the best he could offer. 'The spinach is grown among the poppy,' Sadiq explained. His wife joined them for the meal – a sign not only that they trusted Qais but that Sadiq was not a religious extremist.

Sadiq would insist, 'You know, this is not a war about religion. It's about the freedom of my country.' That was his catchphrase lament: 'My country! My country!'

Not all Taliban were alike. It was obvious Sadiq was a different breed to some of his more extreme brethren. And it was obvious to Qais there were deep suspicions between the groups.

As he travelled to meet Sadiq one time, Qais ran into other groups of Taliban, those who revealed their deep and brutal para-noia. Some appeared to be linked to Dadullah Lang, the leader at that point of the more hardline factions in Helmand. The men showed them mobile phone videos of 'spies' being slaughtered. 'We've killed more humans than chickens,' said one man.

On a hillside in the desert somewhere near Gereshk, Qais also met Abdul Rahim, the Taliban's overall commander in the prov-ince. He kept his face disguised. But he was clearly the boss – a cleaner turban, a neater cut to his trousers – and he spoke with authority. At one point, out in the open, there was a crowd of dozens of armed fighters around them. 'This is the moment the airstrike comes,' thought James Bays, a British correspondent that Qais had brought along.

Sadiq later told Qais he distrusted many of the old Taliban, the ones who had held power before. He also detested Dadullah and his extreme followers. When the press reported the Special Boat

Service had killed Dadullah in early 2007, he was delighted. He declared: 'The dirty spot on the white pure cloth of the Mujahidin has been wiped away.'

Mullah Sadiq and the journalist knew that NATO intelligence was probably intercepting and listening to their calls. But they used to speak constantly. For the journalist, Sadiq provided a window into the rebellion, a chance to understand just *why* this war was happening.

Sadiq's story of how he became a Taliban leader was emblematic of this whole rebellion. The son of a government official, Sadiq was in his forties. He was an educated man, unlike many in his movement. Ever smiling, sometimes confidently, he was mild-mannered, hardly a typical warrior. He was also full of black humour – he saw the irony everywhere. He was a smart fighter too: full of new ideas for tactics, like getting his men between two sets of *angleez* troops and opening fire in a way that made the British fire on each other, or fire on their Afghan army allies, or vice versa.

Asked why he had joined the Taliban, he would weep openly as he described a period 'before the Taliban got strong' and he approached a checkpoint of foreign troops. He had a sick woman in his car and had needed to get to the hospital. The troops just told him, 'Go away! Go away!' Sadiq used to repeat, 'That's what occupation means!'

But the deeper story came back to the same predatory politics that the EU diplomat Michael Semple and British officers had separately described to me: of how the chief of Helmand's secret police appointed when President Karzai took power had turned Sangin into his private fiefdom. Sadiq said the man – nicknamed 'Dado' – had started a private jail, was always drunk or stoned, had raped boys and women and was systematically stealing from the population. Sadiq previously had had a minor role in the old Taliban. This was his call back to arms.

Sadiq and his family, like many in Sangin, crossed the Rubicon of rebellion in the summer of 2006, just as the British arrived. He was involved in the revenge attack that slaughtered members of

Dado's family. There was no turning back now. They blew up Dado's home, although Sadiq used to complain, 'We spent so much on explosives and it is still half there.'

Soon after all this, the Afghan government persuaded Britain to send its paratroopers into Sangin to maintain order. That was the start of the bloody battle of Sangin. As far as Sadiq and most were concerned, the British were there to prop up Dado and his cronies.

Many of the fighters, Sadiq explained, were local villagers. They were paid nothing but fought to defend their families' and tribe's interests. They were also involved in drug production. 'It's the season of drugs. People can't fight very much at the moment,' Sadiq would say. Sadiq acknowledged help from the drug dealers. One of his cars was a gift from them.

There were also many fighters who were sent from the *madrassahs*, the hundreds of religious schools over the frontier in Pakistan. These were not 'foreign fighters' but Afghans, often the children of refugees. They would be paid for service – about 20,000 Pakistani rupees a month (about 300 US dollars at the exchange rate then). But the money was usually sent back to the *madrassah*.

For those who always wondered at the Taliban's apparently suicidal tactics – sending waves of fighters against British machine guns – Sadiq's fighters had the answer. Once they captured some British night-vision equipment. They were discussing what it would fetch in the market. 'Aren't you going to use it?' said Qais. The Taliban just laughed. As one leader explained to the journalist later: 'What you have to understand is that for every fighter who is martyred here, the *madrassahs* will send two to replace him. They become heroes in their schools!' So sending young men forward to die was not just religious zeal, it made a rather cynical, calculated sense.

There were a few genuine 'foreign' fighters – the Saudis or Chechens. Qais never saw any of these. And, according to Sadiq, they had little value. For survival, Taliban fighters depended on village hospitality. When dealing with any coddled Saudi, even a young religious zealot, then hospitality was a heavy burden. 'They don't know the area at all, and it costs more to provide them with hospitality than the value they bring to the fight.' But Sadiq had instructions from Pakistan to look after them well – give them the best food and put them up in the best houses 'so they will go back and tell others to come'. Sadiq believed this war would be won or lost by Afghan fighters, not outsiders – just like the war against the Soviets.

Sadiq complained about the fighting in Kajaki, ironically echoing the complaints of many British soldiers. 'You know we are shooting many of them. But they never announce about their injured,' he said. Despite his status as a mullah, a religious teacher, Sadiq used to swear a lot. He was full of awe of the British medics. 'Even if the *angleez* soldier is in bits then they have a motherfucking doctor who can piece them all together.'

Now, Sadiq was starting to talk to Qais about suspicions of a coalition attack on Musa Qala, which he used to call a 'resting place' for his front-line fighters. Sadiq was offering a trip into the Taliban stronghold. 'Bring your cameras,' he said. 'We will guarantee your safety.'

12. The Battle of 9/11

The Royal Marines patrol from Alpha Company had been out for nearly six hours now, pounding out from the FOB to explore the villages up north. The intelligence reports said up to thirty foreign fighters were lying in wait. But it was no good just sitting in the base and waiting for an attack.

Back at brigade headquarters, staff were reporting a level of Taliban activity across Helmand that had not been seen since the green zone clearances of Operation Palk Wahel in September. New fighters were coming in from Pakistan, said intelligence, and others were slipping down from the north. All in all, the brigade staff thought, it was a clear attempt to divert the British from their pressure against Musa Qala.

All day long the marines overheard the taunts over the Taliban's radio network. Every other moment, they had heard an order to attack and a reply saying, 'I'm ready.' But no one had seen anything. Nothing had happened. So they had started heading home.

Two close combat troops provided the combat strength. 2 Troop was in the lead; 1 Troop had the rear. The company headquarters was in the middle. Everyone was on foot.

About a mile and a half from the FOB, some of the marines had begun to see some strange things, like some well-dressed farmers fiddling with a haystack, just seeming to be moving stalks for no particular reason. They had passed a man whose mobile phone rang and he hadn't even moved to answer it. Then three men were spotted running into the trees with weapons. Most of the patrol were in the open then, stretched along a mud track by the side of a drainage ditch. Everyone started jogging to reach some kind of cover.

'There was a small pause,' recalled Andy Brownrigg, the company sergeant-major. 'It was almost like it was a gentleman's agreement that we will wait for you to get into a hiding place and we will get into our hiding place.'

The opening shot of the ambush that became known as the 'Battle of 9/11' was fired at 16.06.

As machine-gun fire began and RPGs came whooshing over, everyone dropped down. A few men were knocked to the ground by a blast from one grenade. Most of the headquarters ended up in the ditch, pinned down by the gunfire. But they knew they had to reach solid cover to start getting organized. So they dashed one-by-one for a nearby walled but isolated compound. It was a trap. The only entrance, and the roof of the small building inside, were easily raked by enemy fire.

Marine Gary Ogden, a twenty-six-year-old medic with trademark orange-tinted sunglasses, was lying behind another of those little mud banks, firing shots at a couple of Taliban he could see.

'I glanced back at the compound entrance and I could see the rounds striking the wall and a figure screaming for a medic,' he recalled. The man in the entrance was Captain Paul Britton, the twenty-seven-year-old fire support team commander, whose job was to call up guns, mortars and aviation. 'Rounds were hitting the doorway all around him, and I wondered why they weren't hitting him,' said Ogden. With the air filled with the crack and thump of bullets, Ogden picked himself up and charged across the field.

Britton had only just reached the compound after dashing from a ditch. He arrived to see a smear of blood dripping down the walls and a machine-gunner, Corporal James Fletcher, being dragged down with his leg looking lifeless. Fletcher had been on the roof when an RPG blast showered him and his gun team with shrapnel. Marine Matthew Fenwick, an ammo bearer, caught shards of metal in his legs and ankles. Fenwick was a reservist whose job back home was a lifeguard at a Bristol leisure centre.

'As I put my head up on the roof,' recalled Fenwick, 'I could hear the rounds coming over my head. I knew it was going to be pretty intense.'

Fenwick spun round to pull another machine gun on to the roof when he heard a boom and a felt a sharp kick from behind. 'The next thing I know I am on the floor upside down thinking, "What the hell was that?"'

Things then got even worse. A section leader, Corporal Simon 'Si' Greening, moved forward to the compound entrance to yell at his men in the ditches around. They saw him staggering backwards shouting, 'Fuck, I think I've been shot!'

Britton and Major Adrian Morley, the OC of Alpha Company, who was just running in, caught Greening as he stumbled. They ripped off his body armour and clothes and tried to put on a field dressing as Ogden finally came running into the compound. Ogden started going over Greening front and back to look for the entry and exit wounds. He had been shot in the side, bypassing his armour.

'As I rolled Si back he passed out,' said Ogden. 'I think the OC thought he was dead or on his last legs. But I checked his carotid [artery] and found he was fine. His heart was racing like a bastard, but he was still with us.'

Ogden started putting a needle line for an intravenous drip into Greening's arm to give him some fluids to replace the blood loss.

Then Ogden was being called over to treat Corporal Fletcher. 'The RPG took all the muscles off Fletcher's legs, tore his legs to bits. There was lumps of flesh everywhere and so much blood coming out of him,' said Ogden. 'It was fucking chaos. He came down totally out cold.'

Others had put tourniquets on both of Fletcher's legs to block off the blood flow. Without them he would have been dead in minutes. They followed up with field dressings. Ogden found his breathing was OK but was worried about the blood loss. He also checked Fenwick and decided he was stable.

Then Ogden was called back to Greening whose field dressings had come loose and who was pumping out blood again. Blood

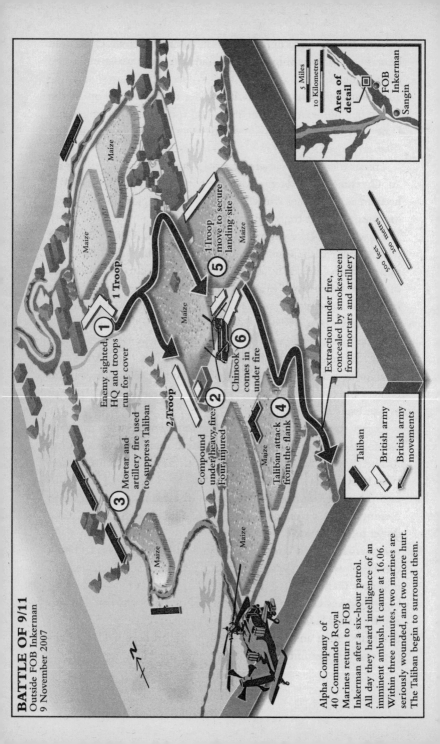

BATTLE OF 9/11
Outside FOB Inkerman
9 November 2007

1 Enemy sighted, HQ and troops run for cover

2 Compound under heavy fire. Four injured

3 Mortar and artillery fire used to suppress Taliban

4 Taliban attack from the flank

5 1 Troop move to secure landing site

6 Chinook comes in under fire

Extraction under fire, concealed by smokescreen from mortars and artillery

Taliban
British army
British army movements

1 Troop
2 Troop

Maize

Area of detail
FOB Inkerman
Sangin

5 Miles
10 Kilometres

200 metres
500 feet

Alpha Company of 40 Commando Royal Marines return to FOB Inkerman after a six-hour patrol. All day they heard intelligence of an imminent ambush. It came at 16.06. Within three minutes, two marines are seriously wounded, and two more hurt. The Taliban begin to surround them.

was also beginning to drain into his lung. Ogden could put a chest drain in, but that would lower his blood pressure massively, so he delayed that option. Greening then woke up and started chatting and 'giving me a load of shit', said Ogden.

It was 16.09 when the watch keepers at FOB Inkerman got the radio message that Alpha Company were three men down – just three minutes after the contact had begun.

Inkerman got on the radio network to Carbon Zero, the operations centre of 40 Commando's Battle Group North. Their day had already been fraught. In the early hours, a vehicle leaving Sangin district centre, 4 miles south of Inkerman, had rolled into a water-filled ditch, killing Lance-Corporal Jake Alderton of the Royal Engineers. Then a Chinook landing at Now Zad narrowly escaped being struck by mortars. And just as the battle outside Inkerman began, a fire fight erupted in the main street of Sangin bazaar. An Afghan soldier was seriously hurt. There were now two simultaneous requests for a rescue helicopter.

Meanwhile, just as it couldn't get any worse, another fire fight began erupting with a US special force unit operating across the river from Sangin. Three serious gun battles were going on at once.

And that was just in the north of Helmand. Down in the southern town of Garmsir, the Gurkhas were just pausing for breath after a four-and-a-half hour battle that had led to serious injuries. It was the most sustained attack down south for the last two months.

Most of Alpha Company were still in the ditches in a storm of bullets, facing Taliban that had ambushed them from multiple directions and was now on the move – threatening a deadly flank through head-high maize and deep ditches. It was hard to spot their firing points. Sometimes it was just the rustling of the corn that gave them away.

The noise was phenomenal. Paul Britton and his mortar controller, Duncan Maddocks, were calling in a barrage of mortar rounds from Inkerman and preparing to bring in artillery. Apache helicopters were also inbound.

Then a flash and bang as another RPG arched down into a wall inside the compound. Shrapnel hit a signaller, Corporal Dave Watts, in the backside. It struck Britton in the arm and hand.

'I knew there was something wrong with my arm,' recalled Britton. 'It hurt and then went numb. I looked across – I saw that my arm was still there, but I couldn't really move it.

'People had jumped on to Corporal Watts because it was obvious he was quite badly injured.' No one noticed Britton had been hit. Britton went up to Maddocks, who was talking on the radio.

'My arm!'

Maddocks didn't even look at him; just raised his hand to say he was busy. Britton repeated: 'No, I want you to see my arm!'

Maddocks looked over. He saw the blood.

'Oh yeah! Your arm!'

He dropped the handset and ripped off Britton's T-shirt and put a dressing on. It felt a lot better and tighter now, but Britton still could not move it. He did not even spot the shrapnel that had gone into his hand. Maddocks offered Britton morphine, but he refused. He had to keep his mind straight.

Ogden had seen Watts drop and he sped across, worried that shrapnel could have severed an artery, but Watts seemed more concerned about his manhood. Ogden checked it out and assured him everything was intact. He patched him up and gave him a cigarette.

By now, it was clear the injured needed a helicopter medevac. Urgently. With so much blood loss from Fletcher and Greening, it would take too long to get them back to the landing site at Inkerman.

Outside the compound, the 2 Troop machine-gunners were running out of ammo. Jim Wright, the troop sergeant, called men forward to resupply with belts of ammunition wrapped round their shoulders like Rambo.

One of them, instead of using the bridge over the ditch, ploughed into the river, which went up to his neck. Wright thought he had seen the last of him. But he came out the other side crawling towards them like a cat. It all seemed in slow motion.

'This is fucking surreal,' thought Wright. Meanwhile, the sergeant-major, Brownrigg, had the task of securing a helicopter landing site. He and 1 Troop started flanking through the thick maize to get to the rear of the compound. The rounds came buzzing through. They couldn't see the enemy. All they could do was use their ears to work out where to fire back at.

The initial attack had been mainly from the east, but the Taliban had flanked now round to the west. And when 1 Troop came out of the maize into open ground again by the planned landing site, they found the Taliban were firing from the south too, from barely 100 yards away.

Two Apaches were now on station and blazed at the tree lines with cannon, rockets and Hellfire missiles. At 16.45, Alpha Company reported the landing site was secure.

It was time to quit the compound, avoiding the fire-raked entrance. A Gurkha engineer tried to crowbar through a wall but gave up. Instead he got out a stick of explosive and blew a 'mouse-hole' through. Fenwick, the injured marine, was told to move. When he got to the wall, he found it was only a tiny hole. 'Oh my God, I'm not going to get through,' he thought. The marines bashed away some more of the mortar, and he managed to squeeze through.

The last to leave the compound was the air controller, Sergeant Michael Garth. With his headphones on he seemed oblivious and was walking, said one marine, 'like nothing was going on, because obviously he was in the middle of telling lies to the AH [Apache helicopters]'. Precise records of what exactly was said to the helicopters were not revealed. But legend has it that Garth, in something of an understatement, told the Apaches the landing site was as 'secure as it will be', and the full meaning of that message never quite made it to the rescue Chinook.

Just before the Chinook came in, Brownrigg saw an Apache hovering over FOB Inkerman and just twirling around and pouring fire from its cannon. Brass shell casings rained down beneath. All at the same time, mortars were whistling down; and shells from Inkerman's battery of three 105mm artillery guns shrieked across and exploded with a *whumph*. Soldiers watching from the base thought it was like a scene from *Apocalypse Now*.

For the past half hour, the Chinook had been circling in the desert near by. At the controls was a Royal Navy pilot, Lieutenant Nichol Benzie, with RAF co-pilot Flight Lieutenant Al Sparks. The pilots had no direct contact with the marines. Sergeant Garth was speaking to the Apaches. And the Apaches spoke by secure radio to the crewmen in the back of the Chinook. And the crewmen relayed the message by intercom to the pilots.

'When you're getting stuff relayed like this, it's a bit like Chinese whispers,' said Sparks. 'It gets a little diluted.' He was on his first tour of Afghanistan. He was feeling pretty wide-eyed. Sometimes it was just as well the information was filtered.

When they got the call that the landing site was clear, the pilots still thought they were heading for FOB Inkerman. It was only when they got 'in amongst the weeds', flying 'ultra-low', said Benzie, that they noticed orange smoke rising in the green zone itself. They took a deep breath. There was almost no protection from gunfire there.

They were coming in fast and had to stop abruptly to get the helicopter down in a small field. As the pilots looked out, they could see guys on the ground tucked into the firing positions. If, like now, no one was looking at the chopper, that meant trouble. 'The more we looked out,' remembered Benzie, 'the more we realized we should lean back and benefit from the Kevlar protection that the aircraft has to offer.'

In the back, crewman Sergeant Scott Todd saw the first casualty – Fletcher – approaching. 'He was losing a lot of blood. I thought it strange straightaway that the casualty was in a poncho, which is like an emergency battlefield stretcher. It means pretty much you're close to the fire fight.

'I was shouting with adrenalin as well, trying to get the guys in fast because the guys in the front were saying, "How long?" I was just trying to call out an estimated time and shouting to the troops to hurry up, to double it.'

They lifted the casualty over the M60 belt-fed machine gun on the ramp and, when Todd went back, he found a solid blood trail over his gun. 'So I knew he was losing blood fast.'

Kneeling in the field, Ogden, the medic, had been preparing the casualties. Looking up as the ramp dropped, he could see the crew had no idea what they had landed into.

'When the Chinook came in, as the back door dropped down, the "doc" [a medic] ran off, all springy and bouncy. As he came out to us a load of bullet rounds came past us. He just seized up. I think it was his first time being shot at. Obviously he tried turning back around towards the helicopter! So I dragged him back and held him. He was listening but not registering.' Ogden handed him a piece of paper where all the conditions of the casualties were written down. 'Eventually he just ran on the back again.' The Chinook pulled away in a choke of boiling dust.

Alpha Company still had to get back home. They moved back in a rolling barrage of white smoke from mortars and high explosive from artillery. Even so, at 17.50, their rear was attacked as they neared the base.

Finally a Dutch F-16 dropped a 500-pound bomb, and after that it went quiet. There had not been a break in the fight for two hours. The Apaches were still circling and watching to see if anyone was following them.

By the time the patrol walked into Inkerman at 18.20, the sun had set more than an hour before and it was almost pitch dark. They heard a round of applause from those back at camp.

For Ogden and the other medics there was still another three hours of work – patching up Captain Britton and pulling out the bits of shrapnel from the others. They discovered that many of the marines had caught bits without realizing. The evening ended with a naked parade as Ogden and the others went down the line, inspecting everyone to check they were unscarred.

The chief of staff, Major Mark Gidlow-Jackson, picked up the ringing phone on his desk. It was Major General Jonathan 'Jacko' Page, Brigadier Mackay's immediate superior in the NATO command, and he rang with orders from General McNeill.

'I've just spoken to COMISAF,' said the general, referring to McNeill's title. 'At this stage there is more political work to be done on Musa Qala.' There was a question mark on Karzai's attitude. But it was now clear an operation to retake the town was on the cards. 'The government will take a kinetic solution if it's required,' he said, using the military's term for a fight.

Already NATO was earmarking forces for a possible assault. The Afghan army's most elite unit, the Commando *kandak*, trained and mentored by US special forces, was being put on notice to move. So was McNeill's own reserve force, the Theatre Task Force, Task Force 1 Fury, led by Lieutenant Colonel Brian Mennes. They would not be available for three weeks, but certainly no later than 10 December.

It was time for some serious planning. 'I want thoughts on the whole Musa Qala piece to me by next Wednesday,' concluded the general.

That night was what Brigadier Mackay would recall as the loneliest moment in his command. As he sat in the office in Lashkar Gah and paced around in the darkness of the base, he had to consider his next move. His forces were now clearly stretched. The pressure on Musa Qala applied by the presence of Chris Bell's Warrior company and its daily skirmishes was having an effect. But the Taliban's own counter-attack was getting stronger by the day. Now there were strong hints from President Karzai not only that Mullah Salaam should be protected but that an attack should be prepared on Musa Qala itself.

But was it right to risk all on the Musa Qala prize? His hope when he arrived had been to get some development going in

Helmand, to move beyond the fighting. The priority had been war-ravaged Sangin, which had been held for the last six months but had seen almost no progress. If the cost of supporting Mullah Salaam and hitting the Taliban in Musa Qala was that Sangin simply dissolved back into violence, the whole venture could be seriously counter-productive. Not to mention the cost in blood for his own soldiers.

Mackay flew to Camp Bastion the next morning to visit the injured from the battle at Inkerman and elsewhere. Lying in bed was Corporal Greening, a man he had met on a visit to Inkerman only five days back. Greening had asked, 'When are we going to get stuck into the enemy?' They had a joke about it now. 'Didn't I say to be careful what you wish for?' he said. Greening said that when he was shot he had thought at first he was winded. 'Then I noticed the blood,' he said.

As he sat in a helicopter heading back to his headquarters, Mackay made his decision. Rather than draw back his forces from the battle, he would do the reverse and ratchet up the psychological pressure on Musa Qala one more notch. 'I had a sense we were actually succeeding,' he recalled.

While the Warriors and their support group were probing the eastern flanks of Musa Qala around Salaam's compound, for now the desert to the west of Musa Qala was unexplored. It was time, decided Mackay, to deploy his own reserve asset – the Brigade Reconnaissance Force (BRF) led by Major Tony Phillips. It would mean taking the BRF out of the green zone – where the Taliban were now gathering strength – and opening a new front: deeper into enemy territory.

As he laid out his orders to staff, there was a sense of the stakes being raised in a game of poker. One adviser told him later his thoughts then were: 'If this goes wrong, Mackay is absolutely fucked. That is a big big call to make.'

PART 4

The Plan

'Playing chess by telegraph may succeed, but making war and planning a campaign on the Helmand from the cool shades . . . is an experiment which will not, I hope, be repeated.'

British officer (anonymous) after the defeat of Maiwand, 1880[16]

Operation Snakebite

At 03.30 on 11 November, the first elements of the Brigade Reconnaissance Force (BRF) leave a patrol base in the green zone near the village of Zumberlay under the command of Major Tony Phillips. They take the road through Gereshk and then turn right into the desert.

The following day, the second half of the force, commanded by Captain James Ashworth, leaves at 04.30 to rendezvous with them to the west of Musa Qala.

The force is mounted in eighteen WMIK Land Rovers and six Pinzgauer trucks, and the total strength of eighty men consists of two fighting troops totalling forty-eight men, a fire support group armed with two 81 mm mortars, snipers and Javelin missiles, a unit that can deploy a small 'Desert Hawk' drone and a headquarters element.

They are travelling light. Everything they need to survive is carried in their vehicles. While Chris Bell's Warrior company, the Mobile Operation Group East, has its own special supply camp – with truckloads of fuel, ammunition and supplies, and a troop of three light guns to support them – the BRF are on their own.

Their destination is to be called Operations Box Inferno, and Major Phillips' orders state: 'Carry out reconnaissance north and west of Musa Qala, find and disrupt the enemy, and influence the civilian population.'

Their camp at night is known as a 'harbour', a place of refuge in a sea of sand and rock. It is to be strictly arranged in the shape of a box, with the fighting troops guarding the corners and the headquarters and fire support team, including mortars ready to fire, arranged in the middle.

13. Camping with Wolves

The desert west of Musa Qala, 11 November
(Remembrance Day)

Major Tony Phillips crawled into his plastic bivvy bag and zipped the top shut over his head. He switched on his red head torch. Then he opened his personal diary to scrawl a brief note. It had been a long day.

A few minutes before, as the last golden light faded beneath the black shadows of the distant mountains, his elite Brigade Reconnaissance Force had been on 'stand to'. That was the centuries-old warrior tradition of standing ready for action at the close and break of day, ready to repel an attack at the classic moments of danger. Then all lights had been put out and all his men had fallen silent. Soon, the only noise was the snores of men and the howl of the wolves that crept around in the darkness. The sentries would see them moving through their night-vision goggles.

As he gathered his thoughts, Phillips could not know then what lay ahead, that this night would be the beginning of what would become an epic three-month adventure and one of the longest British desert patrols in memory. It would be tinged with tragedy. When they were all assembled, the BRF patrol of eighty men that had left the green zone behind would finally come out of the desert with twelve men down – ten injured and two who would be killed in action.

For now, though, Phillips was still filled with the thrill of his mission – the danger of the enemy that lay all around and the large area he was being asked to cover, and the responsibility that lay on his shoulders. His mission was reconnaissance for Brigadier Andrew Mackay, who used to describe the BRF as 'my eyes and my ears'.

But where the BRF went within that mission – and how they did it – was Phillips' choice, and his alone.

'There are no two ways about it,' he wrote quickly, 'this is the brigade commander's baby! It's his idea and we are working directly to Brigade. I have an area of nearly 300 square kilometres in which to do what I want. It's all very exciting. We are in the middle of the desert so should be safe but as Musa Qala has hundreds of Taliban and is their stronghold they could try anything.'

A native of Lancashire, thirty-eight-year-old Phillips had a reputation as something of a rough diamond. By his own description he was 'not exactly your clean-cut nose-clean type of officer' and not infrequently he got into trouble for speaking his mind. Someone once described him as a 'break glass in time of war' type of leader, valued most of all for his physical tenacity and personal courage. Joining the army after a geography degree at Manchester University, he had seen action in Northern Ireland as a troop commander and dealt with the aftermath of an IRA bomb that killed one of his soldiers.

A week ago, Phillips and his men were still in the lush green zone of the Helmand River valley. His force had been manning a patrol base just north of Gereshk. It had been classic counter-insurgency work of the sort that Mackay favoured – getting out to talk to the locals, helping them with some basic medical care and establishing a stable government presence in a village, Zumber-lay, that a year earlier had been Taliban heartland and where my colleague at the *Sunday Times*, Christina Lamb, had been with the Parachute Regiment as they were pinned down by gunfire.

The BRF had already had their baptism of fire. Ironically, the first fire fight had been not with the Taliban but with the Afghan National Police. They had been driving in the night out of Camp Bastion when they came under a volley of machine-gun fire. Only later did they find out who their adversaries were.

Then they had been attacked by a suicide bomber just on the outskirts of Gereshk town. A white Toyota Corolla (*it always seemed to be a Corolla*) came haring towards them. Only quick reactions saved his men. Four of his soldiers had opened fire on the driver, and the car exploded between two vehicles. There were minor injuries, but the main effect was a wake-up call. It made them realize the training phase was over.

The incident that most affected the men down in Zumberlay had been when they tried to help a young Afghan boy. He had burned himself with hot milk that poured all over his skin, and the wounds had been left to fester. The medics had spotted it was a highly serious injury. But appeals to send him to a coalition hospital had been rejected. So the soldiers intervened themselves and collected 300 dollars for him. The boy was driven over to Gereshk and handed over to the Afghan police to take him for treatment. But the next morning he came back wrapped in a carpet. He had died in the night.

Then the orders came through from Brigade to move into the desert. Really the only no-go zone for them was the town of Musa Qala itself. Everywhere else they were to probe relentlessly: testing the Taliban reactions, working out their defensive positions, assessing their strength and figuring out routes for any future NATO advance.

Everyone slept at night by their vehicle on the rocky desert floor, contending not only with fearsome camel spiders, up to six inches long, but also with snakes that might come seeking warmth. Recalled Phillips: 'Nobody was permitted to move outside the "box", so cooking, sleeping, washing and pooing all occurred within a few yards of the vehicle, and its crew. There was no room for shyness.'

This was Taliban country. To his north-west was the town of Now Zad, surrounded on all sides by the enemy. To his east was the Musa Qala wadi, 30 miles of green zone running north to south and entirely in the enemy's hands and the Taliban stronghold of Musa Qala town slap bang in the middle. And throughout the desert in between were small pockets of settlement, each one a potential place from which to be ambushed.

There were also objective dangers. The intelligence maps he was given showed clouds of red – marks that indicated the presence of thousands of mines left behind in the desert by Soviet troops.

They got attacked almost as soon as they arrived. In the desert it was mortars, thankfully missing them by hundreds of yards, but always setting nerves on edge. As they approached the Musa Qala wadi and the villages around, it was gunfire and RPGs that awaited them.

14. War, Tea and Sugared Almonds

The mission of the European Union, Kabul

Michael Semple was at his desk and glancing at his diary. He was halfway through a busy day – nine meetings, beginning with breakfast with a close relative of the elusive Taliban supreme leader, Mullah Omar, and with an office call to a senior official in Afghan intelligence, the NDS, planned for 15.30. His mobile phone rang. It was Naquib, his Afghan partner, calling from a guesthouse in the city suburbs. He spoke in code, something like: 'The Eagle has landed!'

In all his months of meeting with the Taliban, people always wondered how exactly Semple did it. Was he mad or foolish? How could he meet these people safely? Did he have to be disguised or protected? But Semple had a big secret: rather than disappearing off to meet the Taliban, the Taliban came to him, frequently in Kabul. It said something about the nature of this war. The British and Americans wore uniforms, looked foreign and drove about in armoured cars. Moving just 10 miles took hours of planning. But their enemy wore no uniform. They had the freedom of the roads. A Taliban leader could wake up in a Helmand trench one morning, put down his AK-47, get a lift to Kandahar and a bus to Kabul and be up there in a single day.

Semple threw his laptop into his briefcase and jumped into his office car. As his car honked its way through the crowded streets he thought about the man who was waiting for him – a top Taliban commander. He could not but admire his courage. If anyone from his side found out about the talks, he could be hanged. A field worker for Semple had been wooing this man and had tracked him down deep in Taliban territory. After meeting him face to face, the field worker suggested the commander simply jump in a car to meet up with Naquib and Semple. And the commander had agreed.

Meeting Afghans and winning their trust involved rituals – and a language that went beyond words. As he entered the guesthouse, Semple could see that Naquib had placed the commander on a couch, not on floor cushions. 'OK, he is urbanized,' thought Semple, reading the clue.

The commander – whose name Semple still keeps secret – rose up and hugged the Irishman. There was a routine: arms round chest, pull left, pull right, pull left again, lean back and shake hands. The two men looked at each other and compared beards. His was a little longer than Semple's but with no wavy edges, revealing that he trimmed it. 'In local terms that meant he was a liberal!' explained Semple later.

His headgear gave away a little more. It was a simple grey-checked *kefiya* scarf, rather than the rolled-up 9 yards of black silk that hardliners seemed to find essential. He looked Semple straight in the eye through a pair of professorial spectacles without tints. 'Confident!' thought Semple.

The commander got quickly to the point. It was about trust. A high-up Taliban official shared the commander's view that the fighting would have no happy ending. He knew about Semple's and Naquib's reconciliation work. But to end the fighting in his area he needed to trust both foreign forces and the Afghan government. 'Can I trust you? And can I trust them?' he asked.

Semple knew something of this man by reputation and the fighters he led, some of the fiercest and apparently intransigent Taliban groups that were in battle with NATO forces. And yet here he was, sharing with him a cup of tea from a silver-coloured teapot and picking at the sugared almonds and toffees. They jousted over who should pour the tea.

'You are a guest,' said the commander.

'No, you are a guest,' said Semple.

The commander told his story in a few words. That was a good sign. Experience told Semple 'to be wary of those who had too much to say'. This man was a real veteran, one who had fought as a Mujahidin against the Communist regime in Afghanistan in the 1970s – even before the Soviets had arrived. After the Soviets left, he went into business. And when the Taliban came he built cordial relations with them, but was never one of them.

The new government under President Karzai had also given him high expectations. He built a fine house in the local district centre. 'And then his local rivals tricked the Americans into trashing and looting his house, supposedly looking for the enemy,' recalled Semple. After that the man headed for the mountains and joined the resistance. The war had taken hold and before long the government was driven from their area.

Semple quizzed the commander about current details of the fighting, going through the picture village by village. It gave Semple a way of checking if this man was who he said he was. He appeared relaxed – tensing up only when he talked of civilian casualties. 'I felt he was on the verge of tears,' he recalled.

Talking fluently in Pashtu, Farsi and Urdu, the commander voiced his view that any peace settlement would be hard. He did not like the war. It had been forced on him and his people. But the men he led were tough and committed and would carry on fighting 'however long their houses were bombarded'.

'If I could really trust you and the government then it might be possible to find a way out of this,' he said, adding only that, while he could vouch for local Taliban fighters, he could not control the foreigners who joined the Taliban to fight their jihad. 'They have their own reasons for what they do,' he said.

The more the commander talked, the more excited Semple was. It was clear this man was not only a serious player, but also serious about a path to peace. Plying him with questions and bubbling with enthusiasm, he abandoned all thought of taking notes on his laptop. Naquib, who had already done his part, said nothing throughout, ready as the silent umpire to give his verdict afterwards. Semple felt a buzz of adrenalin. 'We really have a chance to do some good, perhaps to save dozens of lives,' he thought.

Semple asked the commander if he would stay the night. 'We would be honoured. It is not good to travel back so late,' he said.

But the commander knew his mind. He had to get back before he was missed. No one knew about his trip.

Semple took his permission to get up and leave. Clambering into his official car, he got out his laptop and rattled off an excited note as his driver, Waheed, pushed through the traffic. He was on his way to his next appointment with Dr Abdullah, the deputy head of the NDS and a small man in a big office of panelled walls. Semple had heard stories of the gadgets the walls concealed.

This afternoon, Abdullah was full of energy and enthused over what Semple was doing. They talked of what lay ahead. As Semple recorded in his computer that night, the spy chief's view was that the main obstacles were 'corrupt ministers' and provincial governors. Looking back, Semple would see those words as prescient.

Semple told Abdullah he was pushing ahead in Helmand province and would tell him if he needed help. He raised the question of backing from President Karzai. Abdullah said that Karzai was positive. 'I suggested it might be useful for us both to discuss it with the president – so I could say nice things about the NDS, and the NDS could say nice things about me!' recalled Semple. Abdullah described that as a 'wonderful idea'.

The meeting with Karzai never happened, though. The commander that Semple had met that day had said pointedly he believed a negotiated peace was possible 'if only we could trust the government'. Did he know something that Semple was ignoring?

15. Alone in Sangin

Outside Sangin bazaar, 14 November, 11.30

There is a blank in the mind of Lance-Corporal Onur Caglar about all that happened in the instant of the explosion. All he remembered was seeing his captain, John McDermid, thrown upwards and consumed in a great fire.

After their patrol was split in half earlier, their mentor team consisted of just the two of them, along with six Afghan soldiers and an interpreter. They were on the outskirts of Sangin, heading back to their base after a patrol through the green zone. Caglar felt the hot wind of the blast press against his face and jolt him off balance. Then, as the smoke cleared, he instinctively jumped sideways into a sort of grass-covered miniature garden as bullets started to crack around him. They were at a road T-junction and beneath a set of electrical pylons. He looked up and saw wires tumbling down in a shower of sparks. All the Afghan soldiers were in front of the blast and in front of him, and he saw it was they who were firing backwards towards him in panic. He shouted, 'Stop, stop,' and they lowered their weapons.

Caglar looked forward at where McDermid had been standing. He had vanished.

'When all the dust had settled,' he remembered, 'all I saw was Captain McDermid's leg, a big massive hole and then the interpreter lying there, and there was like bits of blood and stuff all up the wall.'

The interpreter was shouting for help, but Caglar shouted back: 'No. I can't help you at the moment. I just need to . . . I need to make sure there's no other devices here.'

Out on another patrol in the green zone, Mike Scott, the

117

company sergeant-major for the 2 Yorks in Sangin, heard and saw the blast, and knew it was an improvised explosive device, an IED, but like others he could not quite pinpoint the location. He remembered turning to Colour Sergeant Mark Syron and saying, 'Fuck, I hope that's not a command one,' meaning a command-wire detonated explosive – the worst type because it was hard to detect.

His fears turned out to be well founded. The explosion detonated a concealed 105 mm artillery shell. It had been 'daisy-chained' to connect to two pairs of mortar shells. But, luckily for the rest of the patrol, these had not gone off.

McDermid had set off that morning with a team of seven British soldiers plus the Afghans. But they had been hearing something that worried them as they listened in on the Taliban's radio network.

'Usually they'll say they're watching and they're going to shoot you with their big guns and take no mercy and all that shit,' said Caglar later. 'But it's normally just probably to wind you up. But this time they were saying exactly where we were.' The Taliban were giving names of buildings or clumps of trees they were walking by, and the soldiers turned to each other and said, 'Actually, yes, we are right there.'

McDermid decided to split the patrol in half. It was an old anti-ambush tactic from Northern Ireland called 'satellite-ing'. An enemy will only see one half of the patrol at any one time. And so they will be afraid to attack because they cannot tell if their back is covered. The tactic seemed to work. The Taliban radio went silent.

Unfortunately between McDermid and Caglar, only McDermid had a radio. Now both he and his radio had disappeared. And Caglar had no idea where his other comrades were.

Caglar was trying to work out what to do. He saw the Afghans start to run around in panic. He shouted, 'Stop! There might be more bombs.' The trouble was the interpreter was in no fit state to help to communicate.

He ran forward to try to treat him. 'He had a big chunk missing out of his thumb,' said Caglar. 'There was blood all over his hand.

All his face was bloody, his hair was all matty and dusty and had blood all over it. It was pretty much as if from his waist upwards he'd just been sprayed with shrapnel. There was just little holes all over. His body armour had . . . it was just pierced. And he had one big hole in like . . . just above his collar bone there. In his neck.' Caglar tried to give him morphine. But he realized his own hands were shaking. He got an Afghan soldier to put the needle in and to put on some bandages.

Then a car pulled up about 15 yards from the bomb crater. Caglar shouted, 'Stop,' and then bundled the wounded interpreter into the back. He shouted to the driver, 'DC!' ('DC' was the district centre, the main British base). He hoped he would understand and take him back for evacuation. That was all he could think of doing at that moment.

Turning round, he started looking for McDermid. He noticed part of his body armour. 'It was just like sat there as if someone had just put it there.' And then he saw the top part of his rifle, with the rest torn off. 'It was leaning against the wall. Just like someone had just placed it there.'

In his heart, he knew that, with a leg missing, he must be dead. But he shouted anyway.

'And I tried shouting for him, thinking, you know, that he might . . . he might still be alive. I knew . . . when it first happened I knew that he was dead because from the blast where it was he was directly above it when it went off. But I shouted for him anyway. Just in the hope that he might shout back. But I didn't get any reply.'

Caglar needed to tell someone what had happened. They needed to find McDermid, and he needed to warn others that there could be secondary devices. And he needed to get the Afghan soldiers safely back to base.

But at that moment he was completely alone – out of touch with his own army and alongside soldiers who hardly understood a word he said.

'Anyone got a mobile phone? Mobile phone?' he shouted.

'Uh.'

'Right. We need to go back to camp.'

'Uh.'

'Tangiers [the men's patrol base].'

'Uh.'

'Right. We've got to go!'

'Uh.'

Nothing seemed to register. Caglar realized he needed to go off alone. He got the ANA on to a piece of grass and set up for all-round defence. Then he picked up his machine gun, slung it across his front and started to 'peg it'.

At first he skirted along the walls of the alleyways, trying his best to think of anywhere another bomb might be laid. All he could think of in his head was: 'Boom! Boom! Boom!' Then he was into Sangin's main bazaar, and it was packed with men. It was the middle of the day. Everyone turned and stared at the spectacle of a lone British soldier running through their midst. Most days, the market was friendly territory. But Caglar knew he was vulnerable. In his mind, anyone was now a potential Taliban spy or a kidnapper. He raised his pistol as he ran along, firing shots in the air to clear a path.

'The run felt like for ever! I was totally and utterly blowing out my arse, but I was still running. I don't know how I was still running. I think it was just so much adrenalin pumping through.'

Reaching the Tangiers base, Caglar flung his helmet on the floor and found Sergeant Mattie Lynn in bed. He'd heard the explosion, but then you heard explosions all the time.

'Mattie! Mattie!'

'What? What?'

'Fuck! The boss is dead!'

They found there wasn't even a spare radio at the base. All of them were out with patrols. Together, they jumped in a WMIK and sped down the road to the bomb site. They found the rest of the soldiers from the patrol still hadn't turned up, so they drove on to the main Royal Marines compound at the district centre. Caglar was glad to find the interpreter had made it back. Already by now, a quick reaction force of marines had been sent out, although they hadn't located the blast site. Caglar could now guide them in.

That night, Caglar thought back over his time knowing McDermid. A forty-three-year-old from Glasgow, McDermid was a volunteer for the front line. After twenty-five years in the army, he had risen through the ranks from private soldier to officer, ending up with a staff position at the Sandhurst military academy. But he had volunteered for a tour in Afghanistan. He had told Caglar that morning: 'I am in a good mood this morning, because I woke up and listened to the Proclaimers.'

For the soldiers that worked in Sangin, now, it was the danger of these IEDs that hung heavy over their patrols. The British and Afghans had bases all over the town. They dominated this urban centre. But the Taliban guerrillas in their midst had not departed, merely gone underground. Their tactics were now more subtle and more unnerving.

For Scott, as he tried to motivate his soldiers after McDermid's death, he realized the blast did serve at least one thing positive. 'It might sound a bit callous, but it did give some fucking people a big wake-up call. Until that point, it was becoming a bit more like war tourism than actually doing a job, and that really did focus people's attention.' He remembered briefing young soldiers who asked, 'What can we do to stop these command wires?' And all he could say was, 'Fellas, fucking common sense.' There was no magic gadget to stop them.

But there was ultimately one weapon that could fight these hidden killers: the support of the local people. However ingeniously a bomb might be hidden, it was rarely possible to hide it from the local population. If they came on side and started informing, then the bombs could be found and disarmed quickly. That gave Scott both the chills and a glimmer of hope. While the bombs continued, it meant they had plenty of enemies out there. But it also showed that, if they got things right with the people, there was a way to win in this place.

16. Decision

'Why all this delay? Why have we had so many meetings on this?' said the president at the War Cabinet. He was getting impatient and unpredictable.

Karzai had been speaking constantly to Mullah Salaam, as well as to the former Helmand governor and nemesis of the British, Sher Muhammad Akhundzada. He had spoken too with the Musa Qala elder who had negotiated the truce agreement the previous year that secured the British pull-out. The latter was an uncle of the main Taliban leader in Musa Qala, Mullah Torjan. But all these leaders of the Alizai tribe were right behind an action to seize the town back for the Afghan government. This was a 'historic opportunity', said the president. For the first time that anyone could remember, certainly since the war with Russia, the subtribes of the Alizai were coming together.

The NATO commander was listening. It was time, he thought, to strike a clear deal of his own. Until now, Karzai had been talking endlessly about action but had been endlessly vague about what exactly he wanted.

'So, Mr President, you want me to do this thing?'

Karzai nodded.

'I will be happy to set the right conditions – but I want Afghans to go into the district centre.'

General McNeill said the plan was for NATO forces to surround the town, to bear down with pressure on all sides. That would pave the way for an Afghan force to push through the town itself.

'Yes. We want it like that,' said Karzai.

But McNeill said he wanted Karzai's agreement on two more

things. Firstly, Afghans had to hold the place afterwards. He did not want another beleaguered British force left to defend itself. Secondly, he wanted 'better governance' down in Helmand. It was a strong and clear hint that Karzai should sack Governor Wafa.

'Go ahead, then,' said Karzai. But no civilians should be killed, he said.

'It won't be my aim, Mr President, but I can't make that guarantee. We can do this thing, but stuff will get broken,' said the general. 'And we need some time here, you know.' It would take until December to assemble his forces.

Karzai looked unhappy at that.

Bismullah Khan, the Afghan army chief of staff, intervened. Speaking in Dari, he said Afghan forces were not only ready to go up and reinforce Salaam but could quite easily take Musa Qala on their own.

That just angered McNeill. Five times since he had taken command in Afghanistan, Karzai had rejected the general's suggestion of an operation to recapture the town. Now, after finally giving the green light, the Afghans wanted it done yesterday. There was also delusional thinking going on here, thought McNeill. A 'tribal alliance' might make the people welcome the Taliban's removal. That was crucial to the future. But it was not going to drive a bunch of *jihadi* fighters and narco barons out of town. Nor would the toothless Mullah Salaam help. And nor could the Afghan army do it on their own. They were becoming better trained and more effective. But, if they attacked alone, they would be slaughtered.

None of this was said to Karzai, however. In a gathering like this, no one was going to shatter his pride. In fact, as one senior westerner present at such meetings wondered aloud to me, 'Was the president in his palace ever getting the raw truth?'

McNeill concealed his feelings. Backed by the US ambassador, the general said diplomatically that it would simply be better to wait for all forces to be in place. 'Otherwise the Taliban will simply escape.'

Karzai was still not satisfied. What exactly was the plan to go and rescue Mullah Salaam if his compound was assaulted by the

Taliban? It would be the 'worst possible outcome' to pull out Salaam in ignominious defeat, with his tail between his legs.

The Afghan defence minister suggested a separate plan to protect Salaam. That calmed Karzai.

For all the president's frayed nerves, an agreement was finally in place. Musa Qala would be taken by force. NATO troops would surround the town, but the decisive part of the operation, the seizure of the town itself, was to be done, it was agreed, by the Afghan army.

The meeting that approved an 'Afghan-led' military action had taken place with the British ambassador still away on leave. Cowper-Coles, who had been the voice of caution, was to get a shock when he returned.

McNeill swung rapidly into action. That night he summoned Brigadier Mackay up to Kabul to brief him the following day on how this operation could work. Mackay informed London: 'COMISAF has directed that the conditions have been met to launch decisive operations against Musa Qala.'

The desert west of Musa Qala

They knew they were being watched everywhere. The Taliban had their 'dickers' – as the British called the spotters – on motorbikes or trucks or dug in somewhere. They were shadowing the British forces out in the desert and calling down mortars and rockets to attack their positions.

To the east and west of Musa Qala, the two mobile operating groups, the eastern commanded by Major Chris Bell and his Warrior company and the western by Major Tony Phillips' Brigade Reconnaissance Force, were now in daily battle with the Taliban as they probed the town's outer defences. Raids by US special force Green Berets were also intensifying – targeting Taliban strongholds in villages to the south of the town.

Out to the west, Phillips recalled 'we were the only show in town' for the Taliban. All day long, listening to the Taliban's radio network, his men heard their enemy preparing to attack. 'We could hear them broadcasting a running commentary of what we were doing. And we would later find out why: the enemy had observation points in the high ground.'

As they manoeuvred in the desert, the BRF's contact with local Afghans was sporadic, and those they met were cautious. One nomadic shepherd, wandering alone in a pair of trainers, said it all when he spoke to Captain Duncan Campbell, one of the officers, and threw up his arms in despair. 'You are always coming here to ask about the Taliban. The Taliban come and ask about the British. Me, I'm still looking for my sheep!'

Getting supplied was everything on this desert patrol. Most of it came by parachute – palets pushed out of a Hercules plane on to a drop zone they marked at night. Sometimes it was a Chinook chopper. That was the best because it brought the mail (too risky to drop by air) and maybe some cigarettes. They would feast for a while on parcels from their families. And then it was back to the boil-in-the-bag field rations. For a while, they ate special halal Muslim food. They had ordered some for the interpreters but then got three months' supply for everyone. And no British rations.

Life developed a pattern out here. In the day they approached the Taliban-held villages, always targeting a new place and always by a new route. And at night they retreated back to their harbour, set up camp and cooked their rations. For the moment, even as they fought the Taliban on a daily basis, the BRF seemed to be blessed. They struck no mines and they took no injuries. They remembered how, after the suicide strike, the locals in Gereshk called them the 'warriors protected by God'.

Their life had a certain romance. They looked like the SAS with their long beards and dusty smocks and *shemagh* headdresses. But most just found it plain hard, and sometimes boring.

'I enjoyed it, to be honest with you,' recalled Simon Annan, a thirty-year-old sniper. 'But you have the same conversations with everybody. It's just Groundhog Day. It's almost like you want

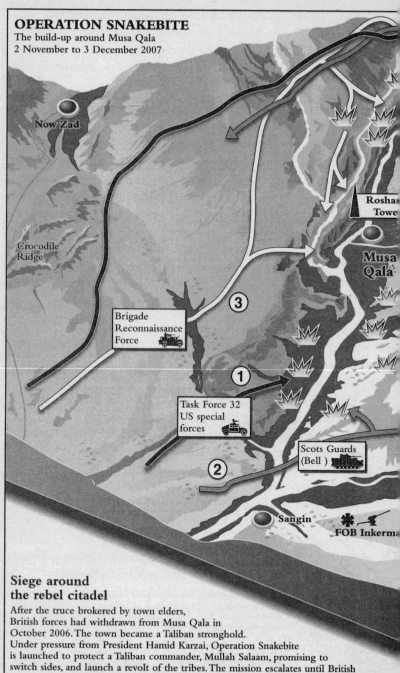

OPERATION SNAKEBITE
The build-up around Musa Qala
2 November to 3 December 2007

Now Zad

Crocodile
Ridge

Rosha
Towe

Musa
Qala

Brigade
Reconnaissance
Force

③

①

Task Force 32
US special
forces

②

Scots Guards
(Bell)

Sangin

FOB Inkerma

Siege around
the rebel citadel

After the truce brokered by town elders,
British forces had withdrawn from Musa Qala in
October 2006. The town became a Taliban stronghold.
Under pressure from President Hamid Karzai, Operation Snakebite
is launched to protect a Taliban commander, Mullah Salaam, promising to
switch sides, and launch a revolt of the tribes. The mission escalates until British
and US forces surround the town from the desert.

Grand Canyon Crossing

(4)

Household Cavalry
C Squadron

▲ Mount
Doom

Helm's Deep

King's Royal Hussars
B Squadron

(5)

Mullah Salaam's
compound

N
5 Miles
10 Kilometres

Ring of Fire

Battles with Taliban forces   Artillery support

(1) Special forces Green Berets begin attack on Taliban defences in the wadi south of Musa Qala from mid-October.

(2) On 2 November, the Scots Guards' Right Flank Company of armoured Warriors begin crossing the Musa Qala wadi with a supply column and artillery guns. Their orders are to patrol close to the village of rebel Taliban commander Mullah Salaam and to launch diversionary attacks.

(3) On 11 November, the eighty strong Brigade Reconnaissance Force deploy in WMIK Land Rovers and trucks to the west and north-west of Musa Qala.

(4) On 21 November, C Squadron of the Household Cavalry, mounted in light Scimitar tanks, cross a canyon 16 miles to the north of Musa Qala, relieving the Scots Guards, who return to base. The squadron is soon in daily battle.

(5) The cavalrymen of B Squadron, The King's Royal Hussars, mounted in Mastiff armoured vehicles, move with the Scots Guards into the desert and then defend the supply camp and mobile artillery troop east of Musa Qala. They also begin their own independent attacks.

something to happen because it gives you something else to talk about. There were periods we sat for two or three days doing nothing, prepping for something. You've just got to try and motivate yourself.'

Much of the fighting involved exchanges of fire at long distance. But some of it was at close quarters. One of the BRF, acting sergeant John 'Matty' Cockburn, would later be awarded a Military Cross, an award for gallantry, for leading a six-man team that charged 200 yards to assault a Taliban trench and captured a prisoner after coming under fire from heavy machine guns.

On the eastern side of Musa Qala, Chris Bell's Warrior company of the Scots Guards, now code-named on the Taliban radio as the 'Desert Devils', kept up a similar routine of camping in hidden positions – often in old Russian trenches – and then moving to the edge of Musa Qala to engage in daily battle.

'It's a wearing thing to do for week after week after week,' said Bell. 'We were disrupting the enemy but we didn't know what effect we were having. We certainly knew that we could drive out to any village in the area and cause absolute chaos – women and children running out, mopeds appearing on hills, the guys in black, who were clearly Taliban, directing. We really didn't know to what degree we were disrupting the enemy. We just knew that we were attracting fire almost every day.'

The squadron of King's Royal Hussars in their six-wheeled Mastiff armoured vehicles were also in action. Deployed primarily to protect the logistics convoy that kept the Warriors going, they played a game of cat and mouse, moving and hiding the soft-skinned logistics trucks away from Taliban spotters. They also began to launch their own independent attacks against the Taliban defences. The Mastiff was the one vehicle the British had that was practically mine-proof. The squadron was to hit fourteen IEDs and mines – and no one suffered a serious injury in one.

For all their attempts to harass the British troops with mines or mortars, the Taliban were powerless to prevent the build-up of a large armoured encirclement, a sort of ring of fire around Musa Qala. By constantly probing the Taliban's defences, they steadily

2. Brigadier Andrew Mackay commanded all British troops in Afghanistan and the multinational Task Force Helmand. He believes there have been too many pointless battles and that the target for British troops is to win the support of the population.

3. Sir Sherard Cowper-Coles, the British ambassador to Kabul, arrived in May 2007 with a determination to avoid misplaced optimism about the war.

4. General Dan McNeill was the NATO commander in Kabul. He believed the mission was 'not to defeat the Taliban but defeat their strategy'.

5. President Hamid Karzai, pictured on a trip to the UK, was not shy of publicly criticizing coalition tactics, most of all the number of civilians killed.

6. Major Jake Little commanded B Company, 2 Yorks, which the author was to accompany in Musa Qala.

7. The promised defection of Mullah Abdul Salaam, a suspected Taliban commander, was the start of it all.

8. Lieutenant Colonel Brian Mennes commanded the American Task Force 1 Fury, a reserve force for Afghanistan. They knew that Musa Qala was somewhere on their horizon. A veteran of special forces, Mennes had forthright views on what was going wrong in the war – and how to fix it.

10. Michael Semple, an Irishman working as a diplomat for the European Union mission, was leading discreet talks with the Taliban across Afghanistan. By the end, he calculated, he might have met more Taliban commanders than the rebel movement's own supreme leader.

9. Sergeant Lee 'Jonno' Johnson, a platoon sergeant with B Company, 2 Yorks, was part of the team mentoring the Afghan army. Once known as 'Mad Dog' and 'Judo' Johnson, he was one of the battalion's most colourful and beloved characters. He had strange premonitions of what lay ahead.

11. British soldiers eat dinner with former Taliban fighters persuaded to change sides by Michael Semple. They were known simply as 'the Group'.

12. Royal Marines in action in the 'Battle of 9/11' outside Inkerman base on 11 November 2007 – the climax of one of the most intense days across Helmand in six months.

13. Mortar line at Inkerman in action in support of troops in contact.

14. Flight Lieutenant Nichol Benzie, who took his Chinook into the 'green zone' on 9/11 in the heat of battle.

15. A *shura* organized by B Company, 2 Yorks, after they were scrambled out of Helmand province and sent to capture a town that had fallen to the Taliban. When B Company returned to base, the Taliban recaptured the town again – an example, says Little, of 'daft orders' from President Karzai.

16-17. *Above*, a Warrior armoured vehicle from the Scots Guards company commanded by Major Chris Bell (*top right*), who led the push into the desert round Musa Qala, at first to protect the rebel Taliban commander Mullah Salaam, whom they soon called Mullah Salami.

18-21. Supplied by frequent parachute drops, the Warriors were joined in the desert by the Brigade Reconnaissance Force (*above left and below right*), who probed far to the north of Musa Qala. Their commander was Major Tony Phillips (*below left*).

22. Taliban fighters photographed in the centre of Musa Qala. One commander declared: 'Our lines are so strong that the foreigners will never break them.'

23. Mullah Sadiq was the Taliban commander in Kajaki. He had doubts about killing and injuring British soldiers, declaring: 'It is their leaders, the politicians and generals, that I would like in the sights of my gun.'

24-5. The small object tumbling from the sky is a satellite-guided JDAM bomb that wreaks devastation when it drops milli-seconds later on to a compound near Garmsir, southern Helmand. The photos were taken by a soldier of the King's Royal Hussars.

26. Soldiers of Task Force 1 Fury from the 82nd Airborne prepare for departure at Kandahar airfield (*left*).

27-8. 1 Fury soldiers head off for the air assault on Musa Qala (*above and left*).

29. A soldier from the Brigade Reconnaissance Force reaches the edge of Musa Qala. The Musa Qala wadi is below, with 'Mount Doom' in the background.

turned up the psychological heat on the Taliban forces in the town. It was what Brigadier Mackay called an 'influence operation'.

Not all activity was productive. Both the KRH and Scots Guards spent days on standby supposedly in readiness to help arrange a secret meeting, instigated by some other agency, between Mullah Salaam and a VIP. They were never told who that was supposed to be, whether it was President Karzai himself or just their brigade commander. 'All we knew of it,' said Bell, was that 'there were people who wanted to speak to Mullah Salami, for whom we were doing all this running around: Every morning it would be "It's on," and then "It's definitely off." That was our life for about a week, and it never happened. And we were doing a lot of reassurance for him, hanging around his village constantly.'

In the weeks that followed, Bell's Warriors were withdrawn to prepare for the attack on Musa Qala itself. They were replaced out in the desert around Mullah Salaam's compound by a squadron of light tanks, the C Squadron of the Household Cavalry Regiment. The handover took place about as far north as British conventional forces had ever reached in Helmand. Circling round through the desert to a point 16 miles north of Musa Qala, the two armoured forces crossed tracks in the stunning scenery of what became called the Grand Canyon Crossing.

Phillips' BRF had scouted the route and remained in position along it. As the vehicles moved across, the Taliban fired over volley after volley of mortars. The soldiers in armoured vehicles could just jump inside and shut their hatches. The BRF, mostly in their open-topped Land Rovers, could only crouch on the ground.

Brigade headquarters, Lashkar Gah

At brigade headquarters, Major Nick Haston, the deputy chief of staff, was staring at a line of figures on a spreadsheet – and it did not add up. The shortage and state of repair of military equipment in Helmand was already bad, but, with a huge operation now on the cards, it was not clear how the troops would get what they needed.

Haston already had some strong feelings on the subject. In public, politicians and generals were claiming the troops were happy with the equipment they had. But he pointed to a yawning gap between the official military estimates of what was needed for this war and the actual equipment in a working state in Helmand.

A few days before, Brigadier Mackay had signed a forthright 'ground truth' memo back to London that warned of a 'grave' situation. The facts at the time were stark. According to brigade staff:

Only one-fifth of the total of heavy machine guns required in Helmand were available.

Only half of the required number of WMIK Land Rovers had been supplied, and many that were working in Helmand lacked crucial fittings.

British soldiers were said to have only half the chance of American soldiers of being equipped with night-vision goggles.

Too many engines were not working among the Household Cavalry Regiment's aged family of Scimitar light reconnaissance tanks. In a perennial problem, many tanks that were declared as 'working' could not even go into reverse gear without restarting the engine, a limitation that was 'not helpful' in combat.

A quarter of the brand new Mastiff armoured vehicles were out of action for weeks because of a missing supply of cheap suspension springs.

Many of the 6 x 6 Vector armoured vehicles in Helmand were out of action because 'the wheels just kept falling off, literally'.

This was not to mention simple design flaws in some British vehicles that, according to some military engineers, made their drivers and front-seat commanders (typically officers or NCOs) uniquely vulnerable to being killed by mine strikes. The continued use of such designs was 'barking mad', thought Haston. In his memo, Mackay was said to have warned of a 'grave crisis' with too much equipment that was 'tired, limited, and failing regularly'.

Time and again, Haston recalled, he and his team found ways to 'manage', but that meant pieces of equipment – from night-vision goggles to machine guns to Land Rovers – were constantly shuffled from one unit to another. Brigade staff, who should have been thinking of the bigger picture, spent time following the fate of an individual set of goggles or even a packet of nuts and bolts.

Held back by a bureaucracy in the UK that was not on a war footing, Haston said he had to bend the rules – buying spares with a credit card on the Internet, for example. And after being kept waiting for weeks for the springs for the Mastiff squadron's vehicles, it took their commander, Major Richard Slack, to pick up a satellite phone from the desert and phone a factory in Coventry to discover and prove that the springs could be easily made in Britain.

As the Musa Qala operation built up, Haston was having to 'beg, borrow and steal' Land Rovers for Helmand from British units based in Kandahar. He would tell them the vehicles he took would be back in a week. 'I kept lying to them for three months! It's awful but we did . . . But that sort of thing creates tension, mistrust . . .'

The complaints to higher command went down badly, Haston recalled, particularly Mackay's tersely worded memo. There seemed to be a feeling that 52 Brigade, with its humble origins, was somehow naive – as if *real* warriors in a *real* war just managed with what they had. All experienced soldiers, the thinking went, had to tailor their suit to fit their cloth. 'I think they thought he [Mackay] was slightly naive to write it,' recalled Haston, 'when he knew damn fine what he was doing. He did not want this issue smothered.'

When he returned from Afghanistan, Haston was to quit the army in disgust. 'I've resigned for a reason – and some of that reason is that I think there are some mediocre, high-level managers who are unwilling to admit and face up to some of the issues we've got . . . I would say that some of the people that procure [equipment] in our Ministry of Defence haven't a clue.'

17. The Manhunt

'The captives of our bow and spear
Are cheap – alas! As we are dear'

Rudyard Kipling, 'Arithmetic on the Frontier'

Forward Operating Base Delhi, Garmsir district centre, 18 November

It was early in the morning when a truck pulled up to the gates of the base. On sentry duty, the Gurkhas of B Company, 1 Royal Gurkha Rifles, could see the bodies of several wounded Afghans slumped in the back. The injured were angry. They claimed that foreign and Afghan soldiers had raided their village by helicopter. At least eighteen people, including children, were dead. Their homes – which the Afghans later identified as the village of Toube – were about twenty minutes' drive to the south, on the Taliban side of the front line. The Gurkhas were surprised. They knew of no operations which had been underway that night. Either the incident was invented or this was the result of something secret, most likely the work of special forces.

There were two hospitals in the area of Garmsir. One was the medical centre at the Delhi base. The other was run by the Taliban. Why had they chosen the British base? the Gurkhas wondered. Some of the injured were men of fighting age. They could be Taliban. Their blast and gunshot injuries suggested a fire fight. But, if they were Taliban, why had they come here?

The doctor on duty was perplexed by some of their injuries. They needed more specialist care. 'It's pretty inconclusive either way,' he told the Gurkhas. He decided to send the injured onwards to the civilian hospital in Lashkar Gah.

No public announcement was made of the incident that day.

No statement was released to the press. But the incident would not be forgotten.

More than three weeks later, a report appeared on the Internet from an international news agency, the Institute for War and Peace Reporting (IWPR). The agency, which works across conflict zones, had received British funding to train journalists in Helmand in the basics of news reporting. Now these same local journalists had their scoop. The headline read: 'Foreign Troops Accused in Helmand Raid Massacre'. The IWPR reported the story of a young baker called Abdul Manaan, who was still lying in Lashkar Gah's emergency hospital with his throat bandaged. He claimed to have survived despite his throat being cut by a group of soldiers – Afghan and foreign – that arrived by helicopter on 18 November. The IWPR reported:

'It was about two in the morning when we heard the aircraft, and I woke up,' said Abdul Manaan. 'My two younger brothers came to me to ask what was going on, but I told them, "Nothing, just go back to sleep."

'Then I heard a noise on the roof, and I looked out and there were armed men up there. They climbed down and came into my brothers' room, and asked them if they were Taliban. One of my brothers said "No, we are shopkeepers, come and search the house. We have nothing, no guns or anything." The soldiers shot him on the spot. My other brother they brought to me, and tied his hands. Then they slit his throat. I could hear him gurgling. He was still making a noise when they got to me.

'They made me stand up against the wall and tied my hands. They put the knife to my neck and cut me three times. Then they threw an old tarpaulin over me and left.

'But I wasn't dead.'[17]

As Abdul Manaan lay under the tarpaulin, holding his hand to his neck wound, he heard the soldiers moving around the house and children screaming. When the soldiers left after about half an hour, he said, 'I got up and went to my brother. He was cold.' He found the women and children alive in another room, together with some who had come from other houses. 'Everyone was screaming and crying,' he said.

In the morning, Abdul Manaan was taken to hospital in Lashkar Gah. 'I survived, but my brothers are dead,' he said. 'What shall I do now?'

For months now the IWPR had documented frequent cases of civilians dying in NATO bombing raids. Often the coalition claimed that Taliban had been fighting from or hiding in the compounds of ordinary civilians. Their deaths were accidental. But this raid appeared different and far more brutal. The report continued:

Abdul Manaan's story is echoed by dozens of villagers from Toube whom IWPR interviewed as they underwent treatment in Lashkar Gah or accompanied injured relatives there. All spoke consistently of soldiers breaking down doors, shooting children and cutting throats. They agreed that the raid began at two in the morning with the sound of helicopters bringing in dozens of armed men, both Afghan and foreign.

Who was really responsible for the raid? And what was the truth of the events that night?

After the injured had left, a phone call came in from a secret unit, asking for the identity of the injured they had treated. Major Mark Milford, the B Company commander, was less than impressed. Why had they not bothered to inform him of the raid? Technically, the target was outside the area he controlled. But only just. And, as night follows day, it was his company of Gurkhas that would be left picking up the pieces – and dealing with any local anger that followed. For the Afghans, the forces involved were simply 'foreign troops' backed by local soldiers. American or British, special forces or conventional troops. They could not tell them apart.

'My complaint was that I wasn't told about it,' recalled Milford. 'You know, we had no details on it. So, we ended up, you know, trying to photograph people, trying to treat them at the same time, trying to figure out what had gone on but not knowing what had happened.

'We treated the people and then released them. And then, all of a sudden, they were saying to us, "Right, what about Omar whatever his name was? Was he in the truck when it came?" Well, I had absolutely no idea. They hadn't left a liaison officer or anything with us. They just hit the target.'

Milford declined to identify the unit involved. But American sources in Kabul revealed its identity: a unit known only by a code-number, Task Force 373.[18] This was not only US special forces, but elite 'tier 1' special forces, the US Navy Seals supported by Army Rangers. The job of 373 was to hunt and 'take down' human beings: the top commanders of the Taliban and Al Qaeda.

The mission that night was code-named Operation Black Carib, the sources said, and it had been successful: it had fatally wounded a Taliban commander, Sher Agha, who had mounted a series of attacks on the British in Garmsir since the beginning of November.

If there was one thing that marred British and American operations in Afghanistan more than anything else it was the persistent reports of the death of ordinary Afghans. Speaking generally about civilian deaths, Mackay would say: 'You can't talk about winning over the population and then be dismissive if you end up accidentally killing part of that population.'

The trouble for regular soldiers was that – again and again – the military units behind these controversial attacks were special force units whose operations were cloaked in secrecy. While Afghans demanded explanations and justice, regular soldiers and their spokesmen were forced to say, 'No comment.'

The use of elite special forces, with the skills to fight in small numbers and survive behind the enemy's lines, had long been seen by America and Britain as at the heart of a strategy to win against a guerrilla army. Just as in Northern Ireland, British army operations had always had their dual components: while regular soldiers did 'framework operations' to take and dominate ground and work with the population, more secretive units made use of intelligence to take the fight to the enemy.

'Don't be deceived by all the hearts and minds and all the open stuff,' one US general told me. 'As big a part of the war is what we call the manhunt: tracking down and getting the bad guys.'

By the winter of 2007, the conventional forces in Task Force Helmand under Mackay's command were augmented by what was becoming a baffling array of different special force teams. None of them came under Brigade's direct command; some of them were not even under NATO command, but rather under America's Operation Enduring Freedom anti-terrorist campaign. And, time and again, the operations they launched came without notice to those who would face the consequences of their actions – sometimes good and sometimes bad.

Britain's most elite forces were the Special Air Service (SAS) and the Royal Marines' equivalent, the less-well-known Special Boat Service (SBS). By 2007, the two key theatres of war were divided so the SAS concentrated on Iraq and the SBS led in Afghanistan. (Likewise, the SAS's sister force, the American Delta Force, also concentrated on Iraq, and the Navy Seals took on Afghanistan.)

Along with the special forces from other European countries like France, Germany and Italy, the SBS had been placed under NATO command. Formed into a 'mobile high-value target team', its activities in Helmand were controlled by the regional headquarters in Kandahar, and ultimately by General McNeill. America's Task Force 373, however, was not under McNeill's command but was working under orders from US Central Command.

British forces had their own special forces base in Helmand, somewhere in the desert, and the backing of the 1st Battalion, the Parachute Regiment, who had in 2006 been re-roled from conventional soldiers into the Special Forces Support Group, operating rather like US Rangers. British special force units were also embedded in training Afghan elite forces. A national counter-narcotics unit, Force 333, was led by British SBS mentors and was in theory under Afghan government command. So was a new reconnaissance force that was training to become a unit to be called the Helmand Scouts.

Also in Helmand was a United Arab Emirates special forces contingent and a reconnaissance force of US marines. The largest American force, however, and the most visible special force presence in the province, was the ubiquitous Green Berets. In Helmand they were operating non-covertly as Task Force 32. Their main global mission – as first defined by President Kennedy, who set them up – was to work alongside indigenous forces, here the Afghan army. But they also worked independently, under the orders not of NATO but of US Central Command.

The logic of using special forces to fight the Taliban was unassailable. The best-trained guerrilla armies melt away before superior forces and the advance of conventional units. They operate in small groups. They stay hidden. They wait for an ambush. They use lightweight kit and they stay mobile. The obvious way to find and to defeat them is to match their tactics. This is where the special forces could excel. At their best, special forces could not only be more devastating to the enemy, they could also be more precise in avoiding killing the innocent.

But working behind enemy lines was dangerous work. In the open, flat deserts of Helmand or the densely populated green zones, there was often little place to hide. The population acted as scouts for the enemy. And a small patrol of special force fighters could easily become overwhelmed. To survive, the patrol would have to call in air power. Then, suddenly, the light footprint became heavy and, with little time to flee from the fight, civilians might get killed by the bombs or crossfire.

The alternative was to strike fast and furiously: to land by helicopter at night, attack the target and then withdraw before the enemy gathered strength. But this too had its drawbacks. A raid was only as good as the intelligence that directed it. And, in a country where ordinary families possessed guns to defend themselves, there was always a high risk that anyone would end up shot. Surprised in his home at night by masked soldiers bursting in, an innocent man might reach for his gun and then be shot instantly by a coalition soldier – acting in self-defence.

Talking of the land round Garmsir, Milford said the people there were jumpy and would defend their homes. 'These people were armed, and yes, they may well have been shooting. But were they protecting their property or were they Taliban?'

Soon after the incident in Toube, a deputation of tribal elders came up to Lashkar Gah to protest at the American raid. They demanded compensation and justice.

In one meeting attended by almost 100 people, the Helmand police chief, Muhammad Andiwal, blamed the Taliban for fighting from the compounds of ordinary families. 'I can feel your pain,' he told the elders. 'Even a heart of stone would melt with these sorrows. I will speak with the foreigners and make them promise not to kill civilians again like this.'

Andiwal told me later: 'They complained there were nineteen or twenty killed, and I'm not sure of the numbers.' But he added, 'It is true. There were casualties.'

Brigade staff who attended the meetings with the elders were suspicious. They wondered if the villagers had been stirred up by the Taliban to make up the allegations of innocent civilians killed. Though supposedly elders from the community, the people involved were unfamiliar. Was this an attempt to turn the Afghan government against the coalition?

Time and again, the facts of these 'civilian casualty' incidents were disputed. The special force units involved would claim that only Taliban or terrorists were killed in the attacks; Afghans would complain that innocents had died too, and the Afghan government – often President Karzai himself – would say he was outraged. Intelligence officers believed the Taliban were being increasingly sophisticated: encouraging the media to report such allegations because they knew what controversy the deaths of civilians had caused.

An investigation was launched by US Central Command into allegations that innocents had died in the raid. The soldiers involved claim that no one's throat had been slashed. And all those killed or injured had been photographed and were accounted for. 'It is clear to us that all of those injured or killed were enemy,' said one US source, speaking only on condition of anonymity.

And yet, when I asked further questions about this incident in Helmand and in Kabul, something still did not ring true about the Allied explanations. Rather than a consistent story, different explanations were offered for what happened.

'This raid was carried out as result of intelligence and against a leadership target,' said another senior coalition source. 'We believe the Taliban may have come back and taken revenge against the villagers they blamed for tipping us off. Then they ordered these people to blame us.'

Major Milford – who knew nothing of the details of the raid but simply had to deal with some of the elders who protested – said he never quite got to the bottom of things. There was something distinctly odd about those who complained. The truck that brought the injured was identified later carrying Taliban fighters. But if they had really been Taliban who were hurt and killed that night, why would they have brought them to the British base? And why would the tribes have protested so vehemently? He didn't know the answer. 'I'm slightly dubious of them, but my personal view is that they were probably smugglers . . . But, I mean, you'll never know. It's just so grey, it's unbelievable.'

For months, the manhunt pursued by these elite forces had been relentless, particularly since the summer. Now, as an attack on Musa Qala loomed, senior US commanders ordered an intensifying of strikes in Helmand.

Military intelligence was producing large diagrams of the leadership of Taliban groups and how they were inter-connected. Names of the important figures were highlighted and became designated as high-value targets, or HVTs.

This was the bread-and-butter work of intelligence across the world in the war on terror. The difference in Afghanistan was that, *provided the information was corroborated by enough sources*, a place on the chart could mean a death sentence. 'It is death by link diagram out here,' one intelligence officer told me. One by one the charts were modified with crosses through the names of those who had been eliminated.

Some soldiers, including some from special forces, felt uncomfortable. They compared all this to the tactics of the Israelis, who systematically assassinated the leadership of Palestine militant groups. It had not won the war there. Or even quelled the violence one jot. It was not that many shed tears for those who were assassinated. Some just wondered where this 'take-down' of enemy leadership was leading, and whether the intelligence was good enough to get it right. Too often the wrong people got killed, as well as anyone who just happened to be around at the time, some said. It was not that innocents were deliberately killed.

One officer, reflecting a minority view, was harshly critical. 'They always say afterwards that the dead were enemy, or they went for the gun. But the reality is that every young man ends up dead.' When attempts were made to investigate afterwards, all involved clammed up.

The same officer, with some direct knowledge of the special forces, continued: 'The routine is something like this. Go to a gym, pump some iron, jump into a helicopter in the dark, jump out and kill all males of fighting age and then go back, get a bit of kip and then back to the gym, pump some iron.'

A more nuanced view, from someone with current special forces involvement, was simply that the balance had gone wrong. Enemy leadership targets needed elite units to hunt them down. But historically special forces had had a much wider role. Time and time again, unconventional wars needed special forces at the heart of the battle. That meant deploying them on long-range deep patrolling, in covert positions, for accurate 'eyes-on' targeting. Above all else they should be working directly and mixed up with local indigenous forces, exploiting their language skills and ability to work with little support or back-up, in small teams. It was their work alongside the Omani regulars in Dhofar in the 1970s that had been the most famous role of the SAS. That was also the reason the American Green Berets were set up by President Kennedy.

'We're too focused on this secret work, too focused on takedown operations,' said the officer. 'The skills of the special forces are the skills needed for assisting the main fight – for the wider effort of getting down among the population and working alongside some pretty wild elements, being lethal but focused. That is what wins these kinds of wars. We have not abandoned this work. We are doing it. But it should be the main effort.'

The elimination of Taliban leadership, others pointed out, appeared to be at odds with the idea of a reconciliation with them. There was a risk of eliminating an Afghan version of the Irish Republican leaders Gerry Adams or Martin McGuinness who could be the ones negotiating a peace. The fear of death might drive enemy leaders to the negotiating table, but it also eliminated some of the few local leaders and strongmen with whom the Afghan government and NATO forces might eventually have to make a deal. One senior British intelligence source pointed out to me that the lessons from the battle against the IRA were that terrorist leaders only entered into meaningful talks once they grew tired of the fighting. 'To some extent, these people have to grow old. There is not much you can do when their rage is still young.'

Senior commanders argued that no one would be targeted if there was a belief they might cross sides. A rigorous targeting process meant that all options were considered before a strike. But the Taliban being killed were the same ones who were planning bomb attacks or ambushes on British or American troops. All would be replaced eventually, but the death of every leader was a setback for the enemy – and those who replaced them were generally not as capable, they insisted. Though as one Taliban leader after another was eliminated – and the rebellion got stronger – many found it hard not to conclude this was wishful thinking.

For all his belief in reconciliation, Michael Semple also took a sympathetic view of the targeting. From directly talking to the Taliban in Helmand, what he saw was a growing fear of death among these men that might encourage some to start thinking of quitting.

'I found as the target killings continued,' recalled Semple later, 'a stunning sense of mortality was encouraged by that. They were well aware they were about to be targeted. They didn't want to die.'

By the time Sher Agha, the target of Black Carib, was killed on 18 November, the Gurkhas of B Company in Garmsir had been under attack for days. And when he died the attacks stopped. 'That is why I personally didn't kick up much of a fuss because it did give us a breathing space,' said Mark Milford. 'Every time there was some sort of activity further south, we'd have a couple of days' rest, basically.' Milford had also won a new concession. Next time there was a raid near his patch, he was promised at least several hours' notice.

Whoever was killed in the attack – in addition to Agha – it was obviously a blow to the Taliban. But the respite earned was just four days. Then the attacks on the Gurkhas started up all over again. Wave after wave of Taliban continued to push forward against the British lines, mostly to meet an ignominious death. 'The cull continues,' reported Lieutenant Colonel Ed Smyth-Osbourne, the commander of the Household Cavalry Regiment headquarters that then ran the battle in the south.

18. The Yanks Are Coming!

Lieutenant Colonel Brian Mennes, commander of Task Force 1 Fury, looked down on the floor of the tent and studied the British plan marked out on a huge map, and he was not best pleased. In fact, he was horrified. The forty-one-year-old led an elite force of paratroopers who had been fighting in Afghanistan for almost eleven months now. Much of it had been in Helmand. They had launched air assaults up in Kajaki and down in Sangin, and in the green zone north of Gereshk. And he was not going to let his men down now by agreeing to something foolish.

It was Thanksgiving – three days earlier – when his battalion had been driving south, and he had got the call to proceed to Lashkar Gah. His higher command said the Musa Qala op had the green light. It could happen within a week. And his soldiers would be in the teeth of it. Mennes did not know Brigadier Mackay and he did not know his views or reasons. But what he saw was a plan from Mackay to split his forces with *two* air assaults. And, as he put it mildly later, 'I was adamantly against it.'

Task Force 1 Fury was the name used on deployment for one of America's most famous airborne assault units, the 1st Battalion of the 508th Parachute Infantry Regiment of the 82nd Airborne Division – also known as the 'Red Devils' or simply the 1-508. They had dropped into Normandy on D-Day and fought in the Ardennes in the Second World War, and then fought later in Vietnam, Panama and, more recently, Iraq. Since January they had been in Afghanistan as the theatre reserve, effectively a strike force under the personal control of the NATO commander, General Dan McNeill.

Originally from Buffalo, New York, Brian Mennes, the 1-508

commander for the last year, was a veteran of US special forces. He had been one of the first to deploy on the ground in Afghanistan when the 'war on terror' was launched after 9/11. Running missions against Al Qaeda targets, he had been based at the Rhino airfield in the desert of eastern Helmand. When he returned to Afghanistan in January 2007 as 1 Fury's commander, he had expected to be there for a year. But now American soldiers were serving gruelling fifteen-month tours – in combat zones where the action was relentless.

Ever since they had arrived in the country, his men had known that Musa Qala lay on the horizon. NATO had announced it was not a case of if but when. But, like so many things in the military, when the plans came together, they came in a hurry.

Mennes had misgivings before he even arrived at the British headquarters. His commanders, or 'Higher' as he called them, had told him it was going to be simple: 'You're just gonna go out and support the Afghans. They're going to do the heavy lifting.' He had seen the same talk of Afghan 'heavy lifting' in a PowerPoint slide sent up by the British from Helmand. But, as he flew down, he had thought to himself: 'There's no way this Afghan force is going to take this town.' One of two things was going to happen, he thought. Either they would get into a fight, and the special forces guys would have to bring in 'huge kinetic effects' just to get them in there, in other words heavy air and artillery strikes that brought the risk of killing civilians. Or it would just be a huge failure and embarrassment. The Afghans were 'going to get stuffed and we're gonna have to bail them out'. And trying to rescue a unit in contact was hard 'because the enemy gets bolstered, and then you're in a real bad way'.

Mennes had been worried about the timing too. He knew Karzai was pressing now for action fast. McNeill had even talked of action by 1 December. Just one week away. And if they left it longer – after the moonlight began to fade – then they would have to land by daylight. 1 Fury had done at least six helicopter assaults in Helmand since they had arrived. *None of them were in daylight.*

He had wanted more time for his men to get ready. For the last four months they had been based up in the north-east of the country, doing softer-edged counter-insurgency work. He told Higher: 'I need to get my guys in physical shape.' They needed to train, do target practice and get rested before they did something big.

Arriving now at the British headquarters for an all-day 'war game' for Musa Qala, he was worried he was coming late, when some basic assumptions, including some wrong ones, had already been made, he feared. The British wanted to put half his forces just south of Musa Qala in a blocking formation and another half that would assault the town. Not only would he be splitting his forces 'in two near-simultaneous air assaults', which was 'not prudent', recalled Mennes, but he also disliked the direction of the attack. NATO troops would be coming from the south and south-west – just as the Soviets had attacked the town in 1983.

Of course, the British way of planning was different from the Americans, whose commanders imposed more top-down direction. And, from Mackay's point of view in hindsight, what Mennes had seen as firm plans had only been options.

Mennes believed in working with the Brits. The way he saw it, he had done something unique, even historic, down in Helmand. Time and again, he had put his US troops under the direct command of British brigadiers for their operations. But he also had his bottom lines. As a US commander he was not going to do something that put his own forces at risk or guaranteed some debacle. Either his partners got that message gently, or he would have to draw a line in the sand.

Back in April when his men had led the recapture of Sangin, he had caused a look of surprise on the face of the then British brigade commander in Helmand, Jerry Thomas.

'Are you saying you're subordinating yourself to me?' said Thomas

'Yes!'

'Are you allowed to do that?'

Everyone was always excited about those national caveats – the

145

rules set by each nation's governments that limited what their forces could do.

'Absolutely, sir, I can do pretty much what I want.'

They had sat in Thomas' tent, war gaming for over twelve hours. 'It was sort of like a World War Two thing, you know, Brits and myself around the table sorting out the strategy for Sangin.' Later, when the battle was almost won, the two men shared a *Cohiba* cigar in the bunker at Sangin district centre to celebrate.

Over the summer, he had put his men under British command again, this time under the brigadier who took over, John Lorimer. Under Lorimer's orders his men had swept down the green zone south of Kajaki and down round Heyderabad.

But Mennes hadn't really seen much sign of long-term thinking. 'We ended up mowing the lawn all the time,' recalled Mennes when I met him later. Like everyone else, 1 Fury had gone and 'cleared' Heyderabad. 'Another high-risk air assault, found caches and killed a bunch of guys, but what for?' What was the 'Big Team', as he called top commanders, going to put in place to make the gains worthwhile, to win people over? 'It's not about killing everybody. Killing is just a piece of it, as well as political development and economic development, social development. We struggled with that for a whole year,' he said.

What not all appreciated was that the US army fighting in Afghanistan and Iraq was not the same army that had arrived here in 2001 or had invaded Iraq in 2003. There were still plenty of the old school. But most had learned some hard lessons fast. Chris Bell, the Warrior commander who had been to US staff college, recalled noticing the Americans were now, if anything, more attuned and more adapted to winning in counter-insurgency. 'While the half-educated Brit recalled false lessons from a Malayan and Northern Ireland history he only half-understood, his American counterpart was asking, "What have I got wrong?" and "What do I need to do it right?" The British were well ahead in 2003 – but five years later the Ameicans were streets ahead and moving away.'

Now, in the planning room in Lashkar Gah, Mennes could see

the old Brit suspicion of American war fighting rearing its head – that he was going to land his troops all guns blazing, would leave behind a heap of dead civilians and would play by his own special American rules. That was the trouble with the British system of troop rotations every six months – a system that many who cared about winning the war found ridiculous. Here he was again, dealing with his third brigadier and having to win his trust all over again.

He was not sure at first these British knew who they were dealing with. 'I was sitting in a planning room with them, and they were talking about operations in and around Helmand and Sangin and I said, "I was there." They didn't really know or appreciate that. I said, "I know about this enemy and I think I know how he is going to fight this thing."'

In the end, the plan did become acceptable, said Mennes, but 'it just took a while, a bit of team building'.

Mennes actually drew his own sketch map of how parts of the plan could look, and he handed it over to Mackay's staff. The end result did not look too different.

Brigade headquarters, 26 November

Sherard Cowper-Coles was on the end of a secure phone, and he did not sound too happy. Three days earlier he had returned from England to find out that plans to attack Musa Qala were moving much faster than he had imagined.

'I was very surprised,' he told Andrew Mackay. 'I thought the idea was that Musa Qala would have to come to us, not for us to go to Musa Qala.'

Uppermost in the ambassador's thinking, it appeared, was the imminent visit of the prime minister, Gordon Brown. As things stood, the very climax of the operation would be on the day he arrived. Cowper-Coles could see already how this might play out. Brown was coming – after months of preparation – to put the final seal on a new Afghan strategy. And now there was this vast military operation in the works that could totally divert both the prime minister's attention and that of all the media too. If Musa Qala was captured without a hitch, then Brown's visit could be denounced back home as an act of political opportunism. People would say he had come to gain political capital from the courage of the soldiers. But then if it went badly – if civilians were killed in great numbers, as happened too often – then Cowper-Coles could just picture the scene: Brown standing next to Karzai on a podium in Kabul as Karzai denounced NATO for its callous actions. The press would have a field day when they saw the snub to Brown. And Gordon Brown's speech to parliament to announce the new strategy, planned for when he returned from Kabul the following day, could be completely overshadowed.

Following his conversation with Mackay, Cowper-Coles expressed his fears in an email to London which managed to upset the Brigadier. He quoted Mackay, brigade staff recalled, as having 'given me reassurances that . . . they will make sure it's not overly kinetic while the PM is visiting.' The message had been copied back to the brigade via Permanent Joint Headquarters. Mackay thought it was disingenuous to have his private words quoted back by others, and inaccurately too. He could not imagine altering a military operation just because a politician was visiting. He told PJHQ the email was nonsense.

19. The Final Plan

ISAF headquarters, Kabul, 28 November

The British ambassador was not giving up. 'The concept of this operation seems to have changed,' Cowper-Coles told General McNeill, after he sat down in the general's office. From the initial idea of ISAF working to support Afghan forces and a 'tribal uprising', it was now becoming more and more a coalition-led attack. He repeated what he had told Mackay: that he was worried about political fallout from the Gordon Brown visit. He warned McNeill again: 'It is vital there are no civilian casualties here.'

He was worried too about what plans existed in the long term, of how the Afghans could keep hold of Musa Qala. 'There is not really a credible Afghan plan to hold this place,' he said. On that point both were agreed.

*Task Force Helmand headquarters,
Lashkar Gah, 28 November*

The two brigadiers strode into the tent, and the assembled officers – almost 100 of them, Afghan, British and their allies – stood up to attention. This was the formal delivery of orders, the 'O-Group'.

What had begun as an operation to put pressure on the Taliban and protect a defecting commander, Mullah Salaam, had morphed first into an operation for the Afghan army to support a tribal uprising in Musa Qala and then finally into something much bigger, more 'kinetic'. The scale was going to be huge, a manoeuvre of almost 5,000 combat troops: Brigadier Muhammad

149

Mohaydin's Afghan brigade of 2,500 men, plus a 600-strong battalion of American paratroopers (Task Force 1 Fury), more than 1,200 British troops including a battle group led by the Royal Marines, a battle group led by the Household Cavalry, a battle group of the 2 Yorks regiment, plus two A-teams of US special forces to join the Afghan brigade, and a screen of further special forces, American and British, to hit the Taliban's key leadership. And all was to be backed by a huge armada of aerial strike power.

But one force was missing: after days of vacillation the Afghan government had declined to send its elite Commando *kandak*. The climax of the battle – the central thrust against Musa Qala itself – would largely be on the shoulders of Colonel Mennes and his paratroops. In theory, this whole operation was still to be led by the Afghans, who perhaps for the first time had full access to the secret planning of the mission. Brigadier Mohaydin spoke first at the orders and was consulted throughout, and he ripped up key parts of the plan. But talk of Afghan 'leadership' of the forthcoming battle was a fiction. The primary role of the Afghan troops was not to win the battle but to influence the town's population to believe that it was the Islamic national government who had returned to control the town, and not a force of foreigners. The use of the Afghan troops was also to influence the Afghan government. It had to feel Musa Qala was its victory – and feel responsible for what happened next.

For all the firepower, this was going to be no conventional battle. It was too important. Victory in Musa Qala, Mackay told the audience, would be defined not just by driving the Taliban away, but by how it was taken and what happened afterwards. Musa Qala had to be captured with little damage. 'It became necessary to destroy the town to save it,' a US major was quoted as saying about the assault on Ben Tre in Vietnam in 1968. No one seriously thought like that these days. But from the Israeli attack on Jenin in Palestine in 2002 and the US attack on Fallujah, Iraq, in 2004 there had been too many big-scale battles that had recaptured a town from a rebel force, but half destroyed it in the process. Musa Qala had to be won back long-term from the

Taliban. That meant securing the support of the people of the town – by doing the operation without killing them or destroying their homes. And as or more importantly, it meant a plan for the follow-up, 'stabilization' phase, when Mohaydin's Afghan troops, it was hoped, could genuinely take the lead.

Lastly, Musa Qala had to be a strategic victory, a blow to the morale and plans of the Taliban and a boost to the morale both of the Afghan nation and of the western nations whose men and women were fighting here. Heavy casualties – whether of innocent civilian or NATO troops – could all turn a tactical victory into a strategic defeat (just as the British prime minister was flying into the country).

The plan Mackay outlined to achieve that victory was not, then, a conventional one. The key emphasis – as it was when Chris Bell's Warriors first crossed into the desert on 3 November – was 'influence'.

To avoid the destruction of an urban battle, the Taliban had to be persuaded to flee the town, to realize their defeat was inevitable. Psychological pressure needed to be ramped up not only through the step-by-step escalation of *actual* combat power but also by spreading the *fear* of NATO strength by using the media, by using deception and ruse, and by using various discreet channels to tell key Taliban commanders it would be suicidal to join this battle. The message to send to the Taliban was the same as when this all started: 'We Are Coming to Get You!'

For the soldiers listening, the pressure was intense – above all, for the combat commanders who were actually going to run the battle. What they heard was not so much a detailed set of orders but more of a vision. There was a clear plan for the build-up to battle, a sense of what should happen afterwards, but, as one key British commander put it, 'there was a big gap in the middle', in other words, how to fight this thing.

After the formalities, a detailed discussion began that quickly became heated. Bell, who was watching, wondered how the Americans would react to this very British scene. 'The Americans are very hierarchical. They've worked it all out. There is not much discussion – and, if there is, it's offline [in private]. But this was very much officers saying, "I don't think that would work."'

As the debate developed, the Americans began pitching in too. The talk came down to the heart of Mackay's vision: of preventing the destruction of the town. Mackay – and his NATO superiors – wanted to put a 'no-go zone' around the town centre into which no heavy weapon or airstrike could be launched without higher approval. The Americans – led by Colonel Mennes – thought it a nonsense. If his troops were fired on from the district centre then they had the *right* of self-defence. No one was going to accuse his men of taking the issue of collateral damage lightly. But the enemy had to be struck where you found it.

'If I was being fired upon from inside Musa Qala, I can use anything and everything to hit that target,' said Major Guy Jones, the 1 Fury operations officer. 'That's not the same Rules of Engagement as the Brits have. So that was a huge friction point,' he recalled. 'General Mackay said, "No, you have to gain approval for us to strike." And Colonel Mennes' point was, "No I don't if it is self-defence, if my guys are taking fire."'

Chris Bell, who was a friend of Jones from staff college, remembered watching a smartly dressed staff officer from Regional Command South, the higher headquarters in Kandahar. He was declaring – again and again – that his boss, the British Major General Jacko Page, would want to authorize each and every air strike on the centre. 'He was standing there saying, "Well, I think my commander, General Page, will want to keep control of the centre of Musa Qala, and he will decide whether you can use certain types of weapons or not." All the commanding officers were saying, "Well that's a crazy idea," particularly the American commander, who was saying, "I promise you, I'm not going to do this." And the staff officer was saying, "No, no!"'

Bell, who was sporting a full desert-grown beard, remembered looking at the officer dressed for headquarters. 'He was there with his little lanyard on – I remember looking at his lanyard thinking, "You idiot!"'

As the discussion degenerated, Bell watched as each of the key combat commanders gradually sloped off and left the staff officer to his argument. 'The whole thing sort of broke down,' he said. 'They gathered in their own corner and began to work out how exactly this battle would be fought.'

Mennes finally ended up speaking to Brigadier Mohaydin. And that was where he finally worked out what the Afghans wanted to do.

'Hey, boss,' said Mennes as they shook hands. 'They say they want me to go in there with you. What are you needing me to do?'

Mohaydin gave him a puzzled look.

'I can't do this on my own. You go in and we'll be partners.'

'I agree we need to be partners. I said we will get you in there. You come up and meet up with us and we will get you in there.'

It was clear, recalled Jones, that Mohaydin wanted the US troops to go much further than the plan on paper actually called for. Mohaydin, it was clear, had no desire or intention to do much fighting. No US troops nor even any NATO troops were supposed to enter the town. But Mohaydin had his own idea: 'I'm not going into town. At night, you all clear it, and make sure it's good, and I'll go in, in the morning.'

'OK, got it,' said Jones.

Mennes for now wasn't spelling out where his men were going. But he told Mohaydin, 'Hey, when I think they're gone, you just walk right through!'

In the next few days, a cabal of commanding officers – Mennes, Smyth-Osbourne, Lieutenant Colonel Stuart Birrell, the commanding officer of 40 Commando and Battle Group North, and Lieutenant Colonel Simon Downey, the 2 Yorks commanding officer – got together at Camp Bastion and worked out a plan for how they would coordinate the manoeuvre of all these thousands of troops. Mackay's planning officer, Major Geoff Minton, was at those meetings. And then Mackay flew over and heard their conclusions – and gave it his backing.

Throughout this process, the Afghans had a way of letting the NATO commanders know who ultimately mattered.

Meeting in Birrell's tent, one of Mohaydin's *kandak* commanders, Colonel Roussal, walked in to demand, 'Who's in charge here?'

'I am,' said Birrell.

'Where's the coffee and tea then?'

20. Camp Shorobak

Sergeant Lee 'Jonno' Johnson was going to Musa Qala. Of that he was certain. But was he going to come back alive? He was getting spooked.

He had come back from Kajaki now and had been due to go on R&R. He had been sitting at the Shorobak camp waiting to go when the news came in of the Musa Qala op. He'd had a night with his brother to mull things over. Lance-Corporal Don Johnson was just out of Sangin and was due up in Kajaki, so his brother gave him a brief.

Jonno took out a map of Kajaki and explained the lie of the land up there and who the main people were. 'It was a really good handover,' remembered Don, 'and then the next morning I flew to Kajaki to take his place, and that's how it worked.' Before he left that night, Jonno talked about himself.

'I've got the option of going to Musa Qala rather than going on leave. So what do you think I should do?'

He always used to come like that and ask Don for advice. Don thought of his elder brother as a little immature, however good a soldier he was. As kids, thought Don, they had hardly known each other. It was being together in the army that had made them close. That night, for the first time in their lives, they said they loved each other.

'What do you think I should do?' said Jonno.

'It's up to you. This is the biggest battle the Battalion has ever had, and if you missed out on it, you would kick yourself for ever and ever . . . If you do go and you get hurt, you're probably going to regret it for the rest of your life . . . You can't ask me what I think, I only tell you what you need to hear.'

Jonno said, 'Yeah. Musa Qala. I need to take Musa Qala.'

'I know you do; you just wanted to ask me.'

'I'm going.'

'You need to be sure you want to go.'

'Yeah, I'm going.'

'OK.'

That was how the conversation ended. As he went to bed, Don thought Jonno was always going to go, no matter what he had said.

When Private Lawrence Fong and the rest of Jonno's team up at Kajaki came back to camp, they were surprised to find Jonno still at Shorobak. He hadn't gone on his R&R. They also learned he had started going to church. Someone said he hadn't been to one for seventeen years. 'Things change,' said Jonno.

Having Jonno in the camp was a pain for some people. He was getting a little concerned about his brother and seemed to hover round the Ops Room. Every thread of news about Kajaki was turned into a question about Don. One night he heard there had been a mine strike up in Kajaki, and his brother was involved. He shook a friend of his, Corporal Lee Brook, awake in his cot to tell him.

'What the fuck are you doing, Jonno?'

'Guess where our kid is now?'

'Kajaki.'

'Yeah, and guess what he's doing.'

'I don't know. What's he doing, then?'

'He's in a minefield. He's poking for mines.'

'You're fucking joking . . . but what are you doing up at four o'clock in the morning?'

'How did Jonno know to be up when it happened?' his brother Don wondered later. 'How was he up? He shouldn't have been out of bed at all. That's just the way it was. How did he find out? He just knew. He knew.'

The mine strike at Kajaki was a horrible event – and it made Don realize how unprepared he had really been for the reality of war.

It was in the middle of the night, and the 2 Yorks mentoring team and their ANA patrol were moving fast down a dry riverbed to meet an H-Hour for an operation with the Royal Marines. There was a section that was in front, sweeping for mines, and Don's section was right behind. Don had stopped suddenly because a battery alarm in his day sack started to go off. 'Right, go firm,' said Don, and he and his men got down on one knee. And then 'for some strange, random reason' an interpreter behind him ran straight past, right in front of him and stepped on a mine about 3 yards away and got blown up.

'There was no explanation of why he was running past,' remembered Don. 'He had no reason to be. He should have been with his section commander. He ran past and he just got blown up.'

Don knew it should have been his own head blown off. 'If there was ever a time when I thought I do not fucking want to be here then that was it.' The incident only lasted about twenty minutes, and he gathered his thoughts again. 'We tried to treat him but he'd lost his . . . his left hand had been completely blown off. Lost a few of his fingers, he had a big hole in his chin, I think his eye had popped out. It was a mess, his nose, you could see where he had been cauterized . . . It was a total mess. Me and the combat medic tried to save him, but I think we broke most of his ribs trying to give him CPR [resuscitate him], he was an absolute mess. We got him back to the helicopter landing site, but he couldn't make it. If that had happened to me, I wouldn't have wanted to make it.'

That whole thing made Don wonder about his luck. Back in Sangin he had walked right past a pressure-plate IED that had hit Sergeant Eddie Nicholls and he had been saved on that occasion too. And it also made him think that next time – if and when he returned to Afghanistan – he would tell all the young lads all the worst stories and show them the worst videos to prepare them for the horror.

'I think it hit a lot of the lads, situations like that. I was not ready to see someone with so many missing body parts and trying to save him. It will scar me. Daft little things like you need to put rubber gloves on. You need to put them on before you treat him. But my rubber gloves were in the bottom of my medic pouch and probably cost me like two minutes to get them out . . . it probably cost that lad two minutes. But you need to prepare the lads for that, because if that's me or one of them on the floor, or one of their muckers, you need to save his life. You need to save his life!'

Over in Kajaki, Don was reading electronic messages from Jonno like 'I think I've made a really bad decision' or 'I don't think I should go' or 'I've got a bad feeling'. But Don told him, 'It will be all right, we will be laughing in a few months' time in the pub.'

PART 5

The Battle

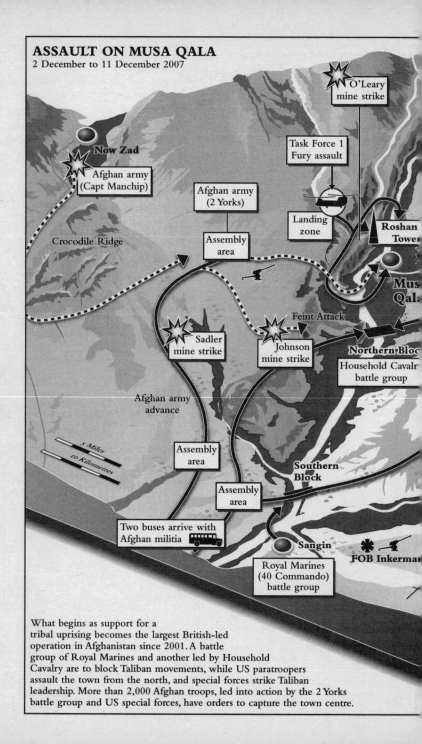

ASSAULT ON MUSA QALA
2 December to 11 December 2007

O'Leary mine strike

Task Force 1 Fury assault

Now Zad

Afghan army (Capt Manchip)

Afghan army (2 Yorks)

Landing zone

Roshan Tower

Crocodile Ridge

Assembly area

Musa Qala

Feint Attack

Sadler mine strike

Johnson mine strike

Northern Block

Household Cavalry battle group

Afghan army advance

5 Miles
8 Kilometres

Assembly area

Southern Block

Assembly area

Two buses arrive with Afghan militia

Sangin

FOB Inkerman

Royal Marines (40 Commando) battle group

What begins as support for a tribal uprising becomes the largest British-led operation in Afghanistan since 2001. A battle group of Royal Marines and another led by Household Cavalry are to block Taliban movements, while US paratroopers assault the town from the north, and special forces strike Taliban leadership. More than 2,000 Afghan troops, led into action by the 2 Yorks battle group and US special forces, have orders to capture the town centre.

An aerial armada circles above the battle, striking targets, jamming and intercepting Taliban radios and feeding live surveillance pictures to the ground troops.

▲ Mount Doom

Taliban HQ

Final Block

Mullah Salaam's compound

Militia

Assembly area

DEC 2	Royal Marine commandos cross Helmand River from Sangin to establish Southern Block at the base of Musa Qala wadi.
DEC 5	Afghan militia arriving in school buses are sent to protect Mullah Salaam – but he turns them away.
DEC 6	Armoured battle group led by Household Cavalry establish the Northern Block across the wadi just 5 miles south of the town. Meanwhile, a 12-mile convoy of Afghan forces, with 2 Yorks battle group and US special forces, advances through the desert.
DEC 7	B Company, 2 Yorks, lead Afghan army's diversionary attack to the south-west of Musa Qala while American paratroopers land by helicopter to the north and attack the town from three sides.
DEC 11	Afghan army forces enter the Musa Qala centre, led by 2 Yorks and special forces.

Crowded skies

Keyhole spy satellite
200 miles orbit

E-8C JSTARS
(ground surveillance)
at 35,000ft

KC-135 inflight tanker
at 30,000ft

Rivet Joint RC-135
(electronic intercept)
at 30,000ft

||||||||| Artillery ceiling |||||||||||

EA-6B Prowler
(radio jamming) at 28,000ft

Nimrod MRA4
(radar surveillance)
at 28,000ft

E-3 Sentry (AWACS)
(command and control)
at 27,000ft

B-1B Bomber
(strategic bomber)
at 26,000 ft

F-15 strike jet
at 23,000ft

F-16 strike jet

Mirage 2000 strike jet

Harrier GR-9 strike jet
at 18,000ft

Reaper (Green Eyes) UAV

Predator UAV
at 16,000ft

||||||||||| Mortar ceiling |||||||||

A-10 strike jet
at 13,000ft

'Spectre' AC-130
Special forces gunship

Command Solo C-130
(Psyops broadcasting)
at 12,000 ft

AH-64 Apache
Attack helicopter
at 3,000 ft

Chinook
Transport helicopter

Black Hawk
Transport helicopter
at 1,000ft

21. The Militia: 4–6 December

On a rocky cliff above the southern Musa Qala wadi, the guards-men of Chris Bell's armoured Warrior company scanned the horizon. It was a piercing cold early morning, and under a blue sky the view was crystal clear and spectacular.

Bell's men and vehicles were dug into old abandoned Russian trenches while apparently oblivious shepherds wandered the slopes around with sheep and goats. 'The sense of history was palpable,' recalled Bell. There they were, staring up towards the snow-capped Hindu Kush, the latest 'in a long line of foreign military expeditions into this corner of the world'.

In the direction of the rising sun the land dropped sharply down to the wide-open Musa Qala wadi, with its patchwork of green opium and corn fields, sprawling mud-brick compounds and ditches and trees on either side of a wide riverbed of grey pebbles, rocks, small rivulets and water pools. On the nearside bank was a small dirt road that snaked up 20 miles due north to Musa Qala itself. Across the riverbed, a line of cliffs marked the far side of the wadi and beyond that a stony and empty plateau.

Behind him to the west stretched the grey-and-brown plateau of the open desert, broken up by the incisions of the deep canyons that cut through it like the veins of a leaf. Beyond to the north-west lay the dark, brooding snow-capped peaks of what the soldiers called Crocodile Ridge: a barrier chain of mountains that separated the open desert from the hostile town of Now Zad.

It was in that direction Bell first noticed billowing clouds of dust that meant a convoy of vehicles was approaching. As they got closer, it got stranger and stranger. Driving along the hard-packed mud track under escort from some armoured cars were what appeared to be two large coaches, something like the old Grey-hound buses that criss-cross America. Peering through his binoculars, he could see the curtains were drawn. For a moment he had an image in his head of a convoy of strike-breakers under escort.

Bell turned to his second-in-command, Captain Matthew Jamieson, and pointed out the 'comedy coaches'. They laughed as they watched the buses creaking and bouncing through the rocks towards the wadi. 'We'll be called over to recover that lot before too long!' he said.

What Bell did not then know was he was witnessing a secret operation. The coaches were school buses but they contained not schoolchildren but a militia hired in Kabul. Their mission that day was to provide a guard force for Mullah Salaam, the rebel Taliban chief who was claiming he was switching sides to the Afghan government and would help liberate Musa Qala with his dozens of loyal fighters. Quite why he needed such protection, when he boasted of his own militia, was an open question.

Something about those bedraggled buses had to make everyone who saw them grin. Here was Britain's biggest operation in Afghanistan. Everyone was tuned up for high drama, blood and bravery. Yet in its first moments there was already that essential element of high comedy.

Sangin district centre, with tactical headquarters,
Battle Group North, 4 December, 05.30

The operation to retake Musa Qala had begun at dawn and it had begun the way that Royal Marines like it: with an amphibious assault. After marshalling in the safety of the Sangin district centre, a column of tracked Viking armoured vehicles trundled down to the riverside and then plunged into the cold waters of the Helmand. In the front passenger seat of one of the Vikings was Stuart Birrell, commander of Battle Group North. With him was Major Dan Cheesman's Bravo Company (who were leaving their base in Sangin in the care of a company of Gurkhas), as well as several trucks of ANA soldiers.

Emerging on the other side, Birrell's forces turned north. His mission that day was to establish the southern block at the base of the Musa Qala wadi. It was partly the first phase of a deception plan to make the Taliban think the main attack would come from this direction. It was also to start boxing in the Taliban: preventing both reinforcement of Musa Qala from the south and suppressing any diversionary attack by the Taliban down towards Sangin and Gereshk.

The Taliban had known for days now that an offensive was about to start. They were bullish. 'Our lines are so strong that the foreigners will never break them,' one commander told an Afghan reporter. 'The foreigners say they are going to launch a major operation in Musa Qala. We are ready for that. In Musa Qala alone, we have 2,050 armed fighters. It will be very easy for us to resist the attack.'[19]

US special forces were already watching the town and trying to track the movement of the Taliban's key leaders. Two days earlier the first blow had been struck. A bomb hit a compound in the town, and the US announced they had killed a senior commander responsible for the kidnap of an Italian journalist.

Birrell's assault that day took the Taliban by surprise. Not far downriver from his crossing point was the village of Qaleh-e-Gaz, a Taliban stronghold that had never yet been 'cleared'. It wouldn't have been hard for the Taliban to muster forces to oppose the assault. Still, within a few hours, there were mortars and rockets dropping down on their new positions across the river.

Birrell's forces pushed north from the crossing point, taking the high ground to the east and west at the entrance to the Musa Qala wadi. He was joined by his Delta Company as well as Chris Bell's Warrior company, both of which had hooked through the desert to reach the block from Camp Bastion.

Next to arrive near the block that day was a second battle group led by the commanding officer of the Household Cavalry Regiment, Lieutenant Colonel Ed Smyth-Osbourne, who was known to most simply as 'Colonel Ed' or CO HCR. Startlingly tall, charismatic and self-effacing, and with a penchant for quoting the words of Rudyard Kipling, he was a man who seemed to find Helmand one magnificent adventure. 'He's so English . . . he makes my coffee turn to tea,' said one American of him. His enthusiasm was so infectious and his comic irony so disarming that men who had been reprimanded by him were said to walk away feeling grateful. But he also had a steely side. When required, he could be ruthless, not least with his own superior officers.

Chris Bell was sitting in the back of his Warrior that morning, drinking a brew with his sergeant-major. They heard a little knock on the door. They opened it. There, stood in the middle of the desert, was CO HCR drinking a mug of tea – and wearing a knee-length camel duffel coat. The coat reminded Bell of pictures of David Stirling, the founder of the SAS. 'Morning, fellas, what's going on?' asked the colonel.

Under his command, Colonel Ed would have his own C squadron of the HCR, driving their 'antiques road show' of light reconnaissance tanks, the squadron of mine-resistant Mastiffs of the King's Royal Hussars, a unit of the Coldstream Guards reconnaissance force, Bell's Warriors and a small company from the Afghan army.

The desert west of Musa Qala, with the Brigade Reconnaissance Force (BRF), 13.00

The convoy was stationary and waiting. Some people turned off their engines. The cigarettes and biscuits were passed round, and water bottles opened. Moving through the desert was like this.

You powered over the sand or gravel at top speed. And then you came to a VP, a vulnerable point, and it was a delay of minutes, or hours, while you waited for a route to be cleared.

A crossing through a steep-sided wadi was where the danger lay. You wouldn't place a mine in open ground where there were a million routes to choose. You put them where your enemy was channelled – where the terrain forced him to take a narrow path. There were few easy ways across. Often your only route down was where a small tributary valley (known as a re-entrant) cut a gentler slope.

Major Tony Phillips, the BRF commander, was escorting a group of vehicles from the Royal Artillery that had come up from Camp Bastion. They were heading north with a pair of 105 mm field guns to set up a position in range of Now Zad and Musa Qala. With them were some large trucks that carried the artillery's ammunition and supplies. That ruled out some of the crazier routes that the BRF's vehicles could usually power up.

About 400 yards beyond where the main convoy was halted, Captain Duncan Campbell's A Troop was scouting the route and had sent Sergeant Daniel Wagstaff with two WMIK Land Rovers to go and clear ahead. This wadi wasn't an area marked on their maps of potential minefields. But then their mine map was only based on limited intelligence. It wasn't that precise.

Each WMIK had three men on board: a vehicle commander, a driver, and a gunner stood up on the .50 cal in the back. Lance Bombardier Ian Wylie, known as 'Swede', was the driver of the second WMIK. His commander was Lance-Sergeant Glynn Bellman, inevitably called 'Dinger'. Their top-gunner was a twenty-one-year-old Territorial Army soldier named Trooper Jack Sadler, who had joined the BRF a few months previously.

The BRF planned to cross this wadi the same way they had gone the day before. But when Wagstaff looked down, he realized it would be too steep for the trucks. The Land Rovers drove along the contours and found a better route. Then they followed it to the bottom of the wadi and up the other side, looking out for mines and potential ambush sites.

Everything looked good, and Sergeant Wagstaff headed back towards the convoy to lead it through. To make things quicker, he used a short-cut up the route they had planned to take earlier, the steep one. They went up one at a time. The key to getting up such a slope was to gun forwards as fast as you could. Wagstaff powered up the slope, over a steep lip and disappeared over the top. Wylie pushed his accelerator pedal down, revved the engine and followed. He remembered reaching the lip. That was when the rest of the convoy heard an almighty bang and looked over to see a cloud of dirty smoke billowing up.

The chatter on the BRF's radio net was always incessant. A report from here. A question from there. But now silence, an absolute, terrible silence. Just that ominous black–grey plume of smoke rising upwards and a sickening feeling. 'I waited a moment for somebody to actually confirm the situation,' recalled Phillips, 'but nothing came through, nobody seemed to want to utter the words and admit we had fallen victim.' Seconds ticked by. Then Phillips pressed the radio switch and shattered the silence: 'Hello Maverick Zero. This is Hercules Zero Alpha. Contact . . . Mine strike!'

Wylie would not later remember the explosion. 'I was going pretty fast and I thought I'd lost control of the vehicle. I remember Dinger shouting out "Swede!"' He must have blacked out for a second or two. The next thing he knew the vehicle had lifted off, spun round 180 degrees so it was facing downhill and turned on to its left side. Wylie opened his eyes, and he was still inside and staring at the dirt inches away. The vehicle was on fire.

Wylie got himself out and checked himself. He was bleeding from his head, but otherwise he was all in one piece. Then he found Dinger, who was in a lot of pain. Bullets starting to zing about. 'We're under attack!' he thought. Wylie dragged Dinger behind a rock. Dinger asked for morphine, but Wylie knew Dinger was not about to die. He told him to fix himself. He knew he had to find Jack Sadler. He couldn't see him anywhere.

He realized the bullets were coming from the burning vehicle, detonated by the heat.

Sergeant-Major Anthony Richards – the senior sergeant of A Troop – ran to the scene.

'What's happened? Where is everyone?' he shouted. At first he thought it was Wagstaff's vehicle that had blown up. He couldn't see Lance-Corporal Simon Cooper. 'Where's Coops?' he said.

He heard Cooper reply. 'No, no, it's not me. I'm here. It's Jack.'

'Where is he?' said Richards.

Cooper said, 'I don't know. I just saw him get blown up in the air and went over . . . you know . . . the vehicle.'

The ground around the vehicle was hard, sharp rock. It was hard to see how anyone could have hid a mine or booby-trapped bomb in there. Campbell and Richards started searching around for Jack Sadler, walking round the burning vehicle and searching in the rocks. The medic, Pete Langhelt, started treating the casualties who'd been found.

Richards decided to climb up what amounted to a 6-foot cliff to get a better sight. And as he got over the brow, he saw Sadler lying on the ground with his body armour in tatters and blown to one side and his helmet nowhere to be seen. It was clear he was in a bad way, and Richards shouted to Campbell, 'He's here. I found him.' Campbell worked his way round so he could see Richards, who shouted to him, 'Get a medic!'

Sadler was still breathing, weakly, but he was unconscious and so could not feel any pain. His mouth was full of blood, and it was clear he'd suffered traumatic injuries.

By now the wrecked WMIK was burning with an intense flame. More and more half-inch (.50 calibre) bullet rounds were cooking off in the heat, and also phosphorus grenades that spewed molten white-hot metal. Richards lay down next to Sadler and used himself as a shield between Sadler and the vehicle. He put a plate of body armour next to Sadler's head. He wanted desperately to move him but could see it wouldn't be easy. He talked to Sadler, trying to get a response and trying at the same time to keep his airways clear.

The explosions were getting louder. It was hard to tell if it was all coming from the vehicle or if by now they were under some sort of attack. Richards remembered: 'It was just loud, very loud. The whole vehicle was on fire, and there were parts of the vehicle like suspension springs and weapon systems blown everywhere. And the force of the explosion was enough to set everything off; so it felt like, within seconds, all the ammunition was cooking off. It was just whizzing everywhere. So, you've got all the rat-a-tat. You've got the explosion of the Claymore mines on board and the phosphorus grenades, which are particularly nasty. Some of it hit my helmet.' Sadler's clothing even caught fire from something.

It felt like hours that he was all alone waiting for help. It was probably less than two minutes. Even though he had a background in teaching first aid, there was just too much for Richards to deal with alone. Finally the young medic, Peter Langhelt, showed up after moving round from the other two injured. Richards saw Langhelt appear from behind a rock. With all the heat, smoke and flying bullets, he seemed reluctant at first to break cover. Richards shouted out and gestured with his arms. 'You've got to come over. I can't move him!' Langhelt looked as if he was gasping something, but Richards couldn't hear. The medic's eyes were like saucers.

Richards shouted again: 'Pete, look, you've just got to fucking get over here, mate, because he's going to die.'

Langhelt summoned up the courage and sprang into action. 'He was absolutely fantastic,' Richards would say later. They realized they would have to find a way of moving Sadler out of range of the bullets and the heat from the burning WMIK. 'It was the most intense heat that I ever felt because, when I lay down, it was just on my back. It felt as if the whole thing was just melting down.'

A big Fijian, Private Tamani Rabakewa, ran up with a stretcher, and they got Sadler out of the heat and down to the safety of a depression where the battery sergeant-major, Paul Hodgson, had found a place for a helicopter landing site.

Phillips had been busy meanwhile organizing the arrival of the medevac chopper. He had also called for air support after Taliban radio chatter suggested they were preparing to launch an attack on the now-static convoy. An RAF jet dived down and screamed over them in a show of force to the Taliban – and a show of solidarity to the BRF.

It was probably another thirty minutes before the Chinook arrived. Langhelt and Richards fought on desperately to save Sadler. They tried to stop his bleeding and, after many attempts, managed to get a needle into his collapsing veins to start replacing fluids. They worked in the back of a Pinzgauer. Hodgson kept popping his head in, saying, 'How's he doing?'

The other two injured appeared OK. Bellman might have broken his back. He couldn't move but was otherwise lucid. Wylie had a big cut to his face but it was mainly the shock that was affecting him. Both were conscious and able to talk.

The Chinook came in, and they put Sadler on. After it left the BRF still had to clear through what now appeared to be a freshly laid minefield. All they had was a couple of metal detectors that looked to the soldiers 'like something out of the Second World War'. Phillips was just wondering who to order to go first when Cooper stepped forward and said, 'I'll do it.' He went ahead with others, and then the convoy just drove off.

Ministry of Defence, Whitehall, London, 14.30 Afghan time / 10.00 London time

The voice of the Commander of Joint Operations, Lieutenant General Nick Houghton, came booming out of the speakers in the meeting room like the Wizard of Oz.

Houghton, reporting by video-phone from the nuclear bunker at the Permanent Joint Headquarters in west London, was the link to the men on the ground. Today, he was briefing Whitehall on the operation to take Musa Qala. He warned the generals and civil servants present they should prepare for the worst. People could die in the coming days. The operation might just prove to be a walk in the park, or it could be much, much worse. Most likely, it would be somewhere in between, but 'we have to brace ourselves for the extreme of the arc,' he said.

According to several sources who described it later, the meeting was tense, unusually so. Normally sensitive debates would be resolved outside such formal meetings. But today's business was pressing, and troops were already pushing forward. Today, the Whitehall officials were as nervous as cats. The prime minister was due to be heading out to Iraq and then Afghanistan, and then to return home to announce his new strategy for the war. The coincidence of timing was extraordinary. And if Musa Qala went wrong . . .

Two months previously, Gordon Brown had been in Basra during the Conservative Party conference. When he announced that 1,000 troops would be home from Iraq by Christmas, he was roundly condemned for playing politics with the army. Coupled with the perception that he had just bottled out of calling an election, it had sent Brown's popularity nose-diving in the polls.

Houghton, the sources remembered, revealed the H-Hour for the landing of airborne troops was just three days away, and the push into Musa Qala would fall on the day when the prime minister would arrive in Helmand.

'Does it have to be so soon? Can't it all be delayed?' asked an official.

The Foreign Office explained that the ambassador, Cowper-Coles, shared their concerns about the timing. This operation could skewer the announcement of the new Afghan strategy. What if civilians died? Karzai would not hesitate to confront Gordon Brown, even in public.

'This whole thing could be "lose, lose" for the prime minister,' somebody warned. It risked undermining any proper attention being paid to his statement to parliament.

The military explained there were few options available. The cycle of the moon meant that light levels were fading for operations at night. The whole operation was also geared to Afghan politics and timed to exploit something as variable as moonlight – the support of the Afghan president. Moreover, in practical terms, the helicopter assault might not have happened, but the operation was already under way.

Houghton was asked to check back with theatre and see if there could be any slippage, but few expected anything to change. Could Gordon Brown really phone up Karzai and call his visit off, saying, 'Look, this operation is not looking good for me or my visit'?

And then someone raised the media coverage. Two journalists – myself, with the *Sunday Times*, and Rupert Hamer of the *Sunday Mirror* – were already embedded with the troops, it was revealed. (We had just arrived at Camp Bastion from Kandahar but were told it was uncertain when we would move forward due to 'decisions' being made elsewhere.)

'Why have we got two embedded journalists? Who are they? Will they be objective?' asked a Cabinet Office official.

There was a suggestion it might be better not to let us go forward with the troops, but instead report from the desert base at Camp Bastion.

But Houghton was insistent that it was too late to intervene. The journalists were already there.

He pointed out that if you wanted poisonous coverage, or at least articles infected by a certain bitterness, there was nothing worse than holding journalists back. And at Camp Bastion all we would get to report on was the wounded or dead casualties coming back in helicopters.

The desert west of Musa Qala, with the Brigade Reconnaissance Force, last light

At a new camp site in the desert, Major Tony Phillips zipped up his bivvy bag and, under the light of his red head torch, pulled out the diary that he wrote out each night. A little earlier, Phillips had gathered his men round and told them the news he had just received from Camp Bastion. Jack Sadler was dead. And, as he recounted the events of the day over two full A4 pages in the notebook, Phillips tried to recall his brief time of knowing Sadler.

How cruel was the death of someone so keen, so elated to be living his dream. Jack loved the military. He had just finished a war studies degree at King's College, London, and talked about applying to Sandhurst to become an officer. He was a walking encyclopedia on military history and had entertained the lads with comparisons between the BRF's desert manoeuvres and General Montgomery's tactics in the Western Desert in the Second World War.

But something was missing from the BRF now, Phillips realized, and it wasn't just Jack Sadler. They had had their suicide bomb in Gereshk and all had survived. They had been driving in these lightly armoured WMIKs all over the mine-strewn desert at top speed and had never been struck. They did that with confidence because, somehow, they could tell themselves it wouldn't happen to them. 'It was like we were invincible,' Wylie, the driver in Sadler's vehicle, would recall. But now that bubble was burst. Every bump in the track was a potential explosive. Maybe it was just because they were so awfully tired after all those days of sleeping rough. But fear had crept into the BRF, and Phillips knew he would have to dig deep and fight it hard.

As a commander he too had his doubts, even if for now he could share them only with his diary. He believed in God. But, as he asked himself that night, where was He now?

The whole thing is surreal. We have just endured what few will ever have to experience in their lives (thank God!) but are carrying on as if nothing has happened. We boiled our rations and brewed up just like we did last night. We mounted sentries and held a 'bonnet brief' just like we did last night and we are now bivvied up just like last night; yet deep down it's all gone hollow. We know that tomorrow, or the day after, or perhaps the day after that may be worse. The soldiers have performed magnificently as usual. As ever, there are questions we all ask ourselves. Should I have done something else? If so, would it have made a difference? It's horrible; for weeks we have beaten the Taliban and now they get one of us like this.

Jack Sadler need not have been here yet he volunteered. What a brave young man. Very bright, he had fitted in well. We rarely had much opportunity to sit and chat – life was simply too fast. I wish we had. I knew today would be testing so I prayed a lot for me and my men. Yet this happened. After Gereshk I really thought that I was protected and that my men would be as well. I can never fathom out where I stand with God. It surely cannot be right that the Muslim extremists who did this have got away?

Lord, please give me wisdom, strength, courage and happiness and carry the Sadler family through the coming days.

The desert west of Musa Qala wadi, 5 December, 07.40

The 'Greyhound' buses came out of the desert, carrying the militia that was supposed to be going to protect Mullah Salaam. They were escorted by some Czech special forces. Waiting for them was Lieutenant David Warwick, a young officer from the King's Royal Hussars.

The men who poured out the buses looked nothing like fighters: ranging from teenagers to men in their sixties, they looked just like ordinary Afghans, dressed in thick woollen smocks. The militia were angry, hungry and thirsty. They'd been sitting in the buses with no food or water all the way from Lashkar Gah, they said.

In charge of the militia was a man called Nick Muhammad, selected apparently for the mission by the presidential palace. Back in Kabul, Michael Semple had been asked for a briefing on him. Muhammad was 'just some minor thug who was running a police checkpost on the main road, and the only reason to run checkposts on the main road is to steal from people,' he recalled. He told those who asked about him: 'If we need a job for a nightclub bouncer and it's not a salubrious place, then Nick Muhammad's your man.' But as far as the British soldiers had been told, all of these men were former Taliban and dangerous.

'They started shouting, getting angry, and refused to move on with us,' said Warwick. The Czechs started to edge away, but Warwick made them stay for now.

Then Muhammad's men started getting hold of their weapons. 'They disappeared off, lifted up the storage containers on the side of these buses and started getting out AK-47s and magazines and ammunition and loading up these magazines and loading their weapons and making them ready.' Things were soon getting out of hand. At first the KRH had their Mastiffs in a circle, with their guns trained outwards for all-round defence. But they soon had some of their guns pointing inwards.

'We'd been told these guys used to fight for the Taliban, that they'd been fighting against British soldiers only nine or ten months back. This was all pretty threatening. And they were waving their weapons around in my face and the interpreters' faces. One of the interpreters started crying.'

Warwick managed to persuade Muhammad to get the guns lowered, and soon Colonel Ed arrived to help. They persuaded the militia to accept some biscuits and water and to get back in the buses. They were told they could keep their weapons, but they agreed to unload them.

The next trouble was to get them down and across the Musa Qala wadi along a track that only an off-road vehicle could make. They got transferred into the Mastiffs – not something that made their crews comfortable. The plan was to take them up to Mullah Salaam's compound and unload them, but when they reached the outskirts of Shah Kariz, there was no one there to meet them.

'It was embarrassing,' recalled Staff Sergeant Rob Sinclair, a troop leader in the KRH. 'We basically picked up these militia, dropped them off, and went, "Right, someone should be here to collect you." And no one was.'

The British asked around the Afghans to see if anyone had a mobile phone or Mullah Salaam's number. Everyone was waving phones around, struggling to find a signal. Someone reached Mullah Salaam. The British said: 'Where are you? We need to come and drop these guys off.' But Salaam demanded to know who this militia force actually was. The soldiers had been told that Nick Muhammad was some kind of best friend of Salaam. Now they heard he did not know him.

Salaam asked if the militia had heavy weapons like large-calibre machine guns. The militia too were saying, 'We're not fighting if you haven't got any heavy weapons.' At that point, the interpreter handed the phone over to the soldiers. There was an English-speaking voice on the line. There was someone inside the compound with Salaam. 'Oh hello,' he said. 'Can I speak to whoever's in charge?'

The conversations went round in circles. It seemed they would have to take the militia back and 'find a way to get rid of them'. Salaam did not want them. The British were not going to give Nick Muhammad more weapons. Mullah Salaam said, 'Well, I don't want the guys then.' To add to their problems, one of the Mastiffs had now broken down. A fan belt snapped. It was getting dark. Things were edgy. They did not know if the village in gunshot range was really friendly. Had they been lured into an ambush?

At Brigade headquarters, the events were being followed closely. With the plan collapsing into bits, the army was being asked to disarm the militia – and essentially have them arrested.

One officer described watching Brigadier Mackay completely 'losing his rag' with a liaison officer from 'another agency'. The brigade commander was someone who rarely lost his cool but that night was a complete 'cluster fuck', what another senior officer described as a 'monstrous distraction'. One staff officer described the sight of the adviser and the commander arguing it out as 'the highlight of my tour'. If this whole thing had been a training exercise, 'no one could possibly have made this up'.

'It was all their plan,' said one senior military officer, speaking of officials in Kabul, 'and it was hopeless.' They had sent a militia down without supplies or the right equipment, with no decent form of transport and with no means to extract them.

Colonel Ed, whose men had taken the militia up to Shah Kariz, was supposed to be launching an assault within hours. And added to that was a real concern from the troops on the ground that all this could 'kick off' into a nasty violent incident.

In some ways, all the frustration of the last few weeks had come to a head, all that talk from Kabul of a tribal uprising, or all these armed men that Salaam was going to bring over, of this 'tribal solution' to the capture of Musa Qala. For weeks now, said the officer, 'we were being fed a line that we didn't believe and we had to swallow it'. Now the brigade was being told, in the dark in the desert, to ask this increasingly angry group of men to hand back their weapons and ammo, and the 64,000 dollars they had been given for Salaam.

The militia were to be sent back in the Mastiffs to the southern block position under the command of the Royal Marines and Stuart Birrell.

Back at the Royal Marines operations centre in Camp Bastion, a senior officer took a call from Kabul.

'Can you take the militia to the Afghan police in Sangin? They will arrest them,' he was told.

'Are you aware of what that will mean? The police will also take all of your money they are carrying? And do God knows what else,' said the officer, imagining rape and murder.

'OK, so can you disarm them?'

'You are saying that you want our soldiers to take these armed and scared ex-Taliban in our vehicles and take all their weapons and their money away?'

'Yes, that's right.'

'Wrong answer,' said the officer in Bastion.

Now Zad district centre, 10.30

Captain James Manchip and James Fraser were artillerymen: trained in the observation of the enemy and in the direction of gunfire on to enemy positions. Today, their jobs were rather different. Attached to the 2 Yorks battle group, they and their team of just six other men were up in Now Zad not to train, or hardly even to mentor. They were here to lead almost 100 Afghans into battle.

Thirty-five-year-old Manchip and his sergeant-major were standing in a compound in one of the most eerie places in Afghanistan. Now Zad had once been a pleasant market town in a desert oasis. Now, its streets were deserted. It was a ghost town that echoed in the wind to the sound of doors banging on empty compounds, or the barks of wild dogs, or then suddenly to the booms and cracks of explosions and gunfire. The British and their allies held the district centre and a fortified hilltop. But their occupation was symbolic. After months of fighting, the population had voted with their feet and left the town.

There was a time the tall ridges of mountains on either side of the town must have been welcomed for their cooling shadows, giving the place the feel of an alpine resort or hideaway. Now, the mountains seemed just dark and menacing. The chopper pilots had labelled a gap in the peaks where they would dash through to land as the 'gates of hell'. A lot of blood had been shed in this place.

Manchip and Fraser were listening to the sound of a contact. Up to the north, the Estonians were fighting hard. The cracking sound of bullets from the Taliban and the NATO troops were hard to tell apart. Estonia being a former Soviet satellite, these troops were equipped with Russian hardware, a fact that the Taliban used to claim was very useful. (They could steal their ammunition and use it in their own guns, also of Russian design.) Some of the Estonian commanders had even been here before – fighting as soldiers with the Soviet army in the 1980s. On the ridge behind the compound, the Royal Marines mortar lines were busy in support. There was a croak of an Apache helicopter's cannon and the crump of the RPGs being fired up in response. In most places in Helmand, thought Manchip, the helicopter's arrival would have silenced the enemy. 'They're brave here. They're not scared of Apaches,' he figured. A rocket aimed at the ridge came arcing into the town centre. They could hear its whistle as it neared, and it exploded about 200 yards away.

Glancing at his watch, Manchip gave the order to form up and move out. The Estonians had attacked to the north. His plan was to attack to the south. The orders were to disrupt and deceive. Brigadier Mackay wanted the Taliban to take a beating up here – to destroy any idea they might have of coming down to reinforce Musa Qala. Manchip was to fight but not to become 'decisively

178

engaged'. The mission was to divert the Taliban, not NATO. Mackay didn't want to have to send other forces up to rescue them.

The idea of mounting this operation had come at short notice. When the initial orders came through at Camp Shorobak, Manchip had been told he would have just two British vehicles and two platoons from an ANA company in a motley collection of fourteen trucks. They would be driving more than 50 miles up through the desert to Now Zad on their own, without any air controller or any kind of heavy weapons. The night before they moved, things improved a bit. Four American Humvees with twelve men from the Green Berets were chopped over to join them. All would be under Manchip's command. It seemed unbelievable – an artillery captain directing US special forces.

Manchip and the ANA headed off to find the Taliban. Intelligence estimates said there were about 100 hardened fighters out there. Leaving the town, they walked towards the cultivated green zone. They were walking to the fields across flat, open desert shingle. The last time this area had been attacked, a British soldier was killed, they had heard. Manchip was mentoring one Afghan platoon on the right. Fraser took the left one. The plan was to leapfrog, or 'pepper-pot' as the army called it. One platoon would stop and 'go firm' – get into firing positions and be ready to provide cover – while the other platoon would move forward. All the same, it still felt a bit mad. Fraser turned to Sergeant Matty Ling, standing next to him. 'This is absolutely fucking barking,' he said. It was just a case of when, not if, the Taliban would open fire.

Fraser heard a bang behind him and turned round and saw a black puff of smoke. 'Air-burst RPG,' he thought. There was a moment of silence. 'Is that it?' Then things went haywire: AK-47s firing, heavy machine guns firing, mortars landing, and RPGs streaking over. It seemed the mortars were zeroing in. They had to move. By now Fraser and Ling were in a small ditch. His ANA were a few yards in front, in a bigger ditch. Getting into cover meant going forward. Fraser was lying on his left shoulder. Ling was on his right shoulder. They stared across at each other – looking up at tracer going just about 6 inches above them. 'Fuck, what are we going to do here?' asked Fraser. And what was happening to Manchip's platoon meanwhile? The same thought was going through Manchip's mind as he lay in another ditch. What the hell is happening to Fraser and his men?

Fraser managed to make it to the ditch in front, and they started returning fire. But, camouflaged by the bright sunlight, the Taliban's firing points were hard to see. All you could do was just guess where they were. The Taliban bullets felt like a mad swarm of bees. Put your head up and they started buzzing all around you.

Manchip decided to get his men out. This wasn't the moment to start clearing into the green zone on foot. Better to unleash some severe hell, he thought. Taking turns, one platoon opened fire and then the other stood up to sprint. They made it back about 200 yards to a deep wadi and, from behind the cover of its banks, they called in a 500-pound bomb from the air, a barrage of artillery, and more than 150 mortar bombs to 'smash their position regularly'.

Their enemy, however, did not give up. When they got up to pull back – some three and half hours later – they were chased through an orchard by the Taliban rounds. 'You could feel the bullets by your face,' remembered Fraser. 'It was that close.' Yet they made it back to the district centre intact.

Next morning, it wasn't over. Having driven into Now Zad, they now had to drive out. Manchip's orders were to withdraw to the south-east, but he had to drive out at a snail's pace with two trucks carrying engineering plant equipment. That meant a top speed of about 5 miles per hour. Sure enough, as they went through the mountains, they drove straight into a prepared ambush. It wasn't a surprise. They could overhear their convoy's every movement being described on the Taliban's radio network.

At that point the ANA appeared to lose it, desperately trying to escape, recalled Manchip. 'All hell broke lose with the ANA playing wacky races, breaking up the order of march, trying to overtake and using our vehicles as cover while they opened fire around them.'

The fight went on for two hours. Dutch F-16s came over to assist. But they refused to fire, concerned about possible civilians around. The Americans called up some of their own F-16s instead. The pilots said they saw only enemy – and engaged. Manchip led the ANA out of the killing zone while Fraser and three Humvees from the special forces stayed behind to suppress the enemy. Then they noticed one of their trucks had been left behind – right smack in the middle of the killing zone. The driver had simply run away in a blind panic. Fraser picked up a rocket-launcher to blow it up. He wasn't going to leave it for the Taliban.

Then he heard an American pipe up. 'Jimmy, that's *our* truck.'

He looked again and realized it was the truck with all their ammo, all their food and water and American ammo too.

'Fuck,' said Fraser, lowering the rocket. 'Gotta go 'n' get that. We can't leave that there.'

Fraser got into his WMIK Land Rover and sped into the killing zone, with American Humvees riding shotgun. Jumping on the truck, he started up the engine and it seemed to still work, though it moved at a walking pace.

He made it out under fire to where the rest of the patrol was waiting. Manchip moved them on quickly. It was getting dark. As they got over the brow of the hill they looked behind and saw mortars landing, just where they'd been waiting minutes earlier.

Camp Shorobak, in the desert west of Gereshk, evening

Jonno was not happy. He had spent all day trying to fit Kevlar armour plates underneath the cushion of his seat on his Vector armoured vehicle. Everyone 'bastardized' their Vectors. It was almost a kit car. But this change did not work, as, with his own helmet and personal kit on, he could no longer fit into the cab.

Soldiers I met in Helmand hated the design of Vectors and many of the other British vehicles too. They had a crucial design flaw which – unlike American Humvees, for example – made the driver or front passenger (usually the vehicle commander) particularly vulnerable to being killed if the vehicle struck a mine. 'It is an absolute death trap. I don't feel safe in this,' said Jonno. 'You've just to get on with it,' he was told. Everyone knew the problem all too well.

That night, Jonno went to visit Fran Myatt, the 2 Yorks chaplain, and asked for his own copy of the Bible. He placed it beneath his combat armour. Then he sat down and wrote an email, sent at 18.00, to his fiancée, Lisa.

FROM: Lee Johnson
TO: Lisa McIntosh
SENT: Weds Dec 5 2007; 1.30pm (GMT)
SUBJECT: RE:

Well angel, I'm going at 2 in the morning. You might see me on the telly soon or in the Times paper as I have got a film crew with me. This is the biggest thing since D-Day and I am not lying. I am worried . . .

You must understand this could be my last message to you. So I am going to say a few things. You know I love you with all my heart and always will. And I am sorry truly for all the things I have done . . . I want you to put the money from the sale of my house and split it . . .

I know this is a bit upsetting but I need to let you know about this. I really love you and will try my hardest to come home safely. I would like you to play one song for me if it happens and this is *Razorlight* and 'really wish I could be somewhere else'. And I want my photos played at wherever the wake is which are all on the DVD marked up 'Kajaki' and the footage I got from there which is on my camcorder which you will receive in my box. Thanks please do this because I want people to understand how things were over here and why I love the army so much and the buzz.

I want you to get on with your life and live it to the full . . . I only ask your forgiveness in my wrongdoing. The thought of not holding you in my arms again is awful and gets me down but your photos are close to my heart and will be with me forever. I love you. Tell my daughter and son I love them. Love you Lisa my angel forever and a day

Xxxxxxxxxxxx

Camp Shorobak, 6 December, 04.00

The convoy set off in the pre-dawn darkness from the Afghan National Army base near Camp Bastion, and headed down Highway One towards Gereshk. Just before the town, it took a left turn on to a desert track, where, as the vehicles started to struggle in the terrain, it began to stretch out into a 12-mile-long column. The vehicles threw up a cloud of dust, and, as the sun rose, it was impossible for the Taliban scouts who were watching to miss it.

At the heart of the convoy were trucks belonging to the ANA's 3/205 brigade, the force that was charged with the seizure of the centre of Musa Qala, and the one that would take the credit. Its commander, Brigadier Muhammad Mohaydin, was a charismatic former soldier in the Afghan Communist army. He was joined by mentors from the 2 Yorks, including B Company, and by US special forces.

As they were usually confined to static bases, deploying so many hundreds of Afghan soldiers to operate from the desert and live off rations was an achievement in itself. Some of them, as I discovered that day, had already been fighting around Musa Qala in the previous few weeks, working alongside US special forces in surprise raids against their defences. Mohaydin's intelligence officer had even dressed up in civilian clothes and driven into the town to see for himself. Whatever could be said of the Afghan army, they had no shortage of bottle. And while the British came to Helmand for six-month tours, the Afghan soldiers were stuck in the war on a full-time basis. In the time that the 2 Yorks were their mentors, fifteen Afghan soldiers would die in combat.

As they passed through small settlements in the desert, Mohaydin jumped down from his vehicle and spoke to the villagers. 'He held a baby – and even gave it a kiss. What a pro!' wrote Simon Downey in his diary that night.

Just before sunset, as the convoy reached its destination for the night, 10 miles further east, the first part of Lieutenant Colonel Ed Smyth-Osbourne's armoured battle group arrived at objective 'Vulcan' on the ridges and clifftops that overlooked the Musa Qala wadi. They were 5 miles south of the town. This was to be the second of two planned 'blocks' on the wadi after the first one put in two days earlier at the base of the wadi near Sangin by the Royal Marines. The light tanks of Major Paul Bedford's C Squadron of the Household Cavalry took position on the eastern ridge, while the Mastiff armoured cars of the King's Royal Hussars moved on to a spur that led down into the flat wadi bottom. The force had set off at 08.00 from their assembly area just south of Mullah Salaam's village.

In the following hours, they would be joined on the opposite western side of the wadi by Chris Bell's Warrior company, by the reconnaissance force of the Coldstream Guards, and by a force of ANA soldiers, who were to descend to the bottom of the wadi to hold the road and complete the block.

Digging themselves into trenches and shell-scrapes, the armoured force at Vulcan held all the high ground, and it 'would have taken at least a conventional brigade to shift us off', said Smyth-Osbourne, who reflected that perhaps 'we committed the Soviet sin of committing too great a force'. Its effect, however, was powerful – preventing reinforcements reaching Musa Qala up the wadi from the series of hostile villages that lay between the two blocks: the 'meat in the sandwich' as he called them.

South-east of Musa Qala, with 40 Commando, afternoon

On the high ground above Southern Block, a fire support group of Royal Marines from Bravo Company were watching American helicopters in action. There had been little action for them these last two days. It was getting boring.

'All we did for two days was watch the Americans annihilate stuff,' recalled Lance-Corporal Gareth Patterson, who was mounted in a Viking armoured vehicle. One incident stayed in his head – watching an Apache chase a Taliban fighter on a motorbike. 'We watched it just nudging the bike. It was right down low and actually using its tail to try to knock him off his bike, and then the bike turned round and floored it the other way and took off that way, and all the Apache did was turn on the spot, chasing him again. We were in stitches watching it. He did it for about five minutes, and then the bike bloke just gave up and stopped still, and it just seemed like the Apache had had enough and just flew off.' The helicopter appeared to get some radio message and then launched a Hellfire missile into a compound.

Afghan army desert leaguer, west of Musa Qala

After dark, Jonno sat down with his platoon, contemplating the days ahead. Kingsman Lee Bellingham, who was attached to them, remembered it as 'like a silent night to get our thoughts together'. Private Fong said a prayer with them. Jonno started talking about his daughter Lilly, passing round her photo and saying that her birthday was soon. The atmosphere was almost cheerful. Then Jonno turned serious. He steeled his men: 'I've been here before, guys, and you can trust me. Trust me, you know. Just work hard, obviously work hard, but you'll be OK.'

The next day – Friday 7 December – was to be D-Day for the attack on Musa Qala. Leaflets had already been dropped into the town by Psyops (psychological operations) planes. They warned residents to stay indoors. Many were already fleeing into the desert.

Already, the impending attack was being reported in the press. An article posted on the Internet that night by the Kabul correspondent of the *Daily Telegraph* quoted Taliban commanders who vowed to stand and fight, while not ruling out a tactical withdrawal if their lines were breached. 'I have 300 Mujahidin with me,' said one commander, using a pseudonym. 'We have brought our best artillery. We have anti-aircraft guns in place to attack the helicopters.'

The Taliban's website declared:

They are dropping leaflets . . . calling on the people to leave their homes as the area will be bombed and their homes will be rebuilt in a modern style. It is a known fact that wherever they have gone with all their power, their strength has melted, their equipment has been destroyed, their skulls have remained [on the battlefield], and they have left the battlefield defeated and broken. The Mujahideen of the Islamic Emirate are completely confident that the enemy will not be able to advance one step, and with every step their tanks will be set on fire.

For all the news that had been circulating, the role that American troops from Task Force 1 Fury were to play had been kept secret.

Before the US paratroopers would land by helicopter, the plan called for a diversionary attack on the town from the south and south-west. The goal was to deceive the enemy that the main force of Afghan army and coalition troops in the desert would attack from this direction.

The attack would be led by the 2nd *kandak* of the Afghan brigade and their British mentors together with US special forces. 1 Fury's anti-tank platoon would provide cover from an overwatch position on a hill top. They would all be under the tactical command of Major Jake Little.

Stepping on to the roof, Qais picked up his mobile phone and dialled Mullah Sadiq's latest number. The latter kept changing mobile phones. But he would always call after a while and leave a 'missed call', a signal that this was his new contact. They rarely lost touch for more than a few days. Often they talked in snatches – brief bursts of conversation. Talking at length could be dangerous. Sadiq knew that NATO could locate him through the signals.

Qais could see reports on the news wires that an attack on Musa Qala was imminent.

'What's happening?'

'I'm there now. We have some special things prepared.'

Sadiq rang off. He called again a few hours later, reaching Qais on his Thuraya satellite phone. 'I can't talk tonight,' he said, 'but something big is happening up here in Musa Qala.' He called again in the morning.

'There are hundreds of Mujahidin here now. We won't defeat them in the desert but we will fight them when they come into the villages around . . . We held a meeting and have decided to fight to the death to protect Musa Qala.'

22. D–Day: 7 December

To the electric guitar of AC/DC's 'Back in Black' – blared from the loudspeakers of the American anti-tank platoon – the ANA's leaguer in the desert broke camp at dawn on 7 December. At 07.30 it began to head north.

The convoy moved 12 miles north across the desert, passing close to where Jack Sadler had been killed. At 12.30, the main convoy established a new leaguer, but B Company broke off and led 2nd *kandak* away from the main convoy and crept towards Musa Qala. Vehicles were parked about a mile away from a village on the edge of town.

Before the soldiers set off on foot, an intelligence flash message stated simply: 'Enemy will fight.' Together with photographer Nick Cornish, I joined B Company on the attack.

Deh Zohr e Sofla village, 3 miles south-west of Musa Qala, with B Company, 2 Yorks, 12.30

A burst of gunfire erupted in front, and we dived into a shallow ditch for cover. It was no protection. We had little choice but to run. Bullets slammed into the ground around us as, feeling horribly exposed, we raced for the sanctuary of an armoured Humvee.

Captain Andy Breach and his company of ANA were the furthest forward when the firing began. They had a gully to their left and they dived into it. For some reason, it felt quite funny as everyone hunkered down. People were giggling. But Breach knew someone had to poke their head up and start returning fire. 'I would have been quite happy just lying there and not doing anything,' he said. It was just like they had taught him at Sandhurst: 'There is a moment when everyone just turns round and looks at the officer and asks for leadership,' he recalled. Breach looked back at Jake kneeling in a ditch across the road and saw the OC giving him the thumbs up. Jake was opening fire – encouraging the others to get their heads back up. So Breach followed suit and everyone began. It was hard to get the ANA to fire. And it wasn't helped by the fact that the interpreter, Raj, had run away to the rear.

On Jake's side of the road, Jonno and his lieutenant, Craig Dawson, were dealing with an ANA company that was even more in pieces. Amid all the incoming fire, they'd become distracted by another drama that was unfolding. As the gunfire opened up, three vehicles were coming up the road. It was the main route leading south-west out of Musa Qala, and, from what we had already seen further back, there was a steady flow of refugees trying to get out. One of the vehicles, a white saloon car, stopped in its tracks. But the other two – a white Toyota Corolla and a wooden-sided green-and-grey truck – started to accelerate. Their drivers were in a panic trying to escape. To their misfortune, those on board were heading straight for two American Humvees and for British soldiers coming down the road. Many feared these cars were suicide bombers: they had been warned the Taliban might be planning such attacks.

Walking at the rear, Jake's second-in-command, Nick Mantell, and Corporal Gregory 'Cagey' Roberts, who was carrying a radio set, watched the tragedy in slow motion. They watched as the Toyota sped towards them. Cagey thought it was a suicide bomber, and he wanted to open fire, but Mantell was in the way. Mantell thought it was just people trying to flee the fight. But neither was sure.

It was the gun trucks of American special forces that opened fire first. Their .50 calibre bullets ripped through the two moving vehicles: instantly killing the drivers of both car and truck. Jake felt the same threat as the cars surged past him, and he too fired some warning shots. But when he saw the Americans engaging directly, he shouted out: 'Don't shoot! Don't shoot! There are women and children in the back!'

But British soldiers had opened fire too.

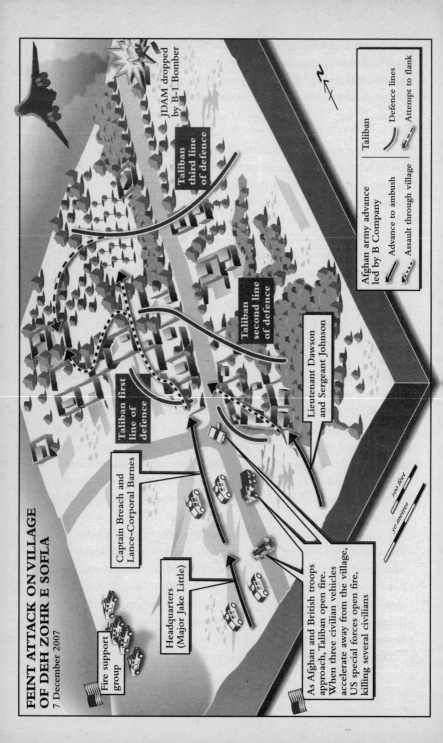

FEINT ATTACK ON VILLAGE OF DEH ZOHR E SOFLA
7 December 2007

JDAM dropped by B-1 Bomber

Taliban third line of defence

Taliban second line of defence

Taliban first line of defence

Lieutenant Dawson and Sergeant Johnson

Captain Breach and Lance-Corporal Barnes

Headquarters (Major Jake Little)

Fire support group

As Afghan and British troops approach, Taliban open fire. When three civilian vehicles accelerate away from the village, US special forces open fire, killing several civilians

Afghan army advance led by B Company | Taliban

Advance to ambush — Defence lines

Assault through village — Attempt to flank

100 feet

50 metres

Lee Bellingham was one of them. Six months later, when we met again and talked things over, he still saw the scene vividly in his mind and still thought of it as he lay awake at night, picturing those children. He, like the Americans, thought it was a suicide attack.

'So the SF [special forces] and us opened fire. They got fifty metres past us, and we just saw the car slip out down and the truck explode in half. When the car landed, it landed on its roof. You could see the hands coming out the windscreen then . . . I'll never forget it . . . there were two kids in the boot because the boot opened up. They fall out and . . . as you're looking you hear a bang next to you, and as you're looking RPGs are flying past you . . . and then you just forget about it because you just get told that you've got to move your men this way, got to move your men that way.'

The first thing I had seen was the Toyota Corolla lying upside down on the road. Its windscreen was covered in blood. Closer still was the truck with two bodies, one dead and one dying, lying by the side. Children were crying and a crowd was gathering. They were looking at the British, shouting, 'Go away! Go away.' They were joined by the ANA *kandak* commander, Rahimi, and Corporal Phil French, the company medic, who tried to save the dying man.

There was a scene I did not know about until months later, one that took the death toll far above the two I initially reported. Further up the hill, where the wounded civilians were being brought, Mantell and Cagey found a pick-up truck with two injured women and about eight children, and a man in the passenger seat who was clearly dying. Matt Hughes, a signaller who was also a team medic, was trying to deal with him. There was also a saloon car with two dead children in the boot, shot through the head, and an injured man in the back, shot in the stomach. And there were two further dead adults.

One of the women was bleeding through her *burqa*. The soldiers wanted to help her, but she would let no one near.

They radioed to get French brought up and Mantell sent a

nine-liner (a casualty report) up to brigade for a helicopter to collect the wounded.

One of the men – whose wife and two kids were injured – said he wanted to drive the group to Gereshk to reach the hospital. But that was a five-hour drive, and Mantell, speaking through an ANA interpreter, urged him to stay. 'There's a helicopter coming,' he said.

Sergeant David McCarrick, who had been looking after B Company's parked vehicles, came across to see what he could do to help. He and Matt Hughes saw the open boot, the dead children and the man laid out on the back seat. The families were refusing to let the soldiers touch the kids. They were persuaded eventually, and Cagey, Mantell and McCarrick started picking off children from the back of the pick-up and undressing the ones that were screaming. 'Sure enough,' remembered Mantell, 'we started finding gunshot wounds on, I think, two of the children. But thankfully the boy's was a graze to the arm, and the little girl's was just a gash.' They would survive.

French and Hughes talked over what to do about the man in the back seat. He had been shot through his liver. They could give him a drip to replace some fluids, but that would only postpone his death. With a battle still raging, they decided they had to conserve their supplies.

Mantell needed to get back with the company in the village, and Jake also needed the company medic, French, to be back with the troops, just in case there were more casualties. Cagey and Mantell took a WMIK and drove French back to the village.

Back at the top, Dave McCarrick was still fighting for the chopper and looking after the wounded, along with Hughes, the team medic.

'We will have a helicopter in five minutes,' they told him.

And then an hour later, he was still saying: 'Where's the fucking helicopter?'

'Oh yeah, it's on its way,' he was told. After about four hours, he heard it definitely wasn't coming. By that time, the man on the back seat had died anyway. It was getting dark and getting cold.

The ANA said, 'Look, they need to go. They need to go.'

'Just go, then,' McCarrick said.

At least seven civilians, including the two children, had been killed so far – more than three times what I had reported.

Back in the village the battle had continued. After all the early mayhem it had been hard to get the ANA back on its feet. Pummelled by gunfire, many of them refused to fight. It was Jonno who helped rally the ANA company on the right flank. He got them up and pushed them forward, and they cleared the compound to the right of the village entrance.

Messages on the Taliban's radio network were saying they were manoeuvring forward, so Breach took a patrol and set up an ambush. At an orchard Breach threw a grenade over the wall – reluctantly, as he was worried about who might be behind it, but Lance-Corporal Alex Temple persuaded him – and they charged in after the impact. It was lucky he had thrown it, as there was a Taliban fighter waiting behind the wall. Initially stunned, he was finished off with a shot. Another fighter, a Pakistani, put his hands up. He was cuffed and dragged away.

The desert east of Now Zad, at 50 feet, 16.15

The armada of twenty-one helicopters was circling at low-level over the desert. Their cargo of paratroopers was already supposed to be on the ground, but a message had come back to say, 'Hold!' So, an impromptu formation was playing chase-the-tail-of-a-snake beneath an orange-tinted sky. They churned around and waited for orders. And all the time they had that sinking feeling that any chance of surprise was gone.

Every spare helicopter in theatre had been scrambled for this moment. The twelve heavy-lift Chinooks with the troops were British, American and Dutch. They had an escort of Black Hawks to provide a communications link. On their flanks they had Apache attack helicopters, armed with rockets and missiles. Circling above them all was the 'C-2 bird' – the command and control Black Hawk with Colonel James Richardson, the American (101st Combat Aviation Brigade) commander.

This was the H-Hour: the moment of highest drama, the moment when the mission and the men were at their most vulnerable.

The Landing Zone was supposed to be in the Wuch Mandah, a dry ravine just west of Musa Qala. But suddenly this landing was in doubt. On a ridgeline above this wadi and on the mountains to the west and north were lines and lines of deep trenches and bunkers. All of which could conceal an enemy in ambush. They were supposed – right now – to be engulfed in flames. Rockets, bombs and artillery were all zeroed and set to go.

When the event was planned, the pilots were told to brace themselves for the blasts. 'This will rock your world!' they were told. But – for all the planning that went on – someone had failed to get the paperwork done. No enemy was in sight. No troops were in contact. So the 'pre-emptive fires' required top-level approval.

There were those in Brigade who could see it coming. The Americans, some said, thought they could just sort out all the approvals once airborne. 'We can use our own rules of engagement,' one said. But the aviation that day was under NATO command. And with the fear of killing civilians uppermost in commanders' minds, it wasn't down to Colonel Richardson on his own authority to unleash hell on the trench lines.

At about 26,000 feet above the desert, an American B-1 bomber was circling. He was close to his decision point, the moment when he had only enough fuel to make it back home. If a decision on the strike wasn't made soon, he would have to return to base.

The choppers took another turn.

They were divided into three groups. The British one had four Chinooks. By some miracle of effort, all were fit to fly that day.

The planning for this moment, the pilots recalled, had gone on for days at Kandahar airfield. This was very much an American show, and for the Brits and Dutch it had taken some getting used to. They had come to see themselves as spectators. And they both enjoyed themselves and worried themselves immensely.

It had begun with an initial planning meeting. 'Well, we've gone back into our archives to find the last daylight heliborne assault we've done,' said the briefer. 'Unfortunately we can't find one.'

Someone at the back of the room had piped up: 'There's a fucking reason for that.'

Flight Lieutenant Nichol Benzie had been deputized to represent the British in the planning. He remembered the obsession of American pilots and planners with organizing a vast volume of pre-strikes. 'It was prophylactic fire they were after. They just wanted to waste the place,' remembered fellow pilot Tristan Jackman. They hadn't seemed to grasp, he thought, that the idea was to liberate Musa Qala for the Afghans, not destroy it.

Benzie remembered a 100-strong gathering when a senior American officer was describing all the bombs that needed dropping just before the landing. In all, they had lined up thirty-four targets to be struck. A British legal officer stood up and said: 'We can't do that. You're not able to do that.'

Just then two American soldiers started hollering from the back of the room: 'Fucking pacifists. Don't they know we're at war?'

A senior officer in the US aviation brigade was a huge bulldog of a man whom the British dubbed 'Al Pacino'. He would end every single briefing, recalled Benzie, by shouting: 'Let's do bad things to bad people.' The classic moment had come just before D-Day, when there was a last-minute run-through of the manoeuvres. People had been shifting paper choppers over a large map. And then someone from the Black Hawks had pointed out they would be low on fuel at a certain point. 'Al Pacino' had replied with a steely calm: 'Right, that's great. We've been fucking planning this for ten days, and you haven't told us that you're going to be running out of fucking fuel. That's pretty fundamental. I'd suggest you all go away and think about this, because at 22.00 hours, the good ideas fucking fairy is dead.'

Then an Apache pilot had said, 'Got anything for us?'

Al Pacino had replied; 'Yeah, go away and learn – and work out how you're going to kill people more efficiently.'

Then there was the Padre who had started to pray: 'Let the Apache pilots rain down fire on the heads of our enemies.' All the Brits could think of was, well, hey, this is a whole different culture.

Benzie had known the Musa Qala operation would come in his last eight days of operational flying. His tour in Afghanistan was due to finish at Christmas, and this was to be his last dose of getting shot at. He had started to get spooked. Everyone he was picking up on the medevac seemed to be getting hurt just before their end of tour.

The intelligence had been fearsome. It had been quite specific. The Taliban were waiting in force. They were looking to shoot down a Chinook. Paul Curnow, the squadron leader, would remember the intelligence officer as a tiny woman with a squeaky voice who was standing up and basically 'telling us that we're all going to die'.

On the eve of D-Day, it had all got even worse. Benzie's girlfriend had rung from home to stay she had spotted a story on the *Daily Telegraph*'s website. The so-called surprise attack was no longer a secret. There was even a detailed map showing a large arrow pointing at Musa Qala from the south-west: exactly the direction where they were intending to fly in. Not good.

They had spent the morning in good cheer though. They had feasted on a special lunch of muffins and fried chicken.

Circling around now, they started to kill time. One of the Black Hawks had a female pilot. As she swept by on the turn, the Chinook pilots started to discuss the female form. Someone suggested to the Black Hawks that they all might pop down to the desert to get a quick coffee break.

The choppers took another turn.

Looking out the window, the soldiers of Task Force 1 Fury knew that something was going astray. Some had been following progress with hand-held satellite-navigation devices. Some watched as they flew right past the supposed landing zone.

Their commander had gathered his men earlier on the sizzling tarmac of Kandahar airfield. When he wanted to look serious, Brian Mennes had an intense and large-eyed stare that grabbed attention. Today, he reminded them, was the anniversary of Pearl Harbor, the greatest surprise attack on America before 9/11. And he 'couldn't be prouder today', than to fight with them on what could be another historic moment. 'Today you will have the might of the best fighter pilots in the world and will arrive in the bellies of aircraft flown by some of the best. Tonight you are the most powerful force on the face of the planet. And when it is time to fight, I know that we will win.'

As they flew out on the choppers, his men had a mix of moods. Some were relaxed. They had seen it all before. Every operation was over-hyped, they felt. It was always 'the big one', and yet the Taliban just vanished. Others nurtured private fears. They had seen the Taliban in Musa Qala on YouTube, on a video shot by Al Jazeera English. They knew the enemy was feeling lucky.

One group of paratroopers had insisted to the RAF that they wanted to sit at the back of the chopper and be the first to get off. 'What's with the ramp? Are you going for the glory?' said Paul Curnow.

The soldiers replied, 'No, we're on a thirteen-month tour here. We all want to get pinged as we come off the boat! The most chance of getting shot is on the first man off.'

If this landing was to be 1 Fury's Omaha Beach, the theory went, then they wanted to be hit in the first hail of bullets. A bullet meant a ticket home and the best bullet was a lazy bullet – the poorly aimed round that injured but didn't take you out. Best take the early bullets before the aim was corrected. 'So, they all wanted to be first off to make sure they got shot but not shot bad,' remembered Curnow. But he wasn't sure how many shared this view.

Another paratrooper, a Sergeant Gomez, had come up to speak to Curnow.

'Sir, can I tell you what an honour it is to fly with the Royal Air Force?'

'Well, it's actually a pleasure to have, you know, TF-1 Fury on board. Would you prefer to be with the RAF than the Americans?'

'Oh, shit, yes, absolutely.'

'Why is that?'

'Well, I'd rather fly with an insane crew than a talented one any day, and you guys are fucking nuts.'

Gomez had described the rescue of a dying soldier in the green zone during the Sangin operation back in the spring. They had been told by every American asset that it was too dangerous to land. Suddenly they had heard a faint noise, and then a British Chinook just plonked down into the fire fight with the pilots waving a big cheerful thumbs-up. From then on they all thought the British pilots were madder than mad, but lucky for that.

The choppers took another turn.

Back in the Brigade Operations Room, the position of the armada was being closely tracked and displayed as contacts or 'blips' on a large TV screen. The assault may have been a mainly American show, but this afternoon all air movements were under the control of Task Force Helmand.

Squadron Leader Simon Tatters, the thirty-nine-year-old brigade air liaison officer, was the master of ceremonies. On a normal day, it was usually just him and his deputy, Flight Lieutenant Rob Quaife, an experienced Tornado pilot, who ran the integration of planes and helicopters for the Task Force. But Musa Qala was extraordinary. Today he had assembled a team of twelve, including three US air force colonels, to run this complex 24/7 operation. They had declared a special air/aviation 'no go zone', known as a HIDACZ, or a high-density airspace control zone. In principle, this was a large 'box' of airspace around Musa Qala into which no one could enter without permission.

Today and in the next few days, Tatters would put at Brigadier Mackay's disposal what one senior RAF officer, Air Commodore Sean Bell, would declare to be possibly the most powerful air package *ever* on call to a British ground commander. His point was that in the Second World War, for example, when a single bomb was on average 2 miles off target, it could take a thousand planes just to guarantee the destruction of one rail yard. These days, with precision weapons, the same task could be accomplished with a single plane. So, even with far fewer platforms in the air, the total *effect* they could deliver was much greater.

Above the helicopters there was a fleet of attack jets and bombers on call – British Harrier GR9 aircraft, Dutch F-16s, French Mirage 2000 jets, American F-15s and A-10 tank busters from Bagram air base, F-18s flying from the USS *Enterprise* carrier in the Indian Ocean, B-1B strategic bombers and Hercules AC-130 'Spectre' gunships run by US special forces aviation. Musa Qala was considered so important than many of these planes were transferred from Iraq.

Those were just the attack planes. Above, alongside and often below them floated electronic warfare planes ready to jam, intercept and triangulate Taliban communications: UK Nimrod surveillance aircraft, Psyops C-130 platforms to broadcast influence messages, JSTARS aircraft that could track the movement of people and vehicles, US 'Rivet Joint' electronic intelligence aircraft to monitor Taliban radio transmission, several air-to-air tankers to refuel everyone, and E-3 AWACS command and control planes to coordinate the flow of so many platforms to and from the HIDACZ area. This huge package was the result of days of detailed planning and coordination, now tightly arrayed into the HIDACZ.

For all the high-tech gadgetry, running the Musa Qala HIDACZ from Lashkar Gah came down ultimately to a whiteboard, some bright pens and a set of stickers. While the radar screen displayed the position of the planes and helicopters, and the many radios provided updated reports, the way to keep them from colliding was to give each one a different height and area to fly in – and mark it up on the whiteboard.

At the climax of this Musa Qala operation, Tatters and his team would have used up every 1,000-foot interval from close to the ground to 35,000 feet. And even then that wasn't the end of it. An F-16 jet might cruise happily at 20,000 feet, but to strafe the enemy it had to screech down almost to the ground. And when the guns, rockets or mortars started firing, all of their rounds curved high into the air. A path from weapon to target needed clearing through the airspace. A pilot might work on the theory of 'big sky, small bullet', assuming the chance of an impact was slim. But with so many aircraft and so much ordnance being fired these days, no one was taking any chances.

In controlling the air space, pilotless drones, or unmanned aerial vehicles (UAVs), proved to be the biggest challenge. The Americans had long used the Predator UAV, armed with Hellfire missiles. The British were also now using the larger and more up-to-date drone known officially as Reaper and nicknamed 'Green Eyes'. American Reapers came armed not only with Hellfire missiles but an arsenal of 500-pound bombs. But the British, for now, were using theirs unarmed. The Americans called the British version 'Reaper Lite'.

Today, at H-Hour, the sky was deluged with UAVs. Everyone, it seemed, wanted eyes on this operation and wanted to control their own view. The Predators were the worst. Task Force Helmand didn't get a downlink from many of them. Nor could Tatters and Quaife often work out just who they actually belonged to. Some were on 'ask no questions' classified missions – the property of special forces or the CIA or whoever. One might belong to some general somewhere who wanted to keep his eyes on the show.

One particular unidentified Predator was in the way, obstructing a pair of fast jets trying to provide close air support to some troops in contact. After several failed attempts to coordinate this UAV with the close air support, Quaife ran out of patience – 'What the fuck are you doing to me? You're in my airspace, YOU'RE IN THE WAY' – and the Predator pilot – in his control room back in Nevada – started getting stressed, telling Quaife to 'Lose your attitude, dude.' The row ended up with an email from a US Air Force 2 star, reminding everyone that Brigade had the 'hammer' – the control authority for the airspace around Musa Qala.

There was also a US air force general who sneaked into the scene without notice in his own personal fighter jet. Nearly crashing with a Predator and a pair of Harriers, he sent back an ugly message afterwards complaining about overcrowding. 'Well, that's exactly why you don't arrive unannounced,' thought Tatters.

The choppers took another turn.

Then finally, the argument on approving the air strikes had run its course. An approval message flashed down from the Combined Air Coordination Centre in Qatar. The on-station B1–B was clear to drop. But it was too late, there wasn't enough time for him to drop his weapons before the helicopters would have either to land or head back. Time had run out.

Some artillery strikes still went in, but they hit only six out of the thirty-four the Americans had originally requested. From his helicopter, Colonel Richardson decided it was not enough. He radioed the choppers: 'Switch to the Alternate LZ.'

All in all the delay had been little more than fifteen minutes. But the switch of landing zone was to change the whole battle. As the crow flies the new zone was less than 2 miles from the original site, but it was one whole valley further away from Musa Qala.

The Chinooks finally began their descent. The British pilots were happy to hear the landing zone had changed. The primary one was in a narrow wadi below a ridge with well-known enemy trenches. Bringing all the helicopters into that space at one time would have been no laughing matter.

The British packet came in second after the Americans – coming as fast as they could with their Black Hawk guides and then flaring in the last seconds in a gut-wrenching twist to cut their speed and bunch themselves up to land side-by-side in the dust and gravel. As the ramp went down, the pilots held their breath. The way they saw it the first packet would wake up the enemy. Enough time to lay on a full Afghan welcome for the Brits.

A stopwatch in the cockpits counted the seconds as the para-troopers unloaded. Paul Curnow just remembered sitting there raising his eyes to the top of the wadi and 'waiting for something to happen, waiting for incoming'. But nothing came. It was all clear, and the ramps went up, and the choppers burst away. They turned south and low. It wasn't quite over yet. They still had to get out of the wadi.

As they pulled themselves out and crested the ridge they finally realized: 'We're going to get through this, all the build-up and all the fear, it had ended up without a shot.' Just then they saw a convoy of British vehicles strung out. It was the Brigade Reconaissance Force on their way into action. In the light of the setting sun they saw a huge Union Jack flapping from an antenna and a soldier standing behind a .50 cal, giving them one incredible wave and shouting 'Yeah!'

The only thing missing, thought Curnow, were the credits for the movie rolling down his screen.

Deh Zohr e Sofla, with B Company, 2 Yorks, 17.00

It was time to withdraw.

We walked slowly back up the dirt road. The body of the Taliban was left lying in the mud, covered in a cloth, as were the bodies of the lorry drivers. It was better that local people, when they felt it was safe, should come forward and give the men a decent burial.

23. Battle for the Wadi: 8 December

One mile south-west of Musa Qala, 05.33

An American paratrooper stood in pitch darkness. He was catching his breath after a long march. As he smoked, he shielded the orange glow of his cigarette in the cup of his hands. He looked upwards, and, as the tobacco burned down, the sky began to change. From the east came the dimmest of lights. One by one, the stars were snuffed out.

Then he heard in the wind the call to prayer. The words came not from some loudspeaker. They were shouted in Arabic, as they had been for fifteen centuries, by a lone man standing on the roof of a town mosque.

> *Allahu Akbar*
> *Ashhadu an la ilaha illa Allah*
> *Ashadu anna Muhammadan Rasool Allah*

> God is Great
> I bear witness that there is no god but Allah
> I bear witness that Muhammad is the messenger of Allah
> Rise up for prayer
> Rise up for Salvation
> Prayer is better than sleep
> Allah is Great
> There is no god but Allah

One hundred yards from the American soldier and his platoon, a group of young Afghan men shook away their thin blankets. They leaned their weapons on the side of a mud-brick compound and prostrated themselves towards the holy city of Mecca. Few of these men doubted God's will that today would be the day of *shaheed*, of holy martyrs.

The paratroopers of 1 Fury had been marching through most of the night, slowed down by their unexpected arrival at a more distant landing site. The absence of a moon did not help. The night-vision goggles they used were high-tech, but they worked by amplifying the ambient light. On utterly dark nights like this, with no illumination but the stars, they had all the clarity of a poorly tuned television set. It all made for hard going as, laden with supplies, the paratroopers had trudged on foot through a series of rocky desert ravines.

As they emerged from the desert, the stage for the battle ahead was to be an altogether different scenery: the cultivated green zone of the Musa Qala wadi. Overlooked by sharp cliffs, it stretched as wide as 3 miles by the town itself. But it was cut in two by a flat gravel riverbed which, as much as 600 yards across in places, was the town's most natural defence. A small but fast-flowing and treacherous stream snaked through the middle, and the town of Musa Qala lay on the far, western bank.

Brian Mennes, the 1 Fury commander, proposed to defeat the Taliban in Musa Qala by sweeping towards it from three sides. His Bravo Company would cross the riverbed and come down from the north. Charlie Company would also cross and then sweep up from the south, and Alpha Company would seize the high and low ground opposite the town itself.

By first light on 8 December, the slow march had put them behind schedule. Bravo was across the riverbed but had established only a toehold, and Charlie, who had the furthest to walk, had yet to make it across. But Alpha had successfully taken the Roshan Tower, a mobile telephone mast on a twin-peaked hill that over-looked and dominated the town and where Mennes had now established his command post.

So far, apart from pre-emptive strikes from the air, 1 Fury had not been in contact with the enemy. Nor did they know where the enemy was.

★

The Battle of Musa Qala wadi began shortly after dawn with a single round from an AK-47. Captain Adam Wehrle, the acting commander of 1 Fury's Charlie Company, thought at first it was a negligent discharge by one of his soldiers. Then came incoming RPGs and automatic fire.

The Taliban were firing from all around Charlie, trying as much as the Americans were to find out exactly where *their* enemy had appeared from. They were scattered in positions throughout the tree lines, mostly for now on the same western side of the wide dry riverbed as the American paratroopers. They were making use of a deep irrigation ditch that ran in parallel to the riverbank, allowing them to run northwards and southwards as fast as they wanted.

Wehrle called for help from the battalion's mortar line. Jet planes were soon on station and dived past in a show of force. And a bomb was dropped on a position about 75 yards away.

On the Musa Qala side of the river, about 4 miles further north, Bravo Company came under attack shortly after Charlie's battle began. At 06.15, Specialist Brad Malone was on the roof of a little mosque setting up his machine gun when he shouted down, 'Hey, I think I see someone with shovels or RPGs. I can't tell.'

A moment later, he knew for sure. Two RPGs darted in, and a day-long fight began.

Malone was in cover behind two small domes on the roof. But he wasn't protected from behind. The fire was coming from all sides. A bullet went through his Camelback water pouch. Seeing the attackers had crept within yards, Malone pulled out the pin from a grenade and was still holding it as he leaped off the roof, twisting his ankle. He managed not to let go.

Most of his 1st Platoon and the company headquarters were still below, trying to dry themselves off. After eight hours of walking and then crossing through the river and mud, most of the men were drenched.

If they had not arrived so late, Captain Don Canterna, the twenty-eight-year-old commander of Bravo Company, had planned to stretch his forces in a line across the green zone – from the riverbed on the western side to a road on the east. His three platoons would then have leapfrogged south towards Musa Qala centre. Instead, his 2nd Platoon had barely made it across the riverbed and was more than half a mile behind his 3rd Platoon and 1st Platoon. The latter was now in the centre of the green zone and vulnerable to attack from the north, east and south. With his line of attack incomplete, Canterna would at first not be mounting the sweep through the green zone he had planned but rather a hasty perimeter defence.

1st Platoon and Captain Canterna's headquarters had stopped to rest in a mosque and a private home. A small alleyway ran between the two buildings, protected only by a low wall on the eastern side and a tree-flanked canal to the west.

After the attack began, Staff Sergeant Otilio Vasquez and his gunner, Sergeant Daniel Aguto, were the first to run out. The scene was surreal. Bullets were flipping up the dirt. And a camel stood impassively on one side. Vasquez ran beside it.

'Well, I got scared,' he said, explaining why he got to know the camel inside its little shelter. 'I'm like: "OK, I need to get in here. Scoot over." RPGs were hitting the wall; the camel just stood there the whole time eating hay.'

Sergeant Jason Murray was in a pair of shorts in the mosque when the fighting started, and Sergeant Harry Jauert was practically naked. They put their clothes on as the bullets ricocheted in through the door. 'It was an insane scene,' Jauert remembered.

The pair came out and made it to the low wall. Beyond was a field with trees and ditches and little earth mounds. The enemy was creeping up, low-crawling through the cover. Murray and Jauert could see two fighters really close, maybe only 15 yards away. The paratroopers would pop up to look, fire a few bursts and then dive down behind the wall before the enemy could zero in on them. Bullets struck the wall in front, throwing up a cloud of dust.

About the third time Murray got up to fire, a stream of tracer swung towards him. A bullet struck the sights of his rifle: smashing debris into his face. Blood gushed out, and Murray went into shock.

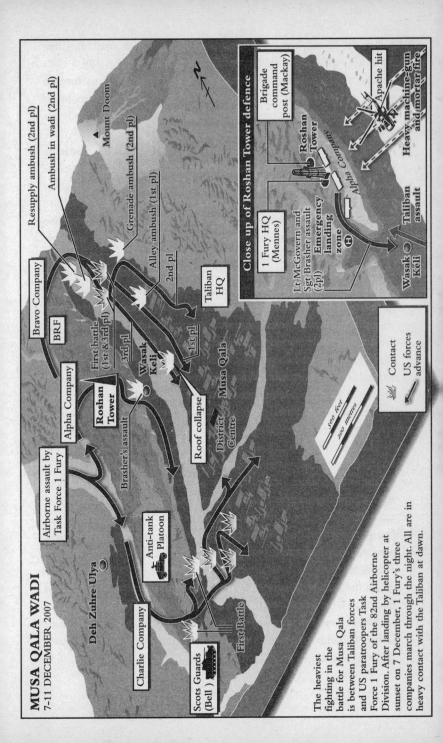

MUSA QALA WADI
7-11 DECEMBER 2007

Deh Zuhre Ulya

Mount Doom

Airborne assault by Task Force 1 Fury

Resupply ambush (2nd pl)

Ambush in wadi (2nd pl)

Bravo Company

BRF

Grenade ambush (2nd pl)

Alley ambush (1st pl)

Alpha Company

First battle (1st & 3rd pl)

Roshan Tower

3rd pl

Wasak Keli

Brasher's assault

2nd pl

Taliban HQ

1st pl

Roof collapse

Musa Qala District Centre

Anti-tank Platoon

Charlie Company

First Battle

First Battle

Scots Guards (Bell)

200 feet

200 meters

The heaviest fighting in the battle for Musa Qala is between Taliban forces and US paratroopers Task Force 1 Fury of the 82nd Airborne Division. After landing by helicopter at sunset on 7 December, 1 Fury's three companies march through the night. All are in heavy contact with the Taliban at dawn.

Contact

US forces advance

Close up of Roshan Tower defence

Brigade command post (Mackay)

Roshan Tower

1 Fury HQ (Mennes)

Alpha Company

Lt McGovern and Sgt Brasher assault (2pl)

Emergency landing zone

Apache hit

Heavy machine-gun and mortar fire

Taliban assault

Wasak Keli

'Jauert, Jauert, they got me. They got me. Oh man, I'm hit. I'm hit.'

Jauert had to grin. Murray's face was priceless, a picture of worry. His face clearly hurt badly. He thought he had lost something important. But Jauert could tell that, for all the blood, the wounds were superficial.

'Oh, it's just – you're fine. You just got caught with plastic or something.'

Robinson, a radio operator, came over to patch him up. Jauert got back on with the firing.

Vasquez had meanwhile got to the other end of the alley. When he looked behind him he saw Murray's head bound in white bandages. He remembered Murray once teasing a squad leader who found it hard to shoot straight. 'I can't see. I can't see,' Murray had mocked. Seeing Murray now bandaged like some First World War gas victim, Vasquez shouted, 'Murray, you can't see, you can't see!'

At his end of the alley, Vasquez had sent a machine-gun team across a waist-deep stream to set up a position under some trees. But a flank was exposed. As Specialist Julian Reyes waded across, an RPG rocket came skimming along like a flat pebble on the surface of the water. But his reflexes were razor sharp and he dived under, the RPG skipped over, and he popped up again, already shooting at the man who had fired. 'Oh, God, oh, my, did this really just happen?' thought Vasquez. And Reyes' eyes were wide open, agog.

By now the attack on 1st Platoon was coming in from almost all sides. About the only safe direction was towards the river, where 3rd Platoon were. Only an assault mounted out of 3rd Platoon's compound spoiled the enemy's attempt to encircle them. As it was, they got perilously close to breaking the company's defences.

Sergeant Brian Reese, the platoon leader, noticed at one point that almost his entire platoon were pinned down, unable to lift their heads for more than a few moments. It meant the Taliban could keep creeping forward and threatening their whole position. Lobbing hand grenades, he killed two men who had got within 10 feet.

Canterna spent much of the fight working with his forward air controller, Keith Mellon, trying to call in air strikes. But they found the fighting was at such close quarters that dropping bombs would risk fratricide. Meanwhile, mission after mission of artillery shells and mortar fire were called in, much of it 'Danger Close', meaning closer to them than normally allowed for safety reasons. 'The situation was that desperate,' said Canterna.

When the attacks eventually died out – for the morning at least – Vasquez looked over at the camel in the stable and a donkey tied up in the field. They were just chewing away like nothing had happened.

The fight that had begun that morning, thought Canterna, had followed months of preparation by the Taliban. Stocks of weapons and ammunition had been spread ready for use all around Musa Qala. With numerous tree-covered irrigation ditches to use like trenches, their manoeuvres were hard to spot at the best of times. But the zero illumination at night, due to the lack of moonlight, had made them virtually invisible to them and even to sophisticated equipment like the Predator UAVs. 'Neither forces' early-warning networks were very effective – ours or the enemy's,' he recalled. As soon as the Taliban learned where the main body of the American force was, they had rushed their fighters over.

Roshan Tower, headquarters of 1 Fury and Alpha Company, 06.45

Sergeant First Class Ronald Strickland was walking down the hilltop trench line where 200 paratroopers were sprawled out. His men were smoked. After hours of humping their gear from the landing zone, of assaulting this hill in darkness and of setting up their perimeter defences, most had barely slept an hour. Strickland hadn't slept at all. But it was light now and he was kicking them all awake.

For the last half hour Strickland, a thirty-five-year-old from Pembroke, North Carolina, had been standing on the ridgeline and watching the tracer down the valley where Charlie Company was in contact. As the light came up, he knew their turn would come soon.

'Hey, man, we better back it up, you know, because we might start getting shot,' he told a fellow sleepwalker.

They got a warning. An EW (Electronic Warfare) sergeant emerged from the command post with a radio intercept. 'We're gonna get mortared. Better spread the word,' he said. Strickland was doing just that with his feet. Within two minutes the rounds started coming in.

The Taliban had opened up not with mortars but with a Dushka, a nickname (meaning 'sweetie' in Russian) for the DShK 1938 machine gun used by the Red Army in the Second World War and in the decades after. Like the American and British .50 cals (which entered service just after the First World War and have changed little), it fired half-inch calibre rounds. They were accurate, dinging on the metal of the red-and-white tower and smashing into the walls of the concrete hut underneath.

The men started putting their gear on. Villagers could be seen fleeing along the road beneath the cliff. A full-scale attack was on.

The fire was coming from multiple directions: from the Dushkas straight across the wadi but also now from the green zone just below the tower. 'The Taliban were trying to manoeuvre on us. They wanted to take the tower back,' recalled Captain John Pelikan, thirty-two, the Alpha Company commander.

Anyone with a military mind had always known the hill around the Roshan Tower was the key to controlling this town. In the 1983 Soviet attack on Musa Qala, the Mujahidin had kept hold of it and kept the Red Army at bay for seven days. The trenches were still there. And still just as useful. The surprise was the Taliban had not defended it the previous night. But holding a high feature was always a double-edged sword. You could aim your guns from here at everywhere. But everyone in the valley had clear sight of you. The mobile phone mast was a perfect target marker.

Strickland was organizing his men. The biggest threat he knew by now was from the south, where a steep road snaked up the hill from a village through which fighters were already sneaking up. Grabbing a team with a 240 machine gun, Strickland moved down the old trench lines. In some places they were dug deep, in other places only shallow scrapes were left. But the worst thing was a little dip between the two high points on the summit. The Dushka gunners were watching the gap. You just took a deep breath, shouted 'OK, ready? . . . Go,' and had to run across with the rounds cracking by.

Reaching the far position, overlooking the village, he found a team leader crouching for cover. He had just popped his head up . . . and dived promptly back down.

'Where's it coming from?' said Strickland. The soldier leaned back and pointed over his shoulder. 'From right down here somewhere, right at these compounds.'

Strickland crawled up to the edge and looked over. Straightaway he saw a gunman running from a building to a tree and opening fire. A narrow tree wasn't much cover. 'Is he retarded?' thought Strickland as he shot him, knocking him on his backside. The man kept trying to get up. So Strickland shot him five more times. Then another fighter came out and stood behind another small tree. Strickland shot him too, and the fighter fell.

Following Strickland's lead, more paratroopers opened up. They pointed their weapons almost vertically down the cliff. More fighters streamed forward, and soon Strickland was bowling grenades straight down the cliff-face. 'It was like attacking a castle,' remembered their commander, Colonel Mennes, 'and the image I had in my head was our guys are pouring hot oil down the castle walls.'

2nd Platoon of Alpha Company was supposed to be clearing compounds that morning. If 1 Fury had landed at the right landing zone, they would have been down in the green zone already. Instead they were under fire, feeling pumped up, but also sick. They were tired and cold and dehydrated after the long walk with heavy kit and just the snatch of sleep. As they moved out, some of them vomited.

'We were in good spirits,' said Sergeant Tyler Clas later, when I met him back at Fort Bragg. 'It wasn't sick like I am now, where you just feel like crap. You were just completely exhausted and done.'

As the attack started on Roshan, Pelikan had gone up to Mennes and pressed for action. 'Hey, sir, we need to manoeuvre. Let's get them off our backs.' Mennes agreed and Pelikan went down and ordered: 'Hey, 2nd Platoon, you're gonna go counter-attack.'

Heading 2nd Platoon was a young first lieutenant named Joe McGovern, on his first combat tour. At his side, though, was a twenty-eight-year-old platoon sergeant named James Brasher with ten years of army experience, including plenty of combat. Brasher, from Albuquerque, New Mexico, was a hard man who led from the front and was followed.

As Strickland's 3rd Platoon fired downhill from the trenches, 2nd Platoon came down round the side of the hill. The squads started clearing the compounds by kicking down doors or blowing their way in.

The Taliban had not yet realized they were coming. Two of them just came round a corner. They were 6 feet away. Brasher raised his M4 and shot the first one, but he didn't kill him, and then his gun jammed. He was going to rugby tackle him when Clas, who led a squad, came over his shoulder and shot him dead. The other fighter ran off – and they threw a couple of grenades after him.

A bloody and close-quarter fight continued. When the platoon got pinned down behind a wall, Brasher led a squad to flank their assailants. Smashing through a wall that stood in their way, they ran straight into a gunman with a PKM light machine gun. The squad opened fire, and the man dropped his weapon and rolled into a ditch. But he wasn't dead, and he reached out and dragged his gun away.

The squad ran forward, lobbing grenades round a corner. As they ran through the smoke, there were two guys 'just chilling right there' about 10 feet away, recalled Brasher. He and another soldier named Jasen Pruitt shot them dead. Brasher sent Sergeants

Michael Verton and Stephen McBride to push forward. They shot one more gunman, but, as they turned another corner, two RPGs struck a wall by them. McBride was deafened.

Brasher called them back. He went forward. Then he noticed an Apache helicopter that was ploughing up a tree line with its 30 mm cannon. The splashes of dirt seemed to be heading Brasher's way, exploding whole trees to his side. He thought (wrongly) it was a Dutch Apache and started cursing into his radio: 'Hey, tell that motherfucker to cease fire! Tell that motherfucker to cease fire!' He threw out a smoke canister and tried to walk back slowly so the Apache would not think he was running away. But he felt the rounds creeping in on him.

Six months later, as he recalled the scene, Brasher was still angry. 'Eventually, that wooden-shoe-wearing asshole got it through his head what he was doing . . . And he went off to go kill some more friendlies!'

Brasher was determined to press on, but this route seemed like the road of death. He turned the squad round again, and this time found a new alley – leading straight up to the enemy's main compound. As they crept up, Brasher picked up another soldier's grenade launcher and fired several rounds. And he threw a hand grenade through a window.

They turned and reached a knee-height wall that covered a wide courtyard. Brasher pulled his shotgun out and delivered all five rounds. He dropped the shotgun and reached for his M4. At that moment, a gunman emerged from a doorway opposite – the same man who had rolled into the ditch and escaped with his weapon. This time, he was faster on the draw. Brasher had just raised his gun sights when the enemy's bullets leaded across, kicking up the dirt and knocking him back behind the wall. A chunk of his arm was missing. There was bare bone and blood was spurting out. Brasher thought his whole arm had gone.

'2–7 is down. Repeat: 2–7 is hit. We need a medevac,' one of the squad reported, using Brasher's call sign.

'Medic! Medic!' screamed Brasher, whose lungs were still intact. 'Those motherfuckers!' The medic, Specialist Spencer Brooks, was already right behind. He wrenched a tourniquet around Brasher's arm to stem the flow of blood. The bullet had gone through his forearm, shattering the bone, cutting a nerve and then blowing away most of his triceps muscle.

Brasher was still by the wall, and the firing was as intense as ever. 'You gotta get up and move because we're still exposed,' someone told Brasher. He stumbled back down the alleyway with Brooks.

McGovern, the platoon leader, was still with the other squads behind a wall where they had first been pinned down. But he had not needed his radio to hear Brasher's profanities up ahead. He felt his stomach churn. Was Brasher going to die? And, with Brasher gone, how many more was he going to lose? But the worst thing was the sense of powerlessness. He could not see the compound from where Brasher had been hit. He could not tell what was happening up forward. McGovern told one squad to stay behind, and he took the other over the wall to get straight into the battle.

Sergeant Billy Lee, just twenty-one and from Metter, Georgia, was point for the new squad charging forward and counted himself one of Brasher's closest friends. As they approached, Brasher was yelling out: 'Go kill those motherfuckers! Go kill those mother-fuckers!'

But as Lee arrived and looked at Brasher, he was not listening to his words – just reading his mind from his dark, intense stare. Lee got filled with the killing rage. McGovern had told him to take the enemy's compound. Lee looked behind him. His team were following. He ran up to the low wall and leaped across. He was aiming to reach the first door on the left of the courtyard. He glanced back again. He had been running too fast. No one else had made the jump. They were behind the wall and Lee was alone and totally exposed in a courtyard ringed by Taliban in every doorway and at every window. He got shot and fell.

'Hey, I'm hit! I'm hit!' he yelled.

He lay clutching a bleeding hand and getting scared. Everyone else got behind the wall. They unloaded with everything they had

– grenade-throwers, machine guns and their M4s. There was a sheet of lead above Lee's head. It gave him protection but it also meant he could not get up.

'Get me out, get me out, I gotta get out. Stop firing for a second,' yelled Lee.

But it seemed the shooting just carried on and carried on. Then just a brief pause. Lee shouted, 'I'm coming.' He leaped back over the wall.

'Ah, my fucking hand, my hand.'

He rolled into a ditch and shouted again, 'Oh I'm hit, I'm hit, I'm hit.' Lee was losing it. But Doc Brooks told him he was fine . . . calmed him down.

McGovern realized it was time to pull out. They had two men to medevac and they had already pumped the enemy compound full of ammo. Time to finish them off, he thought, with a JDAM bomb – or two.

Sergeant First Class Shane Summers was watching the battle from the clifftop by the Roshan Tower, and he dropped into Brasher's and McGovern's radio frequency so he could help spot targets for them and give them fire support. It was Summers who got his fire team on to the radio to call off the Apache when he heard Brasher's angry calls for a ceasefire.

Summers watched as the medevac began and 2nd Platoon withdrew from the enemy compound. He called down to Sergeant Verton: 'Hey, are you guys all clear?'

'Yeah,' said Verton.

Summers gave the order to the machine gunners. It was time to go *cyclic* – holding the trigger down on fully automatic and just letting the belts of ammunition run through the guns until the guns just couldn't stand any more.

Kingsman Lee Bellingham had not heard the blast. But now he could hardly hear anything. He was in a strange, silent world, and the events taking place were moving weirdly slowly.

Just before they went up the hill, Jonno had shouted back to the men to get down in the back: a standard drill for steep slopes, in case you rolled. 'Top cover, get down halfway but don't close the hatches,' he said. 'That way if we get *contacted* you can reach for your gun.' It was only just mid-morning, but everyone was getting hot, hungry and thirsty. They knew they had hardly made any distance from the camp the previous night, and there was still at least another 9 miles to go. And in a convoy, thought Bellingham, 'that's a long way.'

Up ahead on the track out of the wadi was a big Afghan ammo truck, an International 7000, bogged down and blocking the path with its drive-shaft broken. Captain Nick Mantell was standing next to the truck, trying to think of a way of towing it out. Cagey was there too. Jake Little and Andy Breach had gone off looking for a bigger vehicle that could pull it out. The American gun trucks had already tried and failed. Everyone else in the convoy had either been in front of the truck before it got bogged down or driven past it in the last half-hour. Just two British vehicles – a WMIK with Fong at the wheel and Jonno's Vector – remained stuck behind.

Fong had already tried to get past by taking a steep path to the side of the truck, but his WMIK kept losing power that day. It would not go. 'The thing was my vehicle had been working fine, but that morning I don't know what happened to it. It didn't want to go past the truck.'

Jonno came on the radio: 'If you can't get up there then we're going.'

They were halfway up the hill when the soldiers in the back heard the engine struggling. The Vector was getting bogged down: its wheels were spinning, and it was digging down into the sand.

That must have been how it struck the anti-tank mine, probably one left behind by the Soviets. By now, several vehicles had been round exactly that route. They probably loosened things up.

Bellingham must have been knocked out. When his mind started working, he saw smoke everywhere. He felt a thud when the back of the Vector went into something. He popped his head up out of the hatch and saw his machine gun was in bits, cut in half. A piece of the engine was on top of the vehicle. He ducked back down and looked at the others. The interpreter, Tawfiq, was trying to open the back door. Bellingham grabbed him and shouted out, 'Minefield,' although he couldn't hear his own screams. That was just instinct. He hadn't really thought about it yet. The medic, Matt Hughes, was in a lot of pain, and a soldier on board from the Royal Military Police, Corporal Greg Jeffrey, seemed to have dislocated his shoulder. Both of those climbed out, then Tawfiq, who had hurt his wrist.

Bellingham tried to shout to Jonno up the front. There was lots of luggage – bags and ammunition – between the back of the cab and the front. He tried to clear a way through. But there was black smoke everywhere, and rubber was burning. He could taste it in the back of his throat. But it was still silent. He could see nothing for the smoke, and hear nothing too.

Bellingham climbed back up top and looked forward, and then he saw the driver, Lance-Corporal Christopher Fletcher. He was halfway up the hill with blood on his face and his arms were badly cut. And there was blood coming from his mouth. He put his hand up and his lips were moving, like he was shouting for help but Bellingham couldn't hear him at all.

Just then Cagey appeared, clambering over on to the roof of the Vector from the Afghan truck. The Vector had slid back down the slope with a squeak after the explosion and had come to rest against the truck. That must have been the 'thud' that Bellingham felt. His hearing came back now all of a sudden. He heard Cagey say, 'Is everyone all right?' Bellingham said, 'I can't see Jonno. I can't get to Jonno.' Both of them leaned over the top of the cab and tried to prise Jonno's door open, but it was mangled. Then they sat on the roof and tried to kick open the driver's door, which was slightly ajar. It didn't work. Cagey went off to get Andy, the special forces medic.

Bellingham thought, 'Fuck it!' and jumped on the ground by the driver's side and managed to get the door open, clearing away the rubble and dirt inside. He remembered: 'The first thing I noticed there's no steering wheel, it was just black inside. It was like something went through and just left the outer shell, ripping it to shreds inside.' He crawled through towards Jonno, but when he saw him his heart almost stopped. Bellingham knew instantly what had happened when he opened Jonno's eyelids and he saw only darkness. But it wasn't his job to declare anyone dead. He just did what his training said: applied two tourniquets to stem the flow of blood from his torso and tried to cut some of his clothes away to check out his injuries. By now Hughes, the medic, had climbed in too. They could tell instantly there was no life left. Both of Jonno's legs had been amputated in the blast. No one could survive that. Jonno must have died instantaneously. He had felt no pain.

Bellingham got out of the vehicle with blood on his clothes. By now the chopper was in and flying out the other casualties.

How did he recall that day later? 'The weather was, you know, cold and miserable in the morning. In the afternoon it got hot. And it was that sort of day where you're hungry, you're tired, you just want to get back to the camp, get a hot shower, get a beer and stuff like that. And Jonno just turned around and said, "No, I don't like today, something's going to happen," and you know, for him, it did.'

Of the mine blast, Hughes, the medic, would remember only a big bang and smoke and dust. Then he was flying forward on to the ammunition boxes. He also remembered him and Lee stopping Tawfiq, the interpreter, from getting out the back. Then he was sifting through the bags trying to find his medical kit and trying to see in the front. He could see that Jonno was there, but it was too narrow to get through. He took his bag and climbed on to the roof. He was still looking for Fletch, the driver, but saw him being helped up the hill, bleeding. Hughes clambered over the Afghan truck and got to Fletcher. But by then another medic had arrived, so Hughes turned back and clambered again over the truck back into the back of the Vector to try to reach Jonno. He managed to dig a path through the bags and boxes, and by then Lee Bellingham was already in the front.

'We were talking because I wasn't in a position to manoeuvre around Jonno, whereas Lee was.' Hughes got Bellingham to check the vital signs, like his pulse and breathing. There were no signs at all. They were preparing to leave as Andy, the American SF medic, jumped in.

'How is he?' said Andy.

'He's not with us.'

'Right then, let's go.'

That was how the scene ended, although it stayed in Hughes' mind for months. Those two days – the nightmare in the village and then the blast and finding Jonno dead – were about the worst he could think of. Months later he was getting counselling from the army's welfare team. 'I still think about it now,' he told me back in England. 'There's some times when I just can't sleep or there's some times when I think about it so bad I get myself worked up.' Hughes never spoke to his family about it. It was all too much.

In the desert above, when Jake heard the mine blast, he thought at first maybe Nick Mantell had 'denied' the truck (blown it up and denied it to the enemy). But he felt his stomach churn nevertheless, felt unease.

He sped back through the desert. At his side, as always, was one of Jonno's best friends, Dave McCarrick on the .50 cal, and David Percival, his driver.

On his personal radio Jake could hear now it was a mine strike. And as he approached he could see it was a Vector, Jonno's Vector. He wanted to get down quickly and see what had happened and how everyone was. Mantell knew what Jake wanted but knew he had to stop it. There was no gentle way of doing it.

'Jake. Jonno's dead,' he said.

Jake still wanted to go down there. But Mantell said he had stopped everyone going. It might be a minefield. Jake nodded.

Most of B Company spent the rest of the day up on the ridgeline. All day Mantell wondered if he could have done anything differently, if there could have been a way to save Jonno. But he knew deep down there was nothing. It was just sad and unlucky. B Company were waiting for a chopper to bring a bomb-disposal team in to clear the minefield so Jonno's body could be taken away safely and the Afghan truck recovered or blown up. But the helicopters never came.

Emergency landing zone beneath Roshan Tower, with Alpha Company, 1 Fury, 11.00

The paratroopers wanted the chopper in fast. They feared the injured Brasher could die through blood loss, and they knew the JDAMs couldn't be dropped while the helicopters were around.

Eventually a British Chinook showed up, but the message came through: 'We're not landing. It's too hot.'

'Hey, what do you want me to do? Let this guy bleed out?' replied Shane Summers, who was in charge of the evacuation. He was told to move the landing zone.

'We can't fucking move, and this guy's fucking dying. So are you coming in or not?' was what the Chinook pilots heard of his reply.

The Americans knew they were lying about the landing zone's security. The helicopters, who knew there was a battle going on, were saying, 'This place in not secured,' and Summers was saying, 'Yeah, it is secured.' It wasn't a blatant lie. It was true the actual 100-yard strip where the helicopter would land was secure. But they had to skew the data a bit. Right in front were the Taliban positions, and Musa Qala wadi and the town itself were right in sight – and right in range.

The pilot on the circling Chinook was Nichol Benzie – the same man who had landed under contact for the Royal Marines outside Inkerman on 9 November. In the back of the Chinook were the two injured they had just picked up from the mine strike that killed Jonno. Benzie and his co-pilot made the decision to come in. The last 30 feet of descent were as blind as usual, descending through the brown-out of dust and flying rocks. When their vision cleared, the pilots looked straight ahead and realized there was nothing between them and Musa Qala and their enemy.

Summers took the injured round the back of the chopper. Brasher's pain kept him angry. The other injured soldier, Lee, watched as a medic rushed out to help Brasher – and Brasher stiff-armed him aside with his good arm, knocking the medic on to his backside. As they flew off, Lee knew his friend was still in a bad way and he was worried they were paying attention to him and not Brasher. 'That was a fun ride,' remembered Lee. 'Me, messed up on morphine, cussing out some people.'

Helicopter landing site Broadsword, beneath Kajaki Dam, 11.10

Don Johnson was playing his guitar outside the Ops Room. Since that horrible mine strike that killed the interpreter they had had a couple of days off. It was a bit of a luxury. Someone came out and gave him a phone message.

'You need to be on the helipad, right now.'

Don said it was a mistake. There were others due out on R&R on a helicopter that was supposed to have gone ten minutes ago. The messenger insisted.

'I don't think so,' said Don.

He went into the Ops Room. A phone call came in again from the 2 Yorks HQ.

'Right. It is definite. You need to go.'

'Put me on to the ops officer, because I think you've made a mistake.'

The ops officer came on the line.

'Look, I don't know what it is. But you need to make your way back as fast as you can.'

Don put the phone down and walked away. He knew now. He just knew. He was with two lads called Private Shaun Utley and Lance-Corporal Christopher O'Malley. (O'Malley got hit later in Musa Qala and had his toes blown off, recalled Don.) They helped him pack his Bergen.

'I think something has happened to our kid,' he told them.

Then Sergeant Andrew Morrisson came in. Crying his eyes out. A big bloke. No one would expect him to cry.

'Look, I'm sorry. Your kid's dead.'

He gave Don a cuddle.

It was now about 11.15 a.m. Everyone helped pack his kit. He just took his rifle, his webbing, his ammunition, his night sights and his guitar. And then he walked down to the helipad and waited about ten minutes. While he was there, the Royal Marines sergeant-major, David Layton, came over.

'Is it true?' he asked.

'Yeah.'

'Oh.'

They just sat there. Then Layton said, 'I used to go mad with your kid . . . because it was always the fucking ANA that ran out of ammo first.'

He said Jonno used to come running to the rear in the midst of battle, back to where the sergeant-major had his quad bike loaded up with resupply. The ammunition for the AK-47s and variants the Afghans used was always on the top – because he knew Jonno would want his first. And then Jonno would turn around and go running off with two boxes of the ammunition on his back.

The sergeant-major kept up with the stories, and then the Chinook came in, and Don jumped on.

The flight took them past Sangin district centre. That morning someone had dropped off a badly wounded man at the gates. He told them some lies at first but eventually confessed he was Taliban. He'd been handling a bomb that went off too early. The British soldiers took him on the chopper for medical treatment.

Don took a look at the wounded man covered in burns, and, for some reason, it made him furious. 'The back was open and I honestly really just wanted to kick him out the back.' There was a marine officer next to him. He grabbed Don's leg, as if for reassurance. Don was saying to him: 'Can we just throw him off?' The officer just held him and said, 'It's going to be all right, it's going to be all right.' Don buried his face in his arm.

North of Musa Qala, 16.45

It took a while to work out the gunfire was coming from the rear, from the north-east. 2nd Platoon of Bravo Company, 1 Fury, hit the deck and then took cover as best they could, moving closer to the bank of the gravel riverbed.

They had been trying to link up with the British BRF who had collected Bravo's resupply. But they did not make it. Now the BRF were up on the cliffs, firing in support with their snipers and their .50 cal. Anthony Fusco, the platoon sergeant, took a squad into attack, jumping up over the wadi bank and heading for the enemy's compounds. Fusco had cleared about four buildings before they spotted the enemy getting away across open ground. Fusco recalled: 'They were trying to carry their guys off the battlefield. Two were limping because we had hit them in their legs. I turned around and caught another guy trying to skip town and put one through his lung. And then, the Apaches came on station and basically scared them all away.'

Some of the Taliban moved across and attacked the compound where 1st Platoon was holed up. Daniel Price was behind a 240 machine gun. He looked up to see a man running at him firing. A bullet struck him by the heart. It went through his compass, bounced off his armour plating, cracking it, and then ricocheted off into his arm. Price kept firing though and it took two other paratroopers to drag him away from the fight.

His assailant had jumped behind a corner. He was killed with some grenades. And they killed two more men who came to drag away the attacker's body. That was the pattern the paratroopers noticed. As soon as you killed a Taliban fighter, the rest of them got even braver – charging across to recover their comrade's body.

Ridgeline south-west of Musa Qala,
with B Company, 2 Yorks, 17.00

It was getting close to darkness now, and the waiting was still not over. Jonno's body was still in the Vector, and the promised helicopter had still not come with the explosive experts to clear the site. All day, everyone kept asking Jake, 'When's the fucking helicopter coming?' Three times, remembered Dave McCarrick, a chopper came in and hovered about and said they couldn't see the signal smoke or made some excuse. In the end, Jake said: 'That's it. We'll do it ourselves.'

It was Lance-Corporal John Dickens, an engineer, who went down to do the clearance. He got out his metal detector and scanned the ground around the Vector and around the truck. He came back up in a sweat, but gave the all clear.

Then Jake and Benson, the sergeant-major, took a team of five down – those they thought would cope best: themselves, McCarrick, Fong and French. As Jonno's best friend at the scene, it was hard for McCarrick. Jake had to ask him, 'Are you up for it?' McCarrick said, 'Yeah.' He didn't want any of the young lads to see Jonno. As it was, it was OK. 'He didn't look too bad.' As they prepared Jonno to bring him up the hill they found his bible underneath his body armour.

For Fong, it was some relief to go down the hill again. All day, he'd been praying for Jonno, knowing his spirit was sitting some place close. When the explosion went off, Fong had been just below the truck and heard a squeaking noise in the dust cloud as Jonno's Vector slid backwards from the explosion. He and his boss, Craig Dawson, had been ordered to stay put, rather than risk another mine blast. But he had been wishing he had leaped over and tried to save Jonno. But – seeing Jonno's injuries – his mind

30. Members of an Afghan militia sent to guard Mullah Salaam arrive at the British front line in two school buses.

31. Corporal Darryl 'Daz' Gardiner, with the Brigade Reconnaissance Force, shortly after the death of his comrade, Trooper Jack Sadler, in the desert west of Musa Qala.

32. B Company, 2 Yorks, prepares for action at dawn on the day of assault.

33. Soldiers from B Company, 2 Yorks, and the Afghan army in action in the village of Deh Zohr e Sofla after being ambushed by the Taliban.

34. Sergeant-Major Daniel Benson and medic, Corporal Phil French, try to save the life of a civilian with gunshot wounds.

35. An Afghan soldier confronts a Taliban prisoner.

36. Afghan soldiers recover the body of a dead Taliban fighter.

37. US special force Green Berets in action in the village (*left*). They had earlier opened fire on civilian cars.

38–9. (*Left*), the scene just after the mine explosion under Sergeant Lee 'Jonno' Johnson's armoured vehicle on 8 December. Soldiers are clambering over the damaged Vector to reach Jonno. Corporal Gregory 'Cagey' Roberts (*above*) had been trying to recover the Afghan truck, bogged down behind the damaged vehicle.

40. One of the wounded is helped away

41. Captain Nick Mantell was standing by Jonno's Vector when it exploded; he coordinated the rescue of survivors.

42. B Company watch as Jonno's Vector is destroyed by a JDAM bomb.

43-5. Apache helicopters in action in the Musa Qala wadi (*right and below*), as soldiers from the Brigade Reconnaissance Force fire from the ridgeline in support of US troops (*below left*).

46. Chinook helicopters land in the wadi (*above*) to recover wounded and deliver supplies.

47. Sergeant James Brasher, of 1 Fury, before he led an assault at the foot of Roshan Hill.

48. A special forces Spectre gunship in action at night over Musa Qala.

49-50. On top of Roshan Tower hill, overlooking Musa Qala, and Roshan Tower (*inset*).

51. Brigadier Andrew Mackay in command of the front at the top of Roshan Hill.

52. Four scouts from 1 Fury with their Humvee before it struck a mine, killing Corporal Tanner O'Leary (*far right*).

53. Wounded soldier Rifleman Subash Gurung from A Company, 1 Royal Gurkha Rifles, awaiting rescue from a compound in the green zone outside Sangin.

54. Afghan soldiers with B Company, 2 Yorks, on the morning of the final assault on Musa Qala.

55. Private Lawrence Fong, standing opposite Major Little, leads B Company's prayers before the final assault on Musa Qala.

56. The author pictured in the rubble of the former Musa Qala district centre, phoning the BBC with news of the town's capture.

57. Brigadier Mohaydin (*right*), the Afghan army commander, clutches a flagpole before it is hoisted over the captured centre of Musa Qala.

58-59. Medic Phil French walks past an opium factory being put to flames (*above*) as residents begin to return to Musa Qala (*right*).

60–61. The scene on a ridgeline above Musa Qala after a vehicle of the Brigade Reconnaissance Force strikes a mine (*top left*, the damaged vehicle on the far left of picture), minutes later a second mine explodes (*top right*), fatally injuring Corporal Darryl Gardiner.

62–3. Corporal Gardiner pictured (*right*) just minutes before his death as he helps treat Danny Kay, who was injured in the first mine strike.

64. Royal Marines at their memorial at Inkerman to five British servicemen who had died at or near the base.

65. Few doubt that ultimately only Afghanistan's own army can beat the Taliban.

was put at rest. 'I had felt that I would be able to save his life,' he remembered, 'but then the night when we got his body out and I saw his injuries, and I told myself there was no chance at all.'

It was nearly 6 p.m. when they got Jonno up, just as the explosive disposal team finally arrived on scene. The incident had happened more than seven hours earlier. Even then it wasn't over. Jake and the others took Jonno's body over, ready to carry on to the chopper. The message was: 'We'll be there in five minutes.' Then an hour and a half later, the message came that it was just too dark to come.

McCarrick was furious. 'It was just the way we sat around all day out of the game. And then, all the fucking lies that were coming back. I just wanted to get him out and away.'

Jake knew he had to act to try to restore people's spirits, even though his own were at an all-time low. Under the stars, he gathered the company together in a huddle and gave his little speech. His face was weary and he spoke softly. 'I'm shit at this,' he confessed to the men. He spoke of the gap Jonno would leave behind and how he had died doing what he loved. He praised how the men had fought in the village the day before. 'Jonno would have been proud of each and every one of you,' he said.

He explained the helicopter hadn't come, and tonight the lads would have to stand sentry on the ridgeline over Jonno's body. Emotions, he said, would have to be suppressed in the next few days. However hard, they needed to focus on the mission. There would be a time for mourning later. 'We have to move on,' he said, 'but not forget.'

It was a miserable night. Rain began to pelt down on the ponchos of those who could find sleep. Andy Breach had the pre-dawn shift of 4 to 5 a.m. Normally in the British army, officers did not do sentry duty. But in the mentoring teams many traditions like that were ignored.

Only twenty-four hours earlier, on exactly the same shift, Breach had been sitting next to Jonno in a WMIK. Jonno had been in the driver's seat and Breach in the gunner's seat. Jonno had talked about how he loved what he was doing and how happy he had been to lead men forward in the village. 'If anything happens to me,' Jonno had said, 'I want to die outright. Lisa would kill me if I came back in bits.' Jonno had been fatalistic. That was why he was carrying that bible. He had told Breach how he was going to church. 'I know something will happen,' he had said. But he didn't seem scared or deterred.

After Jonno had died, Jake had sent Breach back to the main desert camp to break the news to the 2 Yorks headquarters. He found the regimental sergeant-major, Richard Hind, was out with a team of soldiers, doing the heavy work of digging slit trenches for B Company's return. But B Company hadn't made it back to the camp, so Breach sat out in the rain, 50 yards from Jonno's body, thinking back to what he had said and done. On the horizon he watched the flash of explosions. He heard on the radio a friend from the Household Cavalry in some battle in the distance. 'It was a miserable night,' he remembered. 'And, for us, that was even before the big battle of Musa Qala had started.'

Camp Shorobak, base of the 2 Yorks battle group, 22.30

Don Johnson started dialling the hardest phone call of his life. He wanted to do it, though. There was no good way to tell the news.

When he had returned, Don had been told Jonno's body would be brought back in a couple of hours, but that passed, and all the time he wasn't allowed to phone anyone. When someone died or was seriously injured a whole procedure went into force across Task Force Helmand. Little red signs announcing 'Operation Minimize' were put up outside the phone booths and Internet shacks, and all of them were shut down. The idea was to cut off all communications between the soldiers and back home to stop news of the latest tragedy from reaching the families or the media before the next-of-kin had been properly informed. But in this case Operation Minimize was enforced on Don also. The problem was that, under the rules, Jonno's parents and fiancée could not be informed until Jonno's death and identity were formally certified.

That required a doctor, a military policeman and a member of his unit to all be there to record a statement of his death. Those were the rules – in place, quite logically, to prevent someone being mistakenly informed about a death – but with Jonno's body stuck all day and all night on the ridgeline, it all seemed rather cruel.

'I wasn't allowed to phone anyone. I wasn't allowed to speak to anyone because they hadn't positively identified him,' he remembered. 'Obviously I was getting a bit upset, because if they had brought me back from Kajaki, they must have been positive. You know what I mean, the lads that were with him, like Jake. They'd been mates for years. They would obviously know it was him.'

By 7 p.m., Don was getting quite distraught. He had known now for about eight hours. He said: 'I need to tell someone.' The reply was: 'But we can't yet because we haven't positively identified him.' It was pathetic, he thought. 'It was like they have little rules in the army that sometimes might need to be broke.'

Then he remembered someone coming in about 10 o'clock at night and saying: 'We can't bring him back. The Americans won't bring him back and the British can't fly.'

'Well, what . . . ?'

'Well, he'll just have to stay out for the night.'

Don's head was full of dark thoughts. He thought he knew what they did with the dead in Afghanistan. He had visions of 'dogs eating the dead in the middle of the night'. It was awful.

At brigade headquarters in Lashkar Gah, Nick Haston, the deputy chief of staff, was trying to follow a rule book that, while well-intentioned, had been written in what he thought of as a 'sterile made-up environment' in the UK.

It had been his call to leave Jonno's body on the hillside, 'the most painful decision' he made in his tour in Afghanistan. Ultimately, he recalled, 'we couldn't find a bloody helicopter to pick up a body because we needed that helicopter to go elsewhere.' The shortage of helicopters was a hard fact, with a total of nine other casualties being dealt with that day by one medevac team. Hard as it sounded, if 'someone is dead that comes low down on the priority list' for being picked up. Those who were dying or severely injured clearly got precedence.

The shortage of helicopters would madden people across the brigade. When ministers came to visit, they would say, 'What would you like more of?' But the message, said Haston, was: 'Don't say helicopters, because you've got enough to do the job!' But it was obviously not true, he thought, and 'about time people understood that'.

Now Haston was in an argument with higher command, who were insisting that Don Johnson could not inform his family until Jonno was formally identified.

At about half past ten, the padre came back to Don at Camp Shorobak and said he 'had convinced the battalion, or whoever it was, to let me phone home'. It was obvious that Don was in agony. 'It was killing me,' he said, and everyone could see that. And then he made the call and 'that was probably the worst time I've ever had in my life, crying down the phone. It was horrible.'

Once approval to bend the rules was given, it was Don's decision to inform his family by phone. Normally such things are done in person by a special welfare team. In this case, the welfare team were waiting round the corner from the Johnson household. 'I think my mum and dad appreciated it coming from me and not anyone else. I don't know, they just let me do it. It was good that they let me do it.'

The padre was sitting next to Don as he made the call. His mother answered.

'Mam, can you put Dad on really fast?' said Don.

She must have known it was something bad.

His dad picked up the phone.

'Dad, there's been an accident. Lee died.'

His dad said, 'Oh God, oh my God.'

And then Don could hear his father telling his mum: 'Lee's dead.'

His mum's screams down the phone were awful. Don would never want to hear such screams again. But then he asked, 'Look, you need to be strong. Will you phone Lisa? I need you to go round and see Lisa.' Don remembered: 'I didn't want them to just phone Lisa and tell her when she was sat at home with his little Lilly, by herself. Imagine her screaming in front of that kid, it wouldn't be very nice. I said, "Look, you need to, don't tell no one, go round and speak to her straight away." And they went round and told her, which I think was the best way to do things. I couldn't have done it anyway.'

After the phone call, things did not get any better for a while. There were more complications with the helicopters, and news came and went about when Jonno's body would come out. But in the end Don went to sleep. Exhausted by the emotion of it all, he slept like a baby, for nine hours straight.

24. Night of the Spectre: 9 December

East of Musa Qala, on Roshan Hill
with Alpha Company, 1 Fury, 0700

Sunrise across the wadi ushered in a day that few in 1 Fury will ever forget.

As the men blinked in the early morning light, the rounds from the Dushka guns started whizzing again over their trenches. Forward observers were ready to coordinate return fire. Suspected firing points were identified. The 81mm mortars were called in from the rear, so were the British 105mm artillery guns, firing from the desert. The scouts in their Humvees on the ridgeline thought they saw the Dushka moving on a truck. They called in a mortar strike. The Apaches now on station thought they saw four men crawling into a firing position. They engaged them with their 30mm cannon. *And this was all in the first hour.*

Then all eyes turned behind after a loud boom. A black-grey mushroom cloud billowed up. Radios crackled. The scout platoon had been trying to push up the back of Roshan Hill. A Humvee had struck a pressure-plate IED. Corporal Tanner O'Leary, twenty-three, from South Dakota, was killed outright. Another soldier was wounded.

There was no time for contemplation. Up on Roshan Hill the firing became more intense. The Taliban Dushkas were getting braver by the minute. Most times, in most contacts in Helmand, the arrival of Apache attack helicopters on station would bring a lull in the battle. The Taliban would hide. But in this battle it just intensified. The Taliban started to fire directly at the choppers.

Some thought the .50 calibre rounds being fired by the Taliban that day were explosive-tipped. They seemed to be blowing up as they made impact. However many guns the Taliban had, it seemed they could take a heavy pounding. The Apaches were firing back at their positions with 30mm rounds and Hellfires. They took out a truck full of weapons. They took out one, perhaps two Dushka positions. But if they flew away and then returned, then machine-gun fire would pour out from a whole new spot.

The desert west of Musa Qala, with B Company, 2 Yorks

The helicopter finally came that morning for Jonno's body. Nichol Benzie, the Chinook pilot, remembered being woken up to go and do the mission. As with all flights in those days, it was not a case of simply going and getting Jonno and coming back. They also picked up some prisoners. And then they were ordered over to pick up both O'Leary's body and the gunner who had been injured in the explosion. As they approached, recalled Benzie, they saw a Humvee that had been destroyed in a really, really bad way. 'And you're always nervous, then, landing because if a mine's blown up the Humvee, then what other mines are there?'

Jonno's departure on Benzie's chopper meant B Company could finally move off the ridge. But first Jake wanted to get rid of Jonno's Vector, as well as the Afghan truck. It was partly to destroy the sensitive equipment and to deny any ammunition left behind inside the twisted wreck to the enemy. But it was also about providing some closure for the lads. So everyone could move on.

Packing up camp, B Company moved off with the American Green Berets and the ANA along the desert plateau. They stopped about a mile away. The American forward air controller was going to call in an air strike: one JDAM on each of the vehicles.

On the ground it seemed a long, long wait – almost two hours of just standing waiting for the plane to drop its bombs. All the time the vapour trails in the sky showed there were plenty of aircraft on station who could do the job. What the soldiers on the ground did not see, however, was how this one request from Jake to deny two vehicles caused one of the biggest rows back at the Brigade HQ of the entire air operation.

It all came down to how air strikes were organized. When troops were in contact – their lives facing an immediate threat – then commanders on the ground like Jake had almost total authority to call in whatever close air support they needed. Every pilot had responsibility for what he dropped, and he would always ask for some double or triple checks. But there wasn't the need for every target to be approved by someone at a higher level. But strikes that dropped bombs when no one's life was in immediate danger were governed by a whole set of different rules. Time and again questions came back from higher command demanding: 'Are there any civilians near by?' and 'Do you know where all the friendly forces are?'

On the ground, Jake was insisting there were neither 'friendly forces' nor civilians near by. Above him, the pilots were getting frustrated. All down the Musa Qala valley, and across Helmand too, there were troops in contact. But these planes were just circling around and burning up their fuel waiting for an OK to destroy two empty vehicles in the desert.

Simon Tatters, the brigade air liaison officer, could work out what was happening. A rogue Predator was wandering around near the scene and collecting pictures to which the brigade had no access. Controlled from Nevada but – apparently – under the control of an unknown commander, it was being used to second-guess the judgements that Jake and the forward air controller and the human pilots were making. The Predator, recalled Tatters, was 'providing, from our point of view, disinformation'. The picture they were building up from the ground was being questioned, and the 'frustration slowly built and built and built'.

Among their augmented air team, the brigade had three American air force colonels, so Tatters was glad it was the American who was typing out the 'fucks' and 'bullshits' on the electronic chat as the frustration grew.

The first aircraft overhead, a pair of F-15s, went away and refuelled from a tanker aircraft, came back, waited around and returned to base without dropping a thing. Now a couple of A-10s were on call. And they too were getting angry. They had been pulled away 'from the fight elsewhere'.

'The aircraft had good eyes on,' said Tatters, 'but it was a time-sensitive target, because we needed to deny these vehicles to allow the ground units to move on. And it just went on and on and on and on, and meantime, there were a lot of things happening elsewhere. This was starting to detract.'

After two and a half hours, the permission finally came through. It came with relief but also derision. Tatters guessed the final word had come from the general in Qatar. Perhaps he was on holiday somewhere and they had needed to track him down.

Bravo Company, 1 Fury, north of Musa Qala, 11.50

1st Platoon were still in the same compound they'd been sitting in for a day and a half, the same one where they'd been attacked on the morning they arrived. After the battles they'd fought, they'd run quickly short of ammo and all this time they had been waiting for resupply and waiting for 2nd Platoon to catch up.

That lunchtime someone else decided to have another go at them, perhaps just one man sticking his weapon up and firing a few rounds. Sergeant First Class Reese remembered: 'I could see this guy being a loser and shooting at us, so I did a little textbook move to go and sort him out.'

One soldier, Sergeant Tuyen Doan, however, 'took an extra step on the outside where he shouldn't have' and caught a bullet in his arm. He was in a lot of pain and couldn't move his hand. The medics did their work and he was moved out for a medevac chopper and, said Reese, 'at the same time, we pushed out to go take down this guy who was being a loser. We killed him. And then, right when we killed him, we were in this big open field, so we stopped and came back and we had to wait all day long for resupply.' It was getting frustrating.

Sometimes you get lucky, sometimes unlucky, and then sometimes someone just does something really stupid.

At 13.36, an American Chinook was coming in with a resupply that everyone in 1 Fury was sorely needing. On board was a team to take back some prisoners from Bravo Company, and also Sergeant First Class Matthew Hatfield, the senior sergeant in the 1 Fury's forward observation team. Hatfield had spent the early battle back in Kandahar, but with the forward HQ now firmly established on Roshan Hill, it was his turn to move forward.

Everyone on the Roshan remembered that moment. All morning they'd been under fire and they had made pretty sure that everyone knew that. The supply helicopters were told to approach from the desert behind, not to fly over Musa Qala itself. That made it pretty surprising to look down to the right and see a Chinook steaming straight down the middle of the wadi – right over Musa Qala town and between Roshan Tower and the Taliban opposite.

It was even more of a shock for those on board the chopper, not least Sergeant Hatfield. The ramp was lowered at the back, and he could see all too clearly when the RPGs started whooshing in – air bursting with a boom and a black cloud of shrapnel in the air just behind. He could hear the Dushka too. The gunners in the Chinook door started returning fire, rocking up and down as the chain-belt ran through their machine guns. 'Hey, this ain't good,' he thought.

Hatfield turned to the soldier next to him and shouted, 'They gotta get this chopper on the ground. We gotta land.' The Chinook started corkscrewing, swerving desperately to avoid the fire, banking left to get up and out of the wadi and back into the desert.

What saved them was an act of heroism. Waiting in the sky above was an Apache helicopter, call-sign Arrow 2–3. The pilot, Tim Slade, and his gunner, Thomas Malone, had spent all morning in the skies around Roshan, playing cat and mouse with the Dushka gunners. Both airmen were reservists with three weeks left of a one-year tour. In normal life, Malone was a bouncer in Tucson, Arizona. They had been over Musa Qala since 7 a.m. and already seen some strange sights – like a group of Taliban fighters jump out of a truck all dressed in women's clothes. When they saw the Chinook flying below, it radioed to say it was taking fire from the Dushka. Slade and Malone came swooping in – putting themselves between the Chinook and the Dushka. 'A Chinook would be more of a target because it doesn't shoot back. So with an Apache you have to get closer than the Chinook, make yourself seem like an easier target,' said Malone. RPGs started airbursting in front of them – little black puffy clouds of flak. They could hear nothing. 'It feels like a video game,' said Malone. But the move was to cost them. Two bullets struck Arrow 2–3. One hit Malone in the leg. It felt like it was blown off, 'like somebody strapped a piece of dynamite to my leg.' Malone's words were preserved by a cockpit recorder. 'I'm . . . My God! I'm hit, I'm hit, I'm hit! I'm shot in the leg, shot in the leg!'

The bullet had smashed Malone's knee into the cyclic, the Apache's main control stick. Arrow 2–3 rolled left and started plunging into a gut-wrenching groundward dive. 'I couldn't move my leg, so I had to grab it with my hands and pull it off the cyclic. My leg was about three times normal size – like a big blob of Jell-O.' Slade fought to correct the roll, slamming hard on his cyclic, a move that automatically separated the two men's controls apart and also shifted the helicopter from mechanical guidance on to computer-controlled 'fly by wire'.

'You all right? You all right?' said Slade. He realized another bullet round had struck and knocked out one of their two engines. The power was dropping. They had got within 80 feet of the ground.

Malone thought the bullet must have hit an artery. He could see he was bleeding badly. He tried to wrap a tourniquet on to stop the flow. But the space was too cramped and the leg was too swollen. Every time he tried to reach down, his leg would hit the cyclic and make the chopper turn again. 'All I could do was stick my fingers in the [bullet] hole and I just shoved my fingers in there as hard as I could and just hoped for the best.'

Slade now had the helicopter to fly, one engine to watch, and radios to work. He had to jettison their weapons in the desert to get more power. But it was slow going. An electronic clock showed a countdown of the time needed to get back to Camp Bastion, the nearest hospital – thirty-three minutes.

'Just keep talking, keep talking,' said Slade.

'Hey man, I'll let you know if I pass out.'

By the time he reached base, Malone had lost two-thirds of his blood.

On the Predator feed, Colonel Mennes and Major Jones could see the desert spot where the Apache's weapons had been dropped. Within five minutes there were motorbikes out there to collect the loot.

'Sir, we need to shoot those guys!' someone said.

Mennes couldn't tell though if they were Taliban or just looters.

'I don't know, I don't like it,' said Mennes. 'I'm not going to shoot those people.'

Bravo Company, 1 Fury, north of Musa Qala, 15.45

Vince Corona, a sergeant from Indiana, was on point again with 2nd Platoon of Bravo Company. They were back out in the open riverbed, moving south after finally getting a resupply. Of course, after waiting so long, when it had finally come, as always, it was too much. First the British BRF had made it across the wadi at first light, driving 'their crazy British vehicles'. And then finally a Chinook had come in, unloading two huge pallets of water and ammunition. There was so much they had to cut open half the water bottles and burn a load of ration packs. They didn't want to leave them for the enemy.

The aim now was to link back up with 1st Platoon, dump some resupply with them and then finally move to what had been 2nd

Platoon's initial objective – right across the other side of the green zone by the main road.

It took only thirty minutes after setting off before the Taliban opened up. They had just reached level with 1st Platoon, who they saw waving from the green zone to their left. Fusco, the platoon sergeant, had by now 'acquired' a couple of pick-up trucks, and he'd thrown the hated quad bikes in the back, along with rucksacks, excess weapons and everything that was weighing people down. It was pretty certain they would soon be in contact. Corona had just spotted a track through the green zone that could take them over to the compound.

The Taliban opened up this time from front, from across the wadi to the south-east. One of the trucks took an AK-47 bullet through the door. The platoon dived for cover behind the trucks and were soon calling for artillery to drive the attackers away.

Finally the patrol could move on again. The trucks rolled into 1st Platoon's compound just as it was getting dark. The men refilled their canteens, and Corona walked up to Fusco and First Lieutenant TJ Tepley to check up on the map and the plans. He was told his next objective and entered the coordinates on to his Garmin GPS. The plan was to head east for 900 yards and then turn round finally south towards Musa Qala centre. 'It had been three days and we weren't even at our first objective,' recalled Corona, 'so we were kind of eager to get in there and start clearing our objective, because, until then, you know, we were just held down by vehicles and sporadic fire, and we hadn't really moved.'

Battalion headquarters and Alpha Company, 1 Fury, Roshan Tower, 16.30

Joe McGovern heard nothing. No pops, thuds nor whistles. Just explosions out of nowhere. Others heard a hiss and then a boom, like a mortar, except backwards. There was confusion – some people shouted 'mortars', others shouted 'RPGs'. Whatever it was, there was plenty of it coming in.

That day Alpha's 1st and 3rd Platoons had been pushing south, clearing down the green zone on the opposite bank of the wadi from Musa Qala centre. After their earlier fight in the village, McGovern's 2nd Platoon had stayed to guard the Roshan Tower and the battalion headquarters.

The day had begun like the day before. Waking up in the cold dawn to the zinging sound of Dushka rounds. The Taliban had been firing Dushkas at the hill all day – and at the choppers too, scoring that hit on the Apache. But most of the fire was just harassing rounds. The big attack came when the sun was beginning to set. This time, they struck home.

Tyler Clas was cooking up some rations on the hilltop. He heard one bang and thought it was a stray RPG. Then after three more booms, he put on his armour vest and ran for the trenches, clutching his half-cooked food. His team was standing there staring at him wide-eyed. 'Aw, it's not that big a deal,' he said. He hadn't seen the explosion behind him, just where he had been sitting.

They lay flat down in the trench for two minutes. Then Clas switched on his radio and heard the call. 'Hey, we got wounded. We got wounded, four guys wounded.' With the rounds still landing, two of his guys ran down the hill to help while Clas looked for stretchers. Then there was a pause. The Taliban waited. They knew the men would run for the wounded. They opened up again when they saw movement. This time – with paratroopers on the hilltop now firing back at what they thought was the firing point – the enemy were firing back more wildly.

Specialist David Goth was closer to the action. His team leader, Sergeant Stephen McBride, had just called him over to help guard the line. He looked across and saw one round hit and then another. He glanced at the weapons squad, all lined up together in a shallow trench. He saw McBride and Jason Strickland, a private just twelve days in theatre. He saw the shadow of a round going right at them and then a bang and smoke and he was thinking 'They're fucking toast.'

That explosion had hit McBride and Strickland; and another

took out Specialists Adam Blackburn and Steven Martinez as the pair ran down the hill to help with the casualties.

It was a scene from hell. Goth recalled: 'Everyone was just getting up, fucking rolling. Strickland's fucking crawling, oh my God, you know, 'cause he can't walk, his feet are fucked. I mean, Marty's bolting down the fucking hill. Everyone's just scattering. And, I mean, I figured that fucking – I figured Strickland was done. But I saw Marty get down the hill. He started bleeding out of his thigh and shit. I'm guessing like anyone, it's pure adrenalin. He fuckin' bolted down the hill. He got about down and he was like "Oh, shit." Same with Blackburn. I mean, all the guys were just like – Sergeant McBride got hit in the arm. He didn't even know it until somebody pointed it out to him.'

Strickland had been lucky. He had been lying flat on his stomach with his legs spread apart, and the round landed right between. It messed up his legs, though. Martinez was hit by shrapnel in both legs; Blackburn got hit on his backside and abdomen.

McGovern, the platoon leader, was by now at the scene. He got the feeling that the enemy must have an observer somewhere close. By now a new volley of rounds was getting close again, like it was being walked towards the target. The men started 'hauling ass' downhill. Strickland and Martinez were on stretchers; Blackburn was hobbling along. Though McBride was hit in one arm and about to be evacuated he insisted on helping carry another casualty with his other, good arm. They got down to the medevac landing site, the same one they had used a day earlier.

Inside the battalion HQ on Roshan Hill, in the hut beneath the metal tower, First Lieutenant Anthony Fera, the fire support team leader, was calling in the artillery for Bravo Company up the wadi when he heard the explosions outside. The Taliban's grenade launcher was being backed up with another salvo of highly accurate Dushka rounds. Some in HQ shared the suspicion the rounds were tipped with explosives.

Fera's team had to run the mortars and artillery, talk to the Apache helicopters and talk to the fast jet bombers on station. It had got busier now than at any time. Fera gave Bravo the British guns for their missions. They were slower to get fired up as the mission requests had to go through more channels. Alpha Company, defending Roshan, was given Red Leg, the American 105mm field guns.

The hut they were working in was crowded. Measuring 15 feet by 10 feet, it had not only the fire team, but Mennes' radio operators and his operations staff, and also a team from EW – electronic warfare. Their classified equipment for intercepting and jamming signals was proving itself.

Matthew Hatfield, the fire team sergeant, was out on the ridge-line when all this was happening. He was in the OP, the observation point, where the job was to spot the firing points. He watched the first of the twenty-odd grenades come flying over the parapet and strike the back of the hill. The next one dropped short of the ridgeline. 'Holy crap,' he shouted, 'they're bracketing us.' Bracketing is a standard military procedure for dropping rounds long and then short before adjusting the range to hit right on target. It was moments later when Alpha 2nd Platoon started taking casualties.

The EW team was now picking up interceptions. Someone close by was acting as spotter for the grenade-launcher team: describing where the paratroopers were moving. As the medics ran down in the open to attend to the casualties, the Taliban radio piped up: 'They're on the back side of the hill now.' Then the fire shifted. 'Oh shit,' said Hatfield.

Hatfield had never seen the Taliban so effective. The firing was accurate. It was being coordinated. And even their ammunition – so often defunct – was working. When he saw the explosion by Blackburn's feet, he thought: 'I don't even want to go down there and see that. This is going to be carnage.' But he saw Blackburn get up and start to run downhill, shouting out, 'Oh, hell, somebody shot me in my ass!'

Inside the HQ, Mennes' operations officer, Major Guy Jones, decided something decisive had to be done. He ordered a smoke mission to smother the battalion's positions. 'We got to win some time,' he thought. If the Taliban had a fire observer, then the paratroopers needed to get themselves hidden while both the firing points for the Dushka machine guns and for the grenade launcher were located for the two Apaches still on station to strike. Jones turned to Fera's fire team, but they were all busy talking to the companies under contact. And the man he asked to raise the smoke mission didn't seem to know what to do. So Jones decided to step out himself and take a grip of the situation. Grabbing a map and compass, he proceeded to climb up on to the mobile phone tower. As he got up he saw an Apache scream down the wadi. And just then, in the fast-fading light, he saw on the far side the flash of a Dushka opening up. Noting the position on the map, he climbed back down to the hut.

Back inside, Fera got the Apaches straight on the target, and they pounded the Dushka team with their 30mm cannon. The Taliban fire came to a halt. The trouble was that they had silenced the Dushkas several times these last two days. But, in a matter of hours, they seemed to start up all over again. It seemed they were killing the gunmen but failing to kill the gun. Fera noted down the grid reference of the strike. He wanted to watch that place closely.

Bravo Company, 1 Fury, north of Musa Qala, 17.15, ten minutes after sunset

It was getting dark fast now, and, as they walked out of the compound entrance, Bravo's 2nd Platoon lowered their night-vision goggles from their helmets.

Corona was on point again, and he had gone just 300 yards into a field before he saw a man in the road. The word from intelligence was the Taliban had banned civilians from the street, and the paratroopers figured that no one was going to ignore the Taliban. That night everyone out and about was a bad guy, fair game. This man in the gloom was a legal target. 'We'd seen all the women and children leave, so you figure all the guys that are left behind are bagging us,' he recalled. 'So we weren't just popping random people at night.'

Silently raising his arm to halt the patrol behind, Corona quietly lifted up his M4 and aimed through the laser sights. The man was walking across the road, but he stopped and looked in the patrol's direction, as if he had spotted them. Corona opened fire. But after his second shot, the gun jammed. He bent down to fix it. As he did, he heard a massive blast and felt a shock wave. He was knocked a step back and felt something hitting him and piercing his skin. It was a grenade about 10 feet in front. An AK-47 started firing too.

Corona winced at the pain, but, correcting the malfunction, he raised his M4 and started firing down the alley. He was firing now blindly. The flash of the grenade had closed off his night vision. Another fire team also started putting down suppressing fire. Then another blast wave hit Corona as another grenade went off even closer.

Corona looked around and saw that his automatic rifleman, Specialist Evan Graham, was on all fours, with blood dripping from his face. Obviously a head wound. But he didn't know how serious it was. So he grabbed him and walked back to where he found William Cochran, the radio operator, and Fusco, the platoon sergeant, taking cover behind a wall.

'What the fuck are you doing back here? You're supposed to be up there,' said Fusco.

'Well, I think Graham's hurt,' said Corona.

'Well, what the fuck are *you* doing back here then?'

'Hey, you know, I think I'm hurt too.'

That's when Corona felt down and found blood on his right thigh and left leg. Corona realized he had left the two other soldiers of his team, Walker and Burgesson, up front. So he crept back up and told them what had happened and that they would be folded into another team.

Then Corona turned round and looked at what was going on. 'Everything had just gone to shit,' he remembered thinking. 'It was like a salmon run in this alley. I mean, there were so many people, and nobody knew what the fuck was going on. I mean, it's funny because you practise the most basic training manoeuvres in garrison, but when the shit hit the fan here, everyone just lost it. It was – I mean, it wasn't funny right then, obviously – because I had just got hit with a grenade, but you know, looking back on it, it was pretty funny.'

Corona and Graham walked themselves back to the rear, back to the 1st Platoon compound from where they'd just emerged, and the 1st Platoon medic, Dustin Jones, helped patch them up. Graham was still fired up.

'Oh, I'm going to get back out there and kick this guy's ass,' he told Corona.

'Hey, Graham, time to sit this one out.'

Graham told Corona the second grenade had actually bounced off the optic of his machine gun before exploding in the dirt. Later, when the surgeons pulled the shrapnel from Graham's face, it was tested and found to have been manufactured in 1947. A modern US high-explosive hand grenade would have wiped out Corona's whole team.

After the casualties went back, Fusco started reorganizing the fight. Both Corona and Graham, Fusco recalled, had wanted to stay in the fight. But Graham had so much blood pouring from his face he wouldn't have been able to see much longer.

But Fusco and the men were now pretty angry. Two Apache helicopters came and fired Hellfires into the compound where the enemy with the grenades had walked into. Cochran, the radio operator, remembered 'the best Fourth of July kind of thing I'd ever seen'.

Then Fusco came up with a plan he put to the lieutenant, TJ. He was setting up the 240mm machine guns on a roof in overwatch and then was going to assault across the field with a series of leapfrogs. TJ said the plan was good. But then he got on the radio and told Fusco to slow things up.

'We've gotta wait until the mortar gets set up and 'til Spectre comes back on station,' said TJ. It was too dark now for the Apaches to fly. They'd gone off back to Bastion.

The orders were coming all the way down from the battalion

up on Roshan. While this was going on, there were other battles going on and more casualties. Things were getting critical. If anyone more got injured, there just might not be a chopper to take him out. So 2nd Platoon got hunkered down behind some walls. At one point they got some intercepts from the Taliban radio saying something like: 'We are going to do some gardening.' So the platoon dropped some grenades into the bushes. 'Everything that looked like a garden to us, we put rounds in,' said Fusco.

They pushed forward to the compound. That was pretty much it. The platoon moved back on the road a bit and found a place to spend the night.

Only in the morning did 2nd Platoon realize that the compound where they had rested was actually divided into two parts. The other part was some kind of medical clinic for children and 'pregnant chicks'. It was empty, but on the floor they found some bloody clothes, some empty packets of pain-killers, as well as a metal pan which looked like it had contained an extracted bullet. It seemed the Taliban had been patching up their wounded just behind the wall where 2nd Platoon had slept. 'That was pretty creepy,' said Cochran.

Roshan Tower, 17.30

Lieutenant McGovern's 2nd Platoon of Alpha Company was shattered. It had lost six men in two days, including their platoon sergeant and two team leaders. They knew they were effectively out of the big battle. 'After that,' said one of the men, 'we were combat ineffective and we didn't have enough people to do anything. So they made us just stay on the tower for the next three weeks until someone came and relieved us. We were on that hilltop for a long time without some of our best friends, knowing that our team leader had gotten hit. And we were just angry, and then it started getting colder and it started raining. It was pretty horrible for morale, so a lot of people were really down.'

It was to this battle scene that, just under an hour ago, Brigadier

Mackay had arrived with a team. Up by the steel structure of the mobile-phone mast, they unrolled their sleeping mats and took their place for the night in a slit trench. Hooking up their radio-sets, his staff established what was probably the most front-line brigade command post in the short history of Task Force Helmand. It was an unusual position for someone who led over 8,000 men and women. He would be up on the hill for a day and two nights as it took incoming mortar and machine-gun fire. One of his own protection team engaged and killed two Taliban fighters. 'If you have a brigadier firing, then you are really in trouble,' he would joke later in an interview with *The Times* newspaper.[20]

They had arrived by helicopter at a busy time – on the busiest night in the entire battle. Brian Mennes, whose 1 Fury headquarters was inside the little concrete building at the base of the tower, was welcoming. Privately, though, he wished Mackay had stayed off 'my hill'. What was the brigadier doing there? Was there an element of mistrust? If the decisive part of winning in Musa Qala was to avoid destroying the town, did Mackay think the American commander would break his promise of keeping the bombs out of the town centre? No one likes their boss sitting over their shoulder, least of all on a night when 1 Fury's fire team – those controlling the aviation and artillery strikes – were going to have to make some tough calls.

Months later, Mennes would still ask the same question: 'We're all looking at the district centre,' he said, 'and we've got the general sitting up on my hill – doing what? Praying? There was nothing happening in Musa Qala proper that I needed help with, and yet the whole brigade headquarters was up there. What were they doing exactly? I don't know. Because all the resources [for the fight] came from my team – our team.'

Mennes said he believed the brigadier should have had better things to do. 1 Fury's battle for the wadi was just the first part 'but not the decisive operation' in Musa Qala. Seizing the district centre was 'part of it' and 'not creating collateral damage, yes, a piece of it', but the key should have been to build a plan for what came afterwards. 'The decisive point should have been building consent from the people to the government.'

He added: 'I got some insights from them, which was great. But, again, what they should've been thinking about was – where's the fucking bulldozer going to come from? That's brigade commander stuff, believe it or not, in counter-insurgency.'

Mackay, when he looked back, said that Mennes never betrayed any sign of his annoyance. 'I had to be there,' Mackay said later. 'I knew that from Roshan Hill I would have the best view of the battlefield.' In the next few hours there were decisions to make such as when to deploy the Afghan army forward. Mackay admitted to me, though, that 'foremost in my mind was that I didn't want to smash the place.' That was a key part of the battle plan for Musa Qala. But he insisted he always believed that Mennes knew his intentions and 'I was not there because I mistrusted him. I wasn't watching over him.'

But Mackay's and his brigade's reputation was being made or unmade, and, to add to it all, the prime minister of Britain was visiting Helmand the next day. It was all perhaps far too important to rely on trust.

Battalion headquarters, 1 Fury, Roshan Tower, 19.45

Fera was staring at his Tough Book laptop, the one he'd dragged in his rucksack from the landing zone. On the screen was an image in green-and-white, downlinked from a Predator circling thousands of feet above. It was looking into the darkness with an infra-red camera. Fera's forward air controller could speak to the pilot of this plane. But the pilot was operating the controls from a computer all the way back near Las Vegas.

All Fury's surveillance and reconnaissance resources were on mission that night to watch across the wadi. There were Predators in the sky above, snipers with infra-red scopes, and other still more classified assets. All were looking at the points from which the Taliban had fired during the day. The chief focus was the compound from which the last Dushka had fired – Fera had kept note of its six-figure grid reference.

It was just before 19.45 when someone in Fera's team called the colonel and Major Jones over. Six men could be seen on screen dragging a Dushka. The anti-aircraft version has a distinctive two-wheel carriage. The officers watched the Dushka being dragged for fifteen minutes. That was about the time it took Fera and his controller to arrange the air strike.

At 20.10 an F-15 dropped a 500-pound JDAM. They could actually see pictures transmitted up on their screens at Roshan from a camera mounted on the nose of the bomb as it fell. And the Predator too recorded the deadly moment. Five men went down, and the weapon, they believed, was destroyed too. But not everyone died. One man appeared to get up and walk into a building. The spy cameras now focused on this building. Soon, it became obvious this was somewhere important. People were coming in and out. It was a hive of activity. The EW team started reporting the Taliban radio was now going wild. Suddenly it seemed they had found what could be their biggest and best target: the Taliban HQ, its command and control or 'C2 node' in military jargon. 'We watched it for a while,' remembered Mennes, 'and the guys were running back and forth to this building and all these people were milling around, and I figured that was their command centre.'

Mennes ordered another strike without hesitation. By now there was more evidence of what was going on. 'I had a signal dude up here who could pick up the coms,' recalled Mennes, 'so it was all being triangulated to a spot.' Luck had it that this building was outside the exclusion zone in central Musa Qala so he didn't have to worry about special clearance or discussions with the British. This time, at 20.20, the F-15 put down a 2,000-pound JDAM: as big a bomb as the plane was carrying – and enough to flatten the entire building.

At least six were killed in the strike, but still more started running around near by.

Voices then came over the forward air controller's radio set. It was the special forces airmen in the Spectre gunships that had now arrived with the darkness.

'Hey, we're keeping track of all these squirters, you know? Can we start engaging?'

Mennes gave the go-ahead. The Spectre started following each group of men in the darkness, and one by one they were gunned down with their cannons. 'It was like nothing you'd ever think about seeing,' remembered Fera, who watched it all on the Predator feed. 'You can't hide from this thing. And these guys – you know, you'd see them. They would run, and then they'd hide under a bush – but it didn't get them nowhere.'

By the end of it all, there might have been fifty people killed by the Spectres – fifteen at least from just that one strike.

Mennes was clear about the impact. This, he believed in hindsight, was the turning point, the moment the key leadership decided the fight in Musa Qala was unwinnable.

When they had planned the Musa Qala operation, Mennes had believed the Taliban's key leadership would have holed up in the centre of the town. But they had ended up outside, to the northeast. He believed the Taliban had made 'a huge mistake' by opening up with their heavy weapons because they had given away their command and control centre. It was the way the Taliban did business: 'Their signature weapons are always near the command and control.' Key leaders kept their key weapons close. But that's what got leaders killed.

The Taliban radio was poignant that night, remembered Hatfield. 'It was them calling and saying, "Dan, where are you, Dan? Answer, Dan." But Dan wasn't answering 'cause Dan was dead. And the funny thing about it was – and, I'll say this, that the Taliban – you know, the key leaders – you know, my key leader, Colonel Mennes, his ass is standing right there with me. Major Jones is standing right there with me. But, the frickin' Taliban? They're cowards.' The EW team said the Taliban signals showed the messages from their commanders were now coming from well out of town, back down the Musa Qala wadi towards Sangin. The leaders were still putting out the message: 'Carry on the fight!' But now they were miles away.

Not every Taliban leader had skipped town, though. And, as the night progressed, control of the battle passed, for a while, into the hands of more secretive American forces.

Special forces operations box, north of Musa Qala

This night like no other was the night of the Spectre gunships. They were hunting in a pair, circling their targets and pounding them from two sides. Up on the ridgeline, Brigadier Mackay stood watching the display. At first there was just a low buzz, as these hunters started closing in on their prey. The Spectre is a low-flying converted Hercules plane that would be an easy target for ground fire by day. But variants are called the 'Spooky' for a reason. They never venture out in the sunshine.

At one time, the existence of the Spectre and its armaments was classified information. Spectre missions were still run by special forces airmen. But the deadly night-time accuracy of its weapons and its ability to linger for long periods had made this plane one of the military's top performers. Carrying both a Gatling gun for rapid fire and a 105mm cannon firing the same-sized shells as the army's artillery field guns, the plane came equipped for devastation. These days, the planes were made available for both conventional forces and the more secretive units. Even when the Spectre started firing there was little that made it visible, apart from the muzzle flash in the sky from its cannon. But its throaty roar was unmistakable and, for those on the ground, deeply frightening.

Like the growling thunder and sparks of lightning of some fierce electric storm, all through the night this invisible machine of death was systematically erasing the enemy left in the green zone. Mackay described what was the most spectacular display he'd seen. 'It really beats the Edinburgh Festival fireworks anytime!' He too had watched on screen the moment when the Taliban headquarters was hit. 'It really was an absolute massacre . . . and they were all armed. You could see that on the screen.'

In the hours before midnight, an operational box was marked on the map that was declared out of bounds to conventional forces. It surrounded a compound not far from Musa Qala centre. The target had been pre-planned – the product of an intelligence cell based in Kandahar airbase. This time two Spectre gunships roared into action at once – pummelling the target as they circled in tandem. The Americans later told the press the Taliban's deputy governor of Helmand was inside the building and had been killed.

Kabul, the bureau of Al Jazeera television

Mullah Sadiq called Qais, the Al Jazeera journalist in Kabul, in the middle of the battle. The commanders of the Taliban had held a *shura* in the desert, he revealed. They had their own ruse up their sleeves. 'There has been a meeting. The foreigners have left a door open, a way to slip out of the town. We're going somewhere else. We're moving in trucks.' Mullah Sadiq, who was there, had volunteered to come with them. Though he would not say it then, the battle would take place in his home town, Sangin.

Bravo Company, 1 Fury, north of Musa Qala, 00.54

Bravo Company was at last making the kind of progress they needed. It was past midnight now, and the enemy had already taken a hell of a pounding, they thought. 1st Platoon were pushing ahead.

There was little noise but dogs barking and a faint hum from their guardian angel overhead, the Spectre gunship. Then Reese, the platoon leader, made a mistake. When he changed the route to avoid a big canal, he forgot to tell the Spectre.

Otilio Vasquez and Bryce Hamilton were ahead on point. They

were 50 yards down a narrow alleyway: about 8 feet wide and with 8-feet-high walls.

Vasquez was on the left side. Up ahead he spotted a man who was crouching down.

'Do you see that?' he asked Hamilton to his right.

'Yeah.'

They crept forward but they lost sight of him. 'Where's he at now?' asked Hamilton. Vasquez had switched a night-vision flashlight on, and he began to side-step across the path, creeping right towards Hamilton to see round a bend. Both men had their eyes peeled forward.

Finally he noticed him about 75 yards away. 'I see him,' Vasquez whispered. The man answered with a volley from a PKM machine gun.

Hamilton would come to wish he had shot the guy on sight. 'Orders said we were allowed to shoot anybody out at night who we thought was a threat.' But no one had told Hamilton.

When the bullet struck Vasquez, he thought at first he had run into Hamilton, but then when he pulled the trigger and fired two shots, he felt a stabbing pain up his forearm. His arm felt numb and heavy. By now there were more bullets flying than he could ever imagine. It wasn't just one Taliban down this ammo tunnel, but a whole gang in ambush.

Hamilton had shouldered the SAW gun – the squad automatic weapon capable of firing 750 rounds per minute. As he stood upright with no cover, he went cyclic – turning the alleyway into daylight with an explosion of bullets.

Dust swirled up, and he began to breathe sand. Hamilton could see almost nothing through his goggles but the bright spark of his tracer rounds cutting through a cloud ahead, and a line of flashes of the enemy tracer coming in.

Vasquez was being dragged back down the line. 'Man, I'm going to die here,' he thought.

Hamilton was in a daze of combat, his ears deafened by his own gun. He'd probably shot more than 200 rounds in the last half-minute. He was walking slowly backwards through the dust, facing forward and firing but kicking out against the wall with his right foot as he moved. He hoped that somewhere was a place to take cover. Finally his foot struck out, and there was nothing solid there. But he heard a cry. He'd booted someone finding shelter.

Hamilton ducked out of the alley. 'Dude, they just shot Vasquez,' he said. 'All those fuckers are going to die.'

Further back, medic Dustin Jones was desperately trying to reach Vasquez. It was like his worst nightmare. He had heard the shouts of 'Medic! Medic!' but now he was stuck down what seemed like a 20-foot muddy embankment where he had dived when the firing started. He kept slipping back down again.

The Spectre was soon back and 'it just laid waste to every moving thing on that ground' said Reese. The gunship was using its cannon and its 105mm shells. By now the Taliban were man-oeuvring – creeping round the side of where the platoon was sheltering. Bravo's air controller, Sergeant Mellon, brought the Spectre strikes to within 150 feet.

The platoon was now hunkered behind walls. They heard the thud of the shells being fired from the gunship and then the dread-filled boom of the explosion, as low-pitched as you can imagine. It was deafening and bone-chilling too. Chunks of mud came raining down on their heads.

Vasquez was still sitting on his rucksack getting bandaged. They had denied him morphine because he was going to have to walk out. 'Oh man, this is really close,' he said. He could see the dust flying to Hamilton's position. 'This is gonna be a disaster,' he thought. 'They're actually gonna hit those guys.'

But when it was over Vasquez felt a sense of wonderment. Looking back, he said later, the Spectre had saved them time and again. They all remembered its infra-red beam that turned the night into day with a kind of religious awe.

'You look up there and you see that light of Heaven,' said Vasquez. 'And you'll say you can do anything you want in the world. I'd walk around naked if I had that thing chasing me.'

The invisible Spectre came on the net. 'Yeah, I think we got all of them.' After it was over they went forward and found about fifteen bodies. One guy was still alive and crawling for his gun. He was shot in the head by a sniper.

It took a couple of hours to get Vasquez out. The only chopper that would come into land was a special operations Black Hawk in the neighbourhood already. Vasquez carried his own rucksack 800 yards to the landing zone. On the chopper, he thought at last he'd get some morphine, but they had none. 'Oh, man!' said Vasquez.

Household Cavalry headquarters, 5 miles south of Musa Qala, 02.00

Lieutenant Colonel Ed Smyth-Osbourne crouched by the radio set inside his Sultan command vehicle. Brigade headquarters was on the line and issuing new orders. US surveillance, he was told, showed signs of large movements to the east of the Musa Qala – the one direction where there were no coalition forces. 'Either the Taliban are reinforcing or they are starting to pull out,' said Mackay, speaking from Roshan Hill. He ordered Smyth-Osbourne to collapse his position and move his battle group up to close the Taliban's last escape route.

By daybreak, meanwhile, all of 1 Fury's Companies were close to reaching their final objectives. What remained was to clear the town itself.

Bravo Company, 1 Fury, north of Musa Qala, 06.00

Specialist Robert Spafford from 3rd Platoon was tired and pissed off. So when he felt a bit of roof falling down he just said, 'Fuck it,' and put his sleeping bag back over his head. Then he felt something bump his head. He was getting even more annoyed and was just getting ready to walk outside and brush it off. But then he realized he couldn't move and began to think he was suffocating. He started to freak and thought, 'Fuck, I'm going to die.' The next thing he remembered was waking up with a tube in his nose and a medic screaming over him and holding a razor, about to cut his throat.

3rd Platoon had arrived in the compound just a couple of hours before. They'd been going all night and just taken over the compound and thrown their kit down to get some rest.

The platoon sergeant, James Knops, a thirty-eight-year-old from San Diego, had been asleep for about an hour when he awoke to screams. A soldier named Nathan Harvey was yelling, 'Get up, everybody wake up, everybody wake up!'

The paratroopers reached for their body armour and weapons, thinking it was a fight. Seeing a gaping hole in the ceiling, some thought it was an RPG or mortar. But Harvey said the roof in the room next door had fallen in. Eight people were buried alive. No one knew how it happened. The only thing above the sleeping paratroopers was a stretch of orange canvas laid out as a recognition panel for friendly aircraft.

More soldiers were running in from outside. 'Oh, my God, help us get these fuckers out,' someone shouted. The room was just a chaos of chunks of the masonry and broken logs. The platoon started to dig like dogs.

As luck had it there were only five people under the rubble. Two others were changing guard shift and another was sleeping outside. A couple of those inside managed to pull themselves out of the dust. Knops started grilling them: 'Hey, look, guys, where are the – you know, who is still in this room? Who was sleeping in this room?'

They gave him a name. Knops said, 'He's outside.' Another name. 'He's outside.' Another name. 'He's outside.' That left three people. They found two of them pretty quickly, Allan Sinanan and Shaun Smith. They were hurt but still breathing. But they couldn't find Spafford at all.

Apart from Spafford, Smith had the worst deal. He was lying in the dirt up to his chest. He couldn't move, his legs were messed up, and now everyone was piling into the room and trampling on him. He was alive and that was enough.

'Oh, I'm hurting,' he said

'Shut up! We've got to get Spafford.'

The soldiers kept digging and eventually found Spafford's sleeping bag. They dug on and found his head. When the hole was big enough they opened the bag up. His head just rolled. He was out unconscious. Knops looked over in horror. Spafford was surely dead. He'd been buried that long now under enough pressure that his lungs must have collapsed. He couldn't spot any breathing. The 'doc' rushed up and started to treat him. The medic was a passionate man. He was screaming: 'Come on, buddy, I love you man, I love you.' Then Spafford started spluttering and opened his eyes. He did what most men might do if they woke up and saw someone apparently about to slit his throat. He reached up and tried to throttle the medic. It took a while for him to calm down. His first words were: 'Let me get a cigarette.'

It had been a close call. Captain Canterna remembered the dread that spread throughout the company. In the last few days they had been through a lot 'but I never heard any shakiness or fear in anyone's voice until then'. Knops added: 'These guys had been ambushed. Everybody had been through fire fights, but that was my scariest moment in the whole fifteen months. It was uncontrollable.'

25. Diversion: 10 December

Sangin, 09.51

The radio message said: 'The helicopter landing site is hot. Helicopter will require an armed escort.'

Major Paul Pitchfork and his A Company of the 1st Battalion, Royal Gurkha Rifles, had been fighting now for nearly three hours. They were almost surrounded. Their ammunition was running low. They had two men who were seriously wounded. He had to get them out. The two casualties – who like all the Gurkha soldiers joined the British army from the hill stations of Nepal – were being treated in a mud compound near the banks of the Helmand River.

A photograph records a scene of serenity as they lay calmly waiting for their rescue. While the battle continued outside, behind the walls of a mud-brick compound, soldiers smoked and chatted quietly. In three days' time, they were supposed to be on R&R. One of the injured, Rifleman Jeevan Shrees, whispered to his platoon sergeant, Bahadur Budha, of his holiday plans. He called him 'Guruji', respected teacher. 'We had planned to hire a nice car to go around Nepal, but unluckily I will miss it,' he said.

The sergeant-major of the company, Shuresh Thapa, tried to keep his spirits up. But he was worried. Jeevan's wounds were getting worse. He had a gunshot wound in his upper thigh, and five bone fractures and his legs were swelling. The rescue that day he remembered as nightmarish. 'Can a helicopter ever land here with all this fighting?' he wondered.

Outside, Pitchfork had the same question on his mind. The night before, his plan made clear sense. All afternoon the centre of Sangin and all the Afghan army bases in town had been pummelled by the Taliban, the first offensive on the town for months. At nightfall, the enemy had slipped away. But intelligence suggested they would be back in strength in the morning. It all seemed like a deliberate and determined diversion, not so much an attempt to draw NATO forces directly from Musa Qala but to strike a psychological blow that would undermine any coalition victory up there.

Gathering his tired officers round a map board, Pitchfork had come up with a plan to catch them off balance. He had not wanted to fight them in the town, with all the destruction and death of civilians that risked. Instead, he and his Gurkhas would slip out along the river southwards in the dead of night and round into the green zone. They might just catch them off balance and hit them from behind at daybreak.

This bright morning, alone in the green zone, he could see the plan was having the right effect. The Taliban were being drawn away from the town. But his own company's situation, he recalled, was looking 'none too rosy'. A Company was being attacked from all sides by a bold enemy, pinned down by accurate fire, hampered by casualties and facing the prospect of an under-resourced 2-mile fight on foot to get back to the Sangin base.

The Taliban had struck first at 06.15, initially hitting not the Gurkhas but a patrol of the Afghan army and their British mentors that was moving to block a canal bridge. Their first volley caught half of the men in the middle of a field, barely 200 yards short of their objective. In command of the soldiers was Captain Duncan Turner, who was attached to the 2 Yorks mentoring team. He was caught in the open up front along with about five Afghan soldiers and two other Britons, Trooper Mark 'Scouse' Higgins and Private Luke Ibbotson.

'Captain Turner was bang out in the middle. Next thing the sky just lit up with tracer and bloody bangs going off right left and centre,' recalled Ibbotson.

Turner dived for cover while Ibbotson and Higgins dashed back and leaped into a ditch on the edge of the field. They looked back at Turner, who wasn't moving.

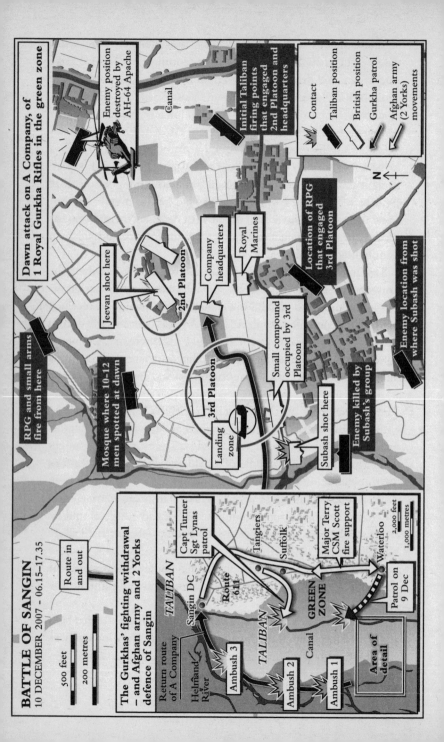

BATTLE OF SANGIN
10 DECEMBER 2007 - 06.15–17.35

Route in and out

The Gurkhas' fighting withdrawal – and Afghan army and 2 Yorks defence of Sangin

Dawn attack on A Company, of 1 Royal Gurkha Rifles in the green zone

Enemy position destroyed by AH-64 Apache

Canal

Initial Taliban firing points that engaged 2nd Platoon and headquarters

RPG and small arms fire from here

Mosque where 10–12 men spotted at dawn

Jeevan shot here

2nd Platoon

Company headquarters

Royal Marines

3rd Platoon

Landing zone

Small compound occupied by 3rd Platoon

Location of RPG that engaged 3rd Platoon

Subash shot here

Enemy killed by Subash's group

Enemy location from where Subash was shot

N

Contact

Taliban position

British position

Gurkha patrol

Afghan army (2 Yorks) movements

Return route of A Company

Helmand River

Ambush 3

Ambush 2

Ambush 1

TALIBAN

Capt Turner Sgt Lynas patrol

Sangin DC

Route 611

TALIBAN

Tangiers

Suffolk

Major Terry CSM Scott fire support

Canal

GREEN ZONE

Waterloo

Patrol on 9 Dec

Area of detail

500 feet
200 metres

2,000 feet
1,000 metres

'Scouse, Captain Turner is down.'

An RPG streaked between them and hit the earth behind. The blast knocked over two more British soldiers – Corporal Craig Johnson (no relation to 'Jonno') and Lance-Corporal Joel Harvey. They were to the rear of the ditch. Behind them was Sergeant Jimmy Lynas. With the captain pinned down, he had to take charge.

For a few minutes, Lynas thought he was dealing with multiple casualties. With the deafening gunfire, he could hear nothing of the shouts of the men upfront, nor could he get them by radio. The two men knocked flat by the RPG picked themselves up, but only when he sent Johnson forward to relay messages did he get to hear from the men in the ditch.

Turner had got up unhurt. He started dragging what the men remembered as cowering ANA soldiers back towards the ditch. One abandoned his rifle. 'How the hell is Captain Turner not getting shot?' thought Ibbotson.

As Turner jumped down beside them, they were beginning to realize the ditch was a trap. It was filled with chest-high water. And the bank behind them was too steep and high to climb out of, particularly with their heavy rucksacks on. The only way out was forward – back into the killing zone. RPGs were now striking the trees that lined the banks above them, showering the water with wooden shrapnel.

Behind them, Lynas was trying to rally the ANA and push them out to cover the sides. A difficult situation would become deadly if the Taliban began to outflank them. They always tried that. 'They're beginning to peel round,' someone shouted.

'Captain Turner said there was no way out of the field,' remembered Ibbotson, 'and with the [radio] coms gone, I was shitting myself . . . because I thought they would come round on us and just shoot us like ducks. This whole thing was the most frightening thing I've ever done.'

'We've got to get fast air in here,' he told Turner.

To be fair to the ANA, who mostly seemed to be frozen in fear, they were not even infantry soldiers. The *kandak* in Sangin had been scratched together from artillery, engineers, mechanics and even storemen and cooks. Half of them were just hiding behind walls. Lynas was shouting: 'Get out here. Get out here.' Most ignored him.

But if some weren't brave, others had a crazed courage. One NCO was standing in the open wildly spraying his PKM machine gun, with a cigarette in his mouth and no helmet nor body armour. Corporal Johnson yelled, 'Get down, mad fucker!' The Afghan just laughed at them and shouted in English, 'Taliban no good! Taliban no good!'

Turner led the escape from the ditch, clawing his way up and then helping drag the others out and back into the fire-raked field. 'This is suicidal,' Lynas was thinking as he watched them. They moved along, trying to reach a small bridge over the ditch that led back to the rear. They alternately kneeled to fire and then crawled onwards. Ibbotson had had enough. He made a run for it over the bridge. 'Well, fuck these bastards!' he thought. He got to a wall and thought, 'I'm safe now,' as he gasped for breath. But he wasn't. The enemy had peeled round too and were shooting straight at them.

Sangin, in the green zone

Nearly all this time the Gurkhas had been in their own battle. After leaving the Sangin district centre base in the early hours and padding south along the Helmand River, they had swung left just before first light. The plan was to form a line between the river and a canal that bisected the green zone. They would then sweep back towards Sangin centre. With the bridges over the canal kept blocked by the Afghan army, the Taliban might be encircled – and be kept out of Sangin town.

They were attacked at 07.05 when they were still getting into position. And they were engaged from the east, the south and the north. Even before the sun was in the sky, the Gurkhas were close to being enveloped. So much for surprising the Taliban.

The Gurkha platoon closest to the river was engaging at close quarters. In the early moments, both Taliban and Gurkha fighters raced across open ground to try to occupy the same building. The Gurkhas got there first, and the Taliban pulled back. They were engaging the Gurkhas from buildings only 50 yards away.

Then one rifleman, Bhim Gurung, spotted that the Taliban were on the move again – trying to creep up the edge of the river and complete the encirclement of the company. If they made it, that would have blocked the only clear exit route. Charging forward – and shouting 'follow me' – Bhim crossed 75 yards of open ground to find a small wall from where he could cover the riverbank. For a few moments he was alone, single-handedly trying to halt the advance. Two machine-gunners soon joined him behind the wall. They killed two Taliban. Rifleman Subash Gurung proudly punched the air in delight – just as a gunman opened fire from an unseen position.

'*Goli lagyo!*' yelled Subash, meaning, 'Bullet struck!' The other two thought he was joking, but then they saw blood seeping from his arm. Bhim tore off Subash's shirt and put on a bandage. Then he threw him on his shoulder and charged back across open ground to the compound where they had come from.

The company sergeant-major, Shuresh, ran over with a medic to assist. When he first saw Subash, it did not look too serious. Subash was joking: 'I may be a casualty but I killed three or four Taliban.' But it became clear his condition was quite serious. It was also clear that, for now, an evacuation was impossible.

Pitchfork, the company commander, was finding it hard to communicate with his troops. A Company was sharing a frantic radio network with everyone in Sangin. To speak to his platoons and sergeant-major, he had to compete for a turn with the 2 Yorks mentoring teams also in combat. A British Apache had turned up. But with no forward air controller to help him, Pitchfork talked to his company on one radio while talking to the helicopter on another.

Around 9.10, half an hour after Subash was shot, Pitchfork heard again on the radio: 'Man down, man down!'

The casualty this time was Rifleman Jeevan Shrees, who was

shot as he kneeled down to fire. He was the radio operator for Second Lieutenant Lou Connolly, who was leading the platoon that was furthest from the river. The bullet spun Jeevan out into the open and on to his back. Again, the Gurkhas thought he was just acting, making fun. The adrenalin had put many in a comical mood. But he really was hurt. Connolly ran out and dragged him back into cover.

The bullet had gone in just below his knee and then shattered his thigh bone. Jeevan was stoic. He hardly said a word. They gave him morphine and put on a splint. He also would need to be got out urgently – and he was not going to be walking.

Sergeant Bahadur Budha, Connolly's platoon sergeant, took six men, and they set off across the fields, carrying Jeevan in a light-weight poncho. They had a 600-yard run ahead – towards where the company sergeant-major was trying to set up a potential heli-copter landing site. 'The ground was totally open,' recalled Bahadur. There was a gap of at least 100 yards between every ditch or piece of cover. 'There was no way to avoid the open ground.' As they ran the fire seemed to intensify.

Camp Bastion

The British prime minister, Gordon Brown, was addressing a group of 150 soldiers who were gathered around him. He had flown direct on a Hercules C-130 from Kuwait, and was exhausted. Sherard Cowper-Coles, the British ambassador, met him at the camp.

Speaking to the soldiers, Brown thanked them for their patriotic service. In an 800-word speech, he said 'thank you' sixteen times. He said, 'I want to thank every one of you for what you have done in what is the front line against the Taliban . . . It is one of the most difficult of tasks. It is the most testing of times and it is one of the most important of missions.' Defeating the Taliban and giving 'strength to the new democracy of Afghanistan' was 'important to defeating terrorism all around the world'.

The soldiers' reaction was subdued compared to the cheers he had received in Iraq a day earlier. 'We have an operation ongoing in Musa Qala, we've just had people die, so it's a different tempo,' Lieutenant Andy McLachlan told a journalist.

Brown had some quick briefs from the few commanders who were left in base then stepped back on to the plane to head to Kabul to meet President Karzai.

The Times newspaper reported that his trip was 'the closest a serving British prime minister had been to front-line ground battle since Winston Churchill visited the beaches after D-Day'.[21] None recorded, however, that since it was constructed in the remote desert, Camp Bastion had never been attacked.

Sangin, Tangiers patrol base

Sergeant Jimmy Lynas and the others changed their kit and restocked on their ammunition. They had broken contact and withdrawn from the green zone. 'We were spanked. There is no way we could have stayed there,' said Ibbotson. But they were happy to have hit the other side hard.

Then Major Barrie Terry, the commander of the 2 Yorks mentoring teams in Sangin, drove into the base and told them, 'Right, you might have to go back out.' There were groups of Taliban moving everywhere, he said. All the men − shattered by the ambush − stared at each other in disbelief. 'No one said owt,' recalled Ibbotson.

As they were waiting, Lynas came round and said, 'Just go and try to get your heads down.'

Ibbo was sharing a room with Lynas, and he was lying on his bed, staring at the ceiling.

'What's wrong with you, Ibbo? Can't you sleep or something?'

'I fucking can't sleep . . . Do you know how lucky we were then?'

Perhaps it was just a hangover from the adrenalin. Before long they did what soldiers do − had a brew and laughed about it. Then they got themselves up into the *sangars* of this little fort – manning the guns as the Taliban attacked.

Jimmy Lynas had been Jonno's best friend. He had got the news of Jonno's death by electronic message a day earlier. When he had last seen Jonno they had given each other a hug. Lynas had gone on to Sangin after the trip with the rest of B Company out to Delaram. Jonno sent him a Christmas package, with a couple of Christmas crackers, some chocolates and a miniature bottle of whisky. 'Have a drink on me!' said the card. That was the last he had heard of him.

For a while, the emotions of the battle these last two days had shelved his thoughts of Jonno.

When Scott, another close pal of Jonno, showed up at the base the day after their fight, he asked Lynas: 'Are you all right?' He meant, how was he coping in his grief?

Lynas replied: 'Yes, fine. I just need some more link [machine gun ammunition].'

'Just for a while I had forgotten about him,' recalled Lynas. 'I just put him in another place in my mind. It was just because of the intensity of what we had done.'

Major Terry sat on the roof with Lynas some time that day watching the Gurkhas moving through the green zone under fire. They talked about Jonno's funeral and whether Lynas could get home for that. But Terry had darker thoughts. He could not help wondering if more people would end up being buried at the end of the day's battle.

Sangin, in the green zone

Pitchfork knew he had to get the helicopter in somehow. The 'nine-liner' radio message that requested a medevac had been sent. But he needed to win some breathing space.

He ran over to Lou Connolly's platoon, which was still under heavy attack. Connolly pointed out where the enemy fire seemed to be coming from. But, between taking cover from incoming rounds and trying to spot gun flashes on what was now a bright sunny day, it was hard to tell exactly where the Taliban was.

To make matters worse they did not even have a proper map. They did have detailed photographic maps, but these covered an area that began 300 yards further north. The night before it was thought they would have reached there in fifteen minutes. But they were still stuck where they started at daylight, and not going anywhere soon.

The Apache finally found his target, and a Hellfire missile bought a brief calm. At 11.05 a Chinook made it in safely and took the wounded away.

There was fighting now going on all round Sangin. Terry and Scott from the 2 Yorks were running up and down the main road in their WMIKs, giving supporting fire to the Gurkhas while they themselves were being attacked. And so was every one of the Sangin's five patrol bases. The larger FOBs at Robinson to the south and Inkerman to the north-east were also being hit. Teams of the enemy were said to have infiltrated Sangin's bazaar and to be trying to lay mines on one of the bridges. This was clearly not just a minor skirmish or the group of fifteen to twenty fighters that the intelligence had predicted. It was an organized offensive.

Scott remembered: 'When we first came to Sangin they told us: "Oh, you'll be very lucky if you ever see a Taliban." Well, we saw dozens that day. They were reorganizing, lining up, doing ambushes, using vehicles to get rid of injured and move weapons.'

Terry's biggest concern was that British forces were over-stretched. To the north of Sangin all the ANA were fighting on their own without British mentors. 'I could hear all hell breaking loose in the north and I couldn't influence that because I was fixed in the south,' he recalled. If the Taliban overran just one of these bases, it would have given them a huge propaganda victory – a devastating counterweight to a victory looming in Musa Qala.

Watching the progress of fighting, 40 Commando headquarters now intervened – issuing a command known as 'patrol minimize'.

It meant all units should return to camp. Sangin was just getting far too hot. Any more casualties on the ground would divert resources from Musa Qala.

Returning swiftly back to base was easier said than done. The Gurkhas had to fight their way back. Pitchfork decided they would return the way they had come. By avoiding the green zone and walking up the gravel riverbed, he could use the riverbanks as cover from ambush. But it also ended any idea of encircling their enemy.

The cover of the tall riverbanks proved an illusion too. It lasted less than a mile. And at 12.30 the Taliban opened up again with machine guns and RPGs. One landed in front of Pitchfork in the gravel.

Everyone had dived into cover and, though now positioned ready to fire back, no one knew where exactly to fire at. Pitchfork ordered Connolly to get someone to stand up in the open and 'draw fire'. It was a textbook way of spotting the enemy. But the textbook missed the hardest part of the drill. Connolly looked around at his men. 'Shit, this is not very easy,' he thought. Who was he going to tell to face the bullets? 'Fuck it. I'll do it myself,' he decided, and began to run along the riverbank. Luckily for him the Taliban declined to engage. They were busy preparing the next ambush.

The Gurkhas reached a fork in the river and had to cross waist-deep water. It was horribly exposed, and, sure enough, just as the headquarters got across, the gunfire began. At the time, Connolly and his platoon were still in the water. They watched bullets skim across like pebbles. The Gurkhas just laughed.

Two Dutch Apaches were overhead to help in theory. But Pitchfork recalled: 'They were offering advice of where the civilians were but not about where the enemy was.'

The same Apaches were also working with the 2 Yorks. Scott remembered begging them to fire but the Dutch reacting with ultra-caution. 'What they wanted us almost to do was to stand on top of a compound and then go: "This is where we want you to fire." Some of these compounds were sticking out like a box on a boulder, and he still wouldn't fire. If it had been the Brits or American, it would have been wasted.'

The mortar line in Sangin and artillery guns at Inkerman were now helping the Gurkhas, firing phosphorus shells to billow a cloud of bright white smoke to cover the men as they continued north.

Just after 16.00, the patrol was finally in range of the guns at the Sangin main base. And when the final ambush came at 16.40, there was a blaze of supporting fire from the .50 cals on the fire support tower. The Gurkhas lay low for a while, waiting for the light to start fading. Then, under a rolling barrage of smoke from mortars, they trudged into base. It was 17.35. A Company had been on patrol for fourteen hours, and in battle for the last ten.

Pitchfork gathered his men. 'There was a tangible buzz, a real energy. I was on a high. I called the boys together for a short chat: I wanted to stress that we had just shared the experience that defines a soldier. A special moment in many ways and an important moment. A coming of age. A day we would all remember.'

Connolly, who had never experienced combat before but had had the lives of twenty-five men in his trust, felt a weird feeling of elation, like he had been 'tested in the ultimate way'. Three days later he was flown away for his R&R and had the surreal experience of walking on Oxford Street in London. 'I found myself after a few days just wanting to be back in Afghanistan, because I suppose you had a taste of something there that you couldn't experience anywhere else.'

If the Gurkhas had felt that 10 December was a test, for the Taliban who fought that day it was a horrific disaster. Their usual tactic was to hit and run, escaping when outgunned. But Pitchfork's apparently risky plan had worked. It cut off their retreat, headed off a successful attack on Sangin and crucially kept the fighting out of the urban area. Intelligence would suggest an estimated sixty-eight Taliban were killed that day. They were being fished out of the Helmand River for weeks.

★

Mullah Sadiq, who had been there all day, called Qais, the journalist, to describe the battle of Sangin. The Taliban had been attempting to divert attention from Musa Qala, but it was a disaster. 'I lost two of my relatives. I was there. The whole thing was a bad idea. We had bad intelligence about where the foreigners were going to be. The enemy had some losses, but ours were very bad. Maybe hundreds killed. It didn't work.' Sadiq was, as ever, paranoid. 'I believe there is a spy in the team . . . the foreigners got the right report and we got the wrong one.'

The desert west of Musa Qala, with B Company, 2 Yorks

Jake and Captain Dan, the special forces A-team commander, took a step away from the line of parked vehicles, out of earshot of the men. Darkness was approaching, but the orders had come through to move forward now to the edge of Musa Qala. This would be the last camp before the entry into the town. Though in Kabul they were celebrating the fact that Musa Qala had fallen and the BBC World Service was already saying that the Taliban had fled, nothing from intelligence had been passed down to the company. They had to prepare for the worst. Jake knew that only a handful of stay-behind hardened fighters could make the Afghan Army's triumphal entry into the centre a bloody disaster. Fighting through an urban area was no joke – even with the best-trained troops.

Dan looked as cool and calm as he always did, and his uniform was as clean and pressed as when he left camp. Some speculated he had an ironing board and launderette in the back of his Humvee. But Dan's unflappable exterior disguised a nervous tension. He was pawing the sand with his right boot, sketching out the lines of the following day's attack and the Taliban lines of defence. 'These people could get decimated,' he said, waving towards the Afghan trucks close by.

But Dan had a plan. He wanted to get the armour involved. One look at a tank, he said, and from his experience the Taliban would flee. Why couldn't Chris Bell's Warriors from the Scots Guards join the attack? They could sweep through the green zone in parallel to the ANA's push northwards through the town. The ANA could still claim credit for taking the urban area but would have armoured protection on their right flank. 'We'll still achieve the IO victory,' he said, referring to the 'Information Operations' value of demonstrating it was the Afghans that took Musa Qala.

Jake agreed. As far as he was concerned, anything that made his troops safer was a plus. 'You push that up your command chain and I'll push it up mine,' said Dan. Jake nodded.

A little earlier Jake had addressed his men. He spoke to his officers and sergeants first. Orders had come in, he said, that the following day they would enter the town. Jake spoke quietly but clearly: 'Brigadier Mackay is concerned about us destroying the town . . . This will not restrict us in doing what we need to do. If blokes are in contact then we will get CAS [close air support] or I won't let you fucking move on!'

Then Jake got the whole company together. It was the first time he'd addressed them since that night on the ridgeline with Jonno's body.

'Fellas,' he said, 'things have gone better today. Tomorrow the *kandak*s will be entering Musa Qala.' There had been news reports that the Taliban were fleeing 'but whatever the situation is, it doesn't mean there isn't going to be a shit load of fighting tomorrow. I need you to put your fear to one side. Be aggressive, fellas and go for it. . . . We will be more controlled. We will take things nice and slowly. But tomorrow morning we have to be on the ball. Get aggressive. I know some of you will be scared. Someone will scare tomorrow. But just switch it on, work hard. It's got to be done tomorrow.'

26. Raising the Flag: 11–17 December

West of Musa Qala, with B Company,
2 Yorks, 11 December

In the hours before battle on Tuesday, the men had risen from their bivouacs and cleaned their kit for the final time. Black smoke belched up from the flames of the paraffin burners that cooked their last hot meal. And the Afghan soldiers crept to the edge of the camp and bent down to say their prayers. Jake Little went round and shook every man's hand. Then the cry went up: 'All on Fong.' Fong was the company's unofficial chaplain. His prayer was spoken in Fijian, a language that no one understood, but everyone knew its purpose and all said, 'Amen.'

'I tried to lift everyone's spirits up,' Fong explained to me later. He had told B Company the story of Joshua and Moses, of how Moses had led his people to the promised land, but never reached it.

'Moses died because he had done what the Lord had told them to do. The Lord told him: "You will never touch the land but you will be able to see." So on the mountain where he died, he had this aide, Joshua, and Joshua was the one that took over. So he took the Israelites over to Jordan. Before they went, the Lord spoke to Joshua and said: "You see the land, Joshua? That's the land I promised Moses, so that's where you'll take my people." He told Joshua that no one would be able to stand against the Israelites. The Lord said: "As I was with Moses, so I will be with you, and I will never forsake you."'

Fong compared this to Jonno's death: 'I said, "We are like God's people; we are going to move on." I told them the Lord was with us and I knew after that prayer everyone was strengthened and had this new spirit in them, and I think it helped us.'

How, I asked Fong, did he reconcile God's word with his soldier's job? 'You have to follow orders in the army,' said Fong. 'But I normally pray about it, and there's times where I had to bear a rifle and fire at the enemy. But I always said to myself before I killed anyone that you have to do these things to save your friends . . . I prayed about it afterwards, but God will be the only judge of that . . . I am thankful that most of us got back alive. But I think everything that happens there has a purpose . . . Even the negative things, everything has a purpose. They happen for a reason.'

Just before we left, one of the survivors from Jonno's vehicle, Lee Bellingham, came and told me he had said a prayer the morning of Jonno's death. 'I never normally pray,' he said, 'but I said something that day. And I feel someone looked after me. I've said a prayer again this morning.'

The convoy move was painfully slow. The vehicles inched forward, their brakes screeching and squealing. The route took them back through Deh Zohr e Sofla – the village that B Company had attacked just four days earlier.

It was 11.30 and baking hot when the vehicles came to a halt. The forming-up point was on the far side of the main stone-filled riverbed through the Musa Qala wadi. But it was concealed from the town by thick copses of poplars that lined a dyke on the bank. This was close to where 1 Fury's Charlie Company had first crossed over. The American paratroops were somewhere in the fields around . . . But they were invisible. There were Humvees visible as miniature shapes on the ridgeline up above, and further along the armoured vehicles of the United Arab Emirates special forces. In theory they might provide fire support.

It was strangely quiet. Small noise carried far – the boots scrunching on the rocks, the muted squawks from the radios and a hum of a propeller high above: an invisible UAV circling in the sky. A message came through the radio. An intelligence report from Higher: 'Taliban Tier One foreign fighters have stayed behind to defend the district centre.' Another message said the ANA had cut a bomb detonation cable.

Andy Breach gathered his platoon to move ahead. 'My day sack is the weight of a small child, a fat American child,' he said.

The soldiers began moving up towards the town. Everyone kept spaced out in single file. About half a mile along the bank swung round to the right at the entrance to the smaller east–west Bagni wadi. The riverbed there was the final open piece of ground before the beginning of the district centre itself.

It was C Company under Major Matt Adams that went over first, with the 1st *kandak* of the ANA. An A-team of US special forces lurked behind the corner in their Humvees – ready to drive up and provide fire support if the Taliban opened up.

Everyone had their theories and suspicions, but no one knew what lay ahead. Adams had been told that across the wadi lay a system of Taliban trenches and bunkers. Everything seemed quiet. No one could be seen. But did that simply mean the enemy was hidden?

Sending his men in broad daylight across this 80-yard width of riverbed into the Taliban's most prized town made Adams feel like he was ordering some kind of First World War attack. One well-placed and well-aimed machine gun could have cut them all to shreds. All the geography gave the advantage to the defenders. Adams was preparing to take significant casualties.

That morning, like Jake, Adams had said a few words to his C Company. They had shaken hands and had taken photos, but it was difficult. There was a feeling that one of their number would not survive. Some felt that, after Jonno's death, it was C Company's turn to lose someone.

The hardest decision Adams made, though it was unavoidable, was ordering the combat engineers over first. They had the job of going in front and checking the crossing for mines. As they walked across with metal detectors, Adams placed a team of machine-gunners behind them and to their flank – poised to fire instantly if the Taliban opened up. The engineers reached the other side, spraying the pebbles with yellow paint to mark a safe route. The main body of Adams' company and the Afghan *kandak* started manoeuvring across. Few were surprised when the Afghans largely ignored the prepared path. It was only when they reached and cleared the first compound on the other side that Adams could allow himself a brief pause to breathe. Still no sign of the Taliban.

B Company then started inching forward. Following C Company's route, they crept through the trees along the riverbank and then reached the crossing of the open east–west wadi. I watched as Afghan soldiers paused to grab clumps of marijuana that was growing freely. After all those days in the washed-out brown colours of the desert, it was pleasant to be back among the lush greenery. One Yorks soldier said it 'reminds me of home after all that sand'.

At 14.20, Jake's B Company started crossing the riverbed. Reports ahead said C Company had not met any resistance. A stash of RPGs had been found.

The southern entrance to the town still lay about half a mile further east. From here the bazaar of Musa Qala stretched 1,200 yards due north to the monument that marked the crossroads of the district centre. The plan called for C Company to clear all the ground and buildings on the left-hand side of the road while B Company would clear the right-hand side.

At 14.40, B Company reached the road and began clearing its sector. There was still no sign of the Taliban. 'It looks like they have well and truly fled,' said Mantell. If they were going to defend the town, he thought, then the edge of the wadi was the place. A motorbike lay abandoned on its side by the metal pole barrier that marked the town entrance. A dead man sprawled near by. He had apparently been shot by 1 Fury from across the wadi a couple of days before. An Afghan flag was raised by the ANA.

Walking through the compounds was disconcerting. Every home was locked up. The shops were shuttered. Vegetables and fruit lay arranged and untouched on the wooden stalls in front. The people had clearly left in a hurry. Apache choppers were still circling overhead. Shots rang out every few minutes. People looked vaguely for where they might jump. But all the bangs were either warning shots or bullets used to break open locks to search the compounds.

The day's objective had been the district centre. But no one was taking chances with booby traps or ambushes. So progress was slow. By sunset, the two *kandak*s had reached just halfway up the road. Jake gathered his soldiers to spend the night in the courtyard of a large garage repair complex.

After the stress of that day, no one really wanted to talk. Most still expected trouble. Even if the Taliban had largely fled, just one bomb left behind or one well-concealed ambush position in the town centre could cause mayhem. Wherever the enemy were, they weren't too far away. The Afghan soldiers and interpreters eavesdropping the Taliban's radio channels reported the Taliban still manoeuvring, still giving orders and talking about where to lay an ambush.

But for others, those far from the front line, the battle of Musa Qala was long over.

In Kabul, the Afghan Defence Ministry spokesman General Mohammad Zahir Azimi announced Musa Qala was now in the hands of NATO and Afghan forces, who were 'strengthening their positions and continuing clean-up operations'. President Hamid Karzai said Musa Qala had been entered following reports of brutality there by the Taliban, Al Qaeda and foreign fighters. 'The successful attack was aided by some local Taliban leaders switching allegiance to the government,' Karzai said. A Taliban spokesman, Qari Yousef Ahmadi, said militant fighters had left Musa Qala because of a strategic decision to avoid Taliban and civilian casualties.

In Musa Qala no one was quite ready to celebrate, even though the Afghan army had wrapped flowers round their rifle barrels.

Just before nightfall, Breach was told by Jake to go out and secure the perimeter by holing up in a compound on the edge.

'What if we get attacked,' he asked. 'Is there a QRF [Quick Reaction Force]?'

'No,' said Jake. 'We're going to sleep.'

An American interrupted.

'Don't worry,' he said. 'Just get on the net . . . We'll reduce the threat.'

The men from Task Force 32 now had a new name: 'The Reducers'.

Musa Qala, 12 December

It seemed colder than the desert had been that first night in Musa Qala. In the morning there was frost on our bivvy bags. I woke up at one point in the darkness, thinking I could hear gunfire. But it was just Nick Cornish, the *Sunday Times* photographer, snoring. I drifted back off to the comforting drone of the Spectre gunship overhead.

'I can't wake up the rats,' Benson, the sergeant-major, was shouting at first light.

The commander of the *kandak*, Colonel Rahimi, had the only armoured vehicle of his unit, a Humvee. He'd installed a bed in it. He wanted to stay there in the warm.

The advance was supposed to start again at 06.30, but no one shifted for another hour. I was with Nuri, the interpreter, who had a radio scanner tuned to the Taliban's frequencies. When we got going, the radio announced: 'The infidel are moving.'

We pushed round the back of the market and through a maze of alleyways. It was quiet again but just as tense. There was a herd of cats that crawled round our ankles. More locks were blown off. A message said somewhere ahead a helicopter had been fired on. The UAVs checked the courtyards in front, but no one saw anything. Taliban radio declared: 'It's your decision if you want to stay.'

A twenty-year-old man, Bagi, was hanging around with the Afghan soldiers and saying that he had stayed behind to mind the shop. He claimed the Taliban always complained about his beard-less face and wanted money from his family. The whole population had left the town about six days before. 'All the Taliban have gone, and all the people have gone north to Baghran. They'll be back soon with their sheep and goats.'

We went down an alleyway, and Nick Mantell spotted some

ANA smoking pot. 'This is a big operation, lads. Hashish no good. Hashish no good!' he told them.

Someone said the ANA had found an old man who said he had already seen people 'with uniforms like yours' moving through a couple of days before. 'Fucking SF!' said Jake, referring to special forces. (Commanders would always later deny there was anyone in the town before us.)

Then we were inching up the final stretch of the main road leading to the district centre, the engineers in the lead with some kind of indestructible truck. But Captain Dan, from the special forces, was worrying again. 'None of these buildings has been searched. This is not clever,' he said, pointing out that everyone was walking past shops that could contain a massive bomb.

At 09.30 we came out to the central crossroads. To the right was a mound of rubble. Welcome to the Musa Qala district centre!

Jake and B Company continued to push on. Their job was to secure the northern edge of the town. A ring of security would then be in place so the generals could arrive to celebrate a victory.

A single mortar round that whistled over our heads was the Taliban's last gasp. Well trained by now, I dived into a ditch. It was full of sewage, and I cut my arm too. Afghan soldiers, who had not flinched, burst out laughing.

I stayed behind in the centre to wait for the flag to be raised. We were all tired now. It was all such an anti-climax. Everyone had wanted one last battle – a few hardened Taliban foreign fighters who could have made a last stand and made all the stress and fears feel like something that would have been *worth it*, made it feel like a prize that deserved to be captured.

Jake was glad he wasn't there for the media event. It fell to Matt Adams and C Company to sort things out for the cameras. Spare Afghan flags were on hand in case the ANA forgot theirs. 'Who has got the Afghan flag?' someone asked. The British hid their WMIKs and Vectors, but Adams also had to get the American Humvees moved away. He found it all very embarrassing, and the Americans at first were unresponsive. They didn't want to collapse their perimeter security. Adams told them there were forces now deployed in depth, and they reluctantly complied. It became something of a farce, though, with gun trucks hidden down alleyways.

Then a convoy of Afghan vehicles came sweeping up the main street and the ever-charismatic Brigadier Mohaydin strode out to take charge. Two soldiers took the flag up a tottering bamboo scaffolding on the central monument, and everyone held their breath as they balanced themselves precariously. Mohaydin made a brief speech and then picked up a telephone and phoned President Karzai to tell him the job was done. 'Three days ago all the terrorists were standing here,' he told me. 'I am sure we have defeated the Taliban in Musa Qala now. They haven't got the authority to come back and fight us.'

The dramatic scene of waving the flag was filmed and broadcast round the world by the Ministry of Defence's Combat Camera Team. They had been with Adams for the last few days but, soldiers claimed, had been under instructions to send back only pictures of Afghans in the operation.

It was at the flag raising that I first met Brigadier Mackay. He did his formal interviews, and then we wandered down the street and sat in a porchway and he told me what this had all been for. 'We could have come here any time and trashed the place,' he said, but then the follow-up – the stabilization and reconstruction – would have been hard. The whole operation to take Musa Qala had been calibrated to minimize the use of 'kinetic force'.

Though the destroyed district centre buildings lay around us, he said it was the Taliban, not the coalition, which had knocked those down.

Musa Qala had been a 'running sore', a base for the Taliban that affected everything in Helmand. When 52 Brigade took over, they had come up with a plan for putting pressure on the Taliban using everything from special force operations to conventional disruption to information operations. Then he had put Chris Bell's Warriors into the equation. 'I took a bet where this would lead us,' he said. The Taliban had reacted to that by putting 'enormous pressure' elsewhere – for example with major attacks down in Sangin. 'We realized what the Taliban were trying to do was draw us back down from Musa Qala so they carry on holding this place. We decided instead that we should increase the pressure on Musa Qala.' That was when he had deployed Tony Phillips' BRF. The Afghan government had also hoped that a tribal alliance could come together and overthrow the Taliban peacefully, but that didn't happen.

That afternoon, as Mackay flew home to Lashkar Gah, the British prime minister, Gordon Brown, stood up to address the House of Commons. He announced a new strategy for the war in Afghanistan, as well as emphasizing that Britain's policy was to kill or isolate the Taliban – not to negotiate with them.

He said: 'Let me on the morning of the capture of Musa Qala praise the professionalism and resolve of our forces who have helped defeat the insurgents and in a vital district of Afghanistan restored peace. And let me make it clear at the outset that as part of a coalition we are winning the battle against the insurgency – isolating and eliminating the leadership of the Taliban, not negotiating with them.'

That night, back in Musa Qala with B Company, Jake turned to Fong and thanked him for his prayers. It felt like a miracle to take the town without fighting. Fong replied: 'Don't thank me, just thank the Lord because he works in mysterious ways.'

In the next few days, the Afghans and the 2 Yorks made use of the fact that homes were empty to do a systematic search of the town. A Taliban headquarters was found with communications gear. Troops also found a factory where IEDs were put together, with enough components left behind to put together several dozen bombs. At least three laboratories were also found for the processing of raw opium.

I joined Jake as he and Sergeant-Major Benson were trying to set light to a large stash of drugs. They were having fun. They'd poured diesel all over the bags and then tried throwing phosphorus grenades to set it all alight. There was a few minutes of intense flame. But it wasn't enough to get the opium itself to burn.

Eventually the engineers stepped in and announced there was a 'proper way' to burn opium – inevitably involving the kind of explosive detonation they liked. All the opium was trucked off and set light together in the wadi. No one knew what it was really worth, but suggestions of an ultimate street value of 500 million dollars were released to the press. It was certainly a big haul, even if it was probably the lower-grade residue that the opium smugglers had not the time or inclination to take with them when they fled. It didn't really matter. It was at least obvious that Musa Qala really had been a centre for narcotics.

Three days after the town was captured, a Chinook's worth of journalists was flown from Kabul to have a whistle-stop tour of the liberated town. Their flight down was delayed and they had barely an hour to get briefed and to go downtown and talk to any of the locals who were starting to appear back. David Loyn, the BBC correspondent, was visibly bristling with frustration both that he had such little time and that the equipment he brought to do a live TV broadcast was not working. His producer, Najib, went to interview some of the locals in the market place. They told him stories that were distinctly off-message. Loyn's report on the main TV bulletins stated:

There is euphoria among those who took the town, but civilians who remained during the bombing told stories of large numbers of civilian casualties . . . This has been denied both by the Afghan government and the MOD . . . and it was impossible to verify in the time we had on the ground . . . This boy, Akhtar Muhammad, says many of his relatives died and their bodies are still under the rubble, while Wali Mohd said that he came on the bodies of fifteen women of all ages in one street.

The British army press team were angry. How could the BBC broadcast such allegations when they'd been in town for such a short time and had carried out no further investigation? Loyn felt it was the army who had restricted his visit to such a short time, and his report had been well qualified. Whether the claims were accurate or not, no one at the time got to the truth of the civilian casualties that had occurred. The soldiers didn't know themselves *then* what *some* would later come to feel: that what David Loyn had broadcast might well have been true after all.

Eight days after Musa Qala fell, Captain Andy Breach from B Company led a patrol back into Deh Zohr e Sofla, the village they had attacked during the feint operation. Surprisingly little had been touched since the moment they pulled out. At the front of the village, the body of the Taliban they had left behind was still lying there. That was how the locals treated foreign fighters. Looking round the place, they discovered the ambush positions that the Taliban had prepared for them further back. There were also strange piles of clipped body hair – reportedly the sign of religious zealots who had prepared themselves for martyrdom.

But there was an uglier sight that also awaited. In the courtyard on which a JDAM had been dropped at the end, there was a stench that made them want to retch. They started picking through the rubble. And what they found was a pile of decomposing bodies. All of them were women and children. There was no sign of any dead Taliban, but there was an impression in the mud in the middle of the compound. 'It was a clear print of the base of a mortar,' said Breach. The Taliban had clearly been firing from somewhere they knew was full of innocent people. It wasn't a place to make you feel good, though: they called that place from then on JDAM House.

Everything that Mackay and all his brigade had done had been designed to try to avoid killing the innocent. They knew that was Karzai's main concern. They knew that civilian casualties would mar their victory. And they knew that – as Mackay kept saying – this war would be won by bringing the civilian population on to the government and coalition side and not by killing them.

But wanting something and doing something were not the same.

The residents of Musa Qala voted with their feet soon after the arrival of the Afghan army. Tractors, pick-up trucks and carts started bringing people home.

Before I left Musa Qala and the 2 Yorks, I interviewed some of those who returned. They described the brutalities of life under the Taliban, including the hanging of four alleged spies and criminals. One 'traitor' had had his head cut off and then placed in the roadway that enters the town. 'They killed him at three o'clock in the morning and then they left his head there for everyone to see,' said fourteen-year-old Gul Wadi. 'They killed both traitors and thieves; the traitors were giving secrets to the enemy.' Others spoke of three others hanged, one left suspended from the entrance barrier to the town, one from the monument in the centre, and another in the bazaar. The Taliban had banned smoking and use of snuff and beaten and thrown into jail those they disliked. Some claimed the Taliban extorted money to fund their jihad, although others said the tax was voluntary.

Speaking at a checkpoint where those coming back were searched for weapons, eighteen-year-old Mahmoud said there had been no school in the town for months. When the Taliban arrived they turned it into a religious *madrassah*, as well as their headquarters. 'No one sent their kids to the school because they were afraid the Americans would drop bombs, and everyone would be killed.'

Camp Bastion field hospital morgue, 17 December

Don Johnson walked into the cool and sombre-looking morgue and saw his brother's coffin laid out on a trestle table and draped in the Union Jack. He was about to join five other pall-bearers to carry the body to the waiting plane to be repatriated back to England. A crowd of soldiers was gathering outside for the ceremony by the aircraft ramp. The 2 Yorks padre had suggested he go in a few minutes before the others to see the coffin and collect his thoughts.

No one had really wanted him to carry the coffin. They feared he would break down. Don, being honest, suspected too that he might break down. And he knew it was going to make it harder for everyone else. But when the regimental sergeant-major had come in and told him, 'I've got six names here,' and that as a courtesy he was checking with Johnson and asked, 'What do you think of them names?' Don had just pointed at one of the names and had said, 'He's not carrying it. I'll carry it.'

They had a little argument.

'Seriously, I'm gonna do it . . . He'd do it for me, he would of,' said Don.

'No, you don't want to break down. It would make a mess of it.'

'Seriously, sir. There's no options in this. I'm doing it!'

He had been practising since, steeling himself to be strong and not let Jonno down. As he rounded the corner into the morgue, he knew everyone outside was nervous for him. 'I needed to get the initial shock out of my system.' It wasn't a nice place – full of the freezers you see in morgues. He saw the coffin draped in the flag.

'I walked round,' he remembered, 'and whew, I think that's when it sank home for me that he had really died. It was really hard. Then for some strange reason I started laughing. I think it put a smile on everyone's face. I don't know, I had a little cry and I had a little giggle. Then I had this real proud feeling. I felt really proud for some strange reason. It was almost as if he'd wanted . . . I cannot get away from the feeling that maybe he wanted it happening. I felt proud of him there.'

What had made Don feel this way?

'He was a big drinker, oh my God he was a big drinker and he was a party animal really. I mean he was the best fucking soldier I've ever met, he really was. He was like Jake and that. They used to go drinking in the day when Jake was only a platoon commander. They were as bad as each other, a different breed, excellent soldiers, but they will drink till five or six o'clock in the morning. And he's . . . I think they've got the most of him and I think if he had a choice of any way he wanted to die, that would have been the one. He would have went that way, maybe not in a mine strike but some sort of way, otherwise he would have been like sixty or seventy years old if he had made it out of there, living in a terrible state. I was just, I was just so proud of him. But he knew it was going to happen. That was the worst bit.'

PART 6

The Aftermath

'One flower is not the spring.'

Afghan Proverb

27. Perfidy

Governor Asadullah Wafa finally switched his gaze to Michael Semple, the EU official sitting next to him. He frowned. 'Michael, what are you up to at the moment?' he asked.

Semple and his party had already been there for some minutes, but Wafa, who took little account of Afghan courtesies, had been deep in conversation with his intelligence chief, Muhammad Naeem. The atmosphere was already claustrophobic. The living room of the governor's residence was long and narrow, and the windows were all shut off. Wafa was clutching a notebook. For someone who never appeared to listen to a conversation, it seemed a rather strange thing.

Joining Semple on the over-ornate couches was his Afghan partner, the former air force chief General Naquib (the man who had first made contact with Mullah Salaam). Also there were his close friend, the UN diplomat Mervyn Patterson, and his assistant, Amini. Judging by the time of their invitation, they could expect to stay for dinner.

Semple, who was following Wafa's lead in switching from Persian to Pashto, tried to think of a way of introducing the idea of the training camp. What were Wafa's thoughts on the follow-up to Musa Qala? He didn't want to present the plan to train former Taliban as a given. But Wafa already knew about Semple's idea. And he had an agenda.

'Do you want to set up a military unit for the Taliban?' Wafa asked.

'No. But we are suggesting some rehabilitation training for them – something to make humans of them!'

Semple tried to expand the conversation, asking those around the room to give a summary of the ideas they had for exploiting the success of Musa Qala. He asked Naquib to speak. Naquib was very measured.

'Nobody wants to set up a military unit, but there is this idea of a training camp to provide a destination for the Taliban who have fought –'

Wafa suddenly interrupted his flow, his face tensing with anger. 'Guards, arrest these men!' he bellowed, pointing at the Afghans in Semple's party.

At this point, Naeem's plain-clothes officers stepped into the room. Silent, they looked in their element and produced metal handcuffs.

Semple turned to Wafa: 'This is out of order. Naquib is an officer; you don't need to handcuff an officer.'

But Wafa burst into a torrent of abuse, calling him a 'fake general' and a 'son of a Pakistani dog'. Semple urged him to calm down. Wafa was still shouting, telling the guards to arrest Amini too. Another man walked in, the cousin of the head of the Human Rights Commission, who had come round to drop off Semple's luggage.

'Arrest him too,' said Wafa.

'But he's from the Human Rights Commission,' said Semple.

'They are all drug dealers, drug dealers!' said Wafa, boiling with rage.

It was not typical Afghan behaviour. Even the cruellest of betrayals are customarily delivered with great courtesy. In a land bedevilled by feuds that last generations, every move of an Afghan chief is calculated, in normal circumstances, to minimize an enmity that may linger.

'It's the president's orders,' shouted Wafa when Semple protested. 'Talk to the president, not me. It's the president's orders. Don't ask me,' he shouted again, as the Afghans were led away.

It was only eleven days since the flag had risen on Musa Qala, but events had been moving swiftly in Helmand, and mostly in the right direction, until this meeting.

Mackay and his headquarters always knew they would be judged by what came *after* the battle of Musa Qala, not by the fighting itself. Above all, Musa Qala should not be 'another Sangin', a town captured with almost no plans for how to rebuild it afterwards. Brian Mennes, whose men had now led the recapture of both towns, agreed. In Musa Qala, a British team arrived the day after the flag-raising to deliver a plan they had indeed prepared earlier. The head of the 'stabilization team' was the second-in-command of the Coldstream battalion, Major Guy Bartle-Jones. Sitting in the garage of a former opium market, his men opened up their laptops, and he spread out an architect's plan for a new mosque.

Next to him was the moustachioed Brigadier Mohaydin, the leader of the victorious ANA force. All that morning, Simon Downey, the 2 Yorks commanding officer, had been struggling with the ANA. As far as Downey was concerned it was all hands on deck to secure a new camp for the Afghan troops in the centre of the town. Downey and his regimental sergeant-major, Richard Hind, had led by example, filling sandbags at dawn. But the Afghans were not interested.

'Heroes don't fill sandbags!' said Mohaydin, with a certain twinkle in his eye. The lack of security had put the Green Berets from Task Force 32 in a spin. They had been warning Downey of suicide bombers that would soon wander in. And before Downey knew it they had pulled away their entire force, claiming their job was over.

Bartle-Jones was outlining 3 million dollars of expenditure. It was to include repairing roads and renovating a medical clinic and the school. There were two options for the mosque – one for 300 worshippers and one for 800. In the following days, those sincere promises of reconstruction became a mantra, used to impress the townsfolk as they drifted back to their homes and shops, and to tell the press. The hard thing was turning it all into reality.

What General McNeill and Cowper-Coles in Kabul had warned about had immediately happened: the town had been taken from the Taliban, but President Karzai had yet to appoint anyone to run the place instead. The idea had been for the Afghan army to take Musa Qala and garrison it under an Afghan governor. To fill the vacuum, Mackay now told Simon Downey to take command in Musa Qala. All of a sudden his 2 Yorks headquarters was not only mentoring an army but running a town.

During the early days, recalled Downey, Mohaydin rose to the challenge, getting his soldiers to win the sort of consent from a sceptical population that western forces could never have achieved. 'They talked to the people, Afghan to Afghan, knowing what buttons to press, how to encourage and how to coerce. The people saw them broadly as a legitimate, Islamic force.' But there was still one man missing from the show: the now legendary man of mystery, Mullah Abdul Salaam, whom almost no one had actually ever seen. He finally appeared without warning on 23 December, the day that Downey and Mohaydin got a large *shura* together. And he was a striking figure, with a wild and bushy black beard and curled slippers: something like a genie from a bottle in an Arabian Nights caricature. Everyone watched anxiously to see how the people would react to Mullah Salaam. The 1 Fury commander, Brian Mennes, noticed the British were particularly nervous, perhaps 'because they were scarred by the initial Musa Qala operations, which had failed so miserably.'

But Salaam spoke like a pro.

'Three weeks ago, I was doing bad things,' he told a crowd of locals. 'And a few years back you and I were killing the Americans. But I'm on board now. You all need to come with me!' Salaam had totally taken charge, said Mennes. 'I've listened to *a lot* of Afghan *shura* speeches – and I was like, "Oh, oh, he's good." He was very good.' Salaam spoke the words the coalition wanted and was prepared to repeat his message to everyone – he was driven round from village to village to tell the people to back the government.

Mennes saw a lot of him later. 'I used to walk into his little court with everyone on the floor, sitting around smoking cigarettes and drinking tea on pillows. They had a little stove, and people were feeding his cat.' They struck up a bond. 'He told me the liberation of Musa Qala was about the most heroic thing he had seen. Because we killed almost no one that shouldn't have been killed.'

Up in Kabul, Michael Semple had been trying to make sense of what had happened in Musa Qala. In the build-up, he had been active behind the scenes, emptying and sharing his contact book with anyone who needed it. The Afghan security agencies had pumped the telephones, trying to cajole Taliban commanders not to join the fight.

'It wasn't my job as an EU political officer to play a direct role in a NATO military operation,' he recalled. 'But I did brief and advise everyone who cared to listen. There was a pooling of effort in putting pressure on the Taliban not to join the fight.'

By the end they estimated the 'reconciliation' process had successfully kept some key Taliban commanders out of the fight. Both the Afghan intelligence service (the NDS) and the Interior Ministry claimed some 800 fighters in northern Helmand had chosen to avoid joining their comrades in the defence of Musa Qala. Semple thought the true figure was more like 400. But it was still a lot.

The stunning Taliban defeats in both Musa Qala and Sangin by NATO forces had also changed the dynamics, thought Semple. The time was ripe to take reconciliation on to another stage, to test the words of some of those Helmand tribesmen and fighters who had vowed to him and Naquib they would reject the extremists. He had been chatting over what to do next, principally with Dr Abdullah, the deputy head of the NDS, and with two deputy interior ministers, Hadi Khalid and Munir Mangal. Ironically, given what followed, it was in a meeting with the latter that the concept of the 'training camp' was thrashed out.

'The idea was simple,' said Semple. 'You needed somewhere to invite people to. An assurance of love and goodwill from them was not enough. But simply recruiting them into a fighting force wasn't either a good idea or something that NATO would accept.'

Semple thought up a six-week 'life-skills' type of course for former Taliban: Afghan history and constitution, some reading and writing and plenty of physical exercise. Mangal suggested getting a private security firm to run it.

The Afghan officials he met in Kabul liked the camp idea, as did the British. The brigade in Lashkar Gah was briefed, and soon the army got to work on the planning for the camp, even finding a place for it. Contractors who were going to start work on a road to Kajaki were interested – offering to give the ex-Taliban work.

On 18 December, Cowper-Coles was in Lashkah Gah. He and Mackay were briefed on the latest ideas. The ambassador – who referred to the camp as the 'boy scout plan' – asked if Wafa had been informed. He was told not. Semple was invited to come down to lay things on the table. That Sunday, Semple arrived on a United Nations helicopter. He had hitched a ride with his friend Mervyn Patterson, who had some separate UN business in Lashkar Gah: nothing to do with Semple or his plans, though Wafa invited them both for a meeting that night.

Arriving at the Lashkar Gah base, Semple and a delegation from the Ministry of Interior were ushered into a briefing room. Patterson did not take part. Semple and Naquib told everyone about the big idea. It was still just a concept – a possible option. Brigadier Mackay was keen.

As Semple drove round to the ill-fated meeting with Governor Wafa at his residence, Khalid, the Interior Ministry deputy minister, rang to ask how things were going. Semple quipped, 'I am going into battle as your soldier, pray for me.' Khalid wished him luck.

The morning after, with General Naquib still in the custody of the secret police, Semple saw Wafa again. He was now dangling a USB computer memory stick taken from Naquib. 'I have his internet, I have got his internet,' he exclaimed.

The memory stick contained a draft of a briefing on the ex-Taliban camp plan, including a draft budget intended to help make a bid for British funding. Wafa had also seized cash from Naquib. Wafa said it was more than 150,000 dollars to be paid to 'terrorists' – a fabrication, according to Semple. In fact it was, he said, 18,700 dollars and it was British Embassy money intended to fund the expenses of the ex-Taliban 'Group' in Gereshk.

Andrew Patrick, the deputy head of mission at the British Embassy, was pouring drinks for Christmas Day lunch when the phone rang. It was the duty officer. With the ambassador away on leave with his parents-in-law, Patrick was in charge of British interests. All ambassadors from the European Union were being summoned immediately before the minister of foreign affairs, Rangin Spanta.

The envoys were given the news: Michael Semple and Mervyn Patterson were being declared *persona non grata* and ordered to leave the country within forty-eight hours. They had taken 'actions prejudicial to the security of Afghanistan' – they had engaged in unauthorized negotiation with the Taliban, were carrying thousands of dollars to pay them off and had even held a meeting, it was later suggested, with one of the most wanted senior Taliban commanders, Mansour Dadullah, brother of the Taliban commander killed by the Special Boat Service.

Telephoned in the UK, Cowper-Coles started to pack his bags to return to Kabul. The idea of Semple and Patterson, who was a UK national, both being expelled seemed extraordinary, a wind-up. While no official statement was made that accused Britain of involvement, the Afghans were telling anyone who asked that Semple and Patterson had been mixed up with British intelligence. Their talks with the Taliban were a plot by the Secret Intelligence Service, a revival of the spy intrigues of the nineteenth-century 'Great Game'. This whole row was not just an accusation by Karzai against EU and UN diplomats, it seemed like an attempt to stir up a row with perfidious Albion.

Afghan officials were spouting public outrage. President Karzai's spokesman, Humayun Hamidzada (whose salary, ironically, was paid by the UN), told a news conference two foreigners were under arrest for 'posing a threat to national security'. Wafa declared to foreign nations: 'It is our duty to defend our dignity,' and he could not 'allow anyone to carry out political activities without the government's permission.' In Ireland the expulsion of two

Irishmen beat the Pope's Christmas message as the top news story.

It was not only the end of Semple's activities and the training camp plan. The whole programme of discreet contacts with Taliban commanders was now suspended. On Boxing Day, Mullah Qassim and his deputy from 'the Group' in Gereshk were summoned to see the governor and arrested. The militia was disarmed and placed under house arrest in Gereshk.

When Captain Rob Sugden heard the news, he phoned up Lieutenant Colonel George Waters, his commanding officer in the Coldstream Guards and the brigade's security sector adviser.

'Fuck, fuck, fuck,' said Waters, when he told him of the Group's arrest.

It did not sound like reassurance. Sugden had been watching *Sky News*, and he heard Gordon Brown's denial that the British were negotiating with the Taliban.

'Are we all going to end up in court?' said Sugden.

'If you are then I'll be joining you there,' said the colonel.

Even less reassuring, thought Sugden. His experiment at least for now was over.

Cowper-Coles got back to Kabul on 28 December and saw President Karzai in the palace the following day. The ambassador had brought with him a sheaf of emails: from both the Ministry of Interior and the NDS. Semple had exchanged more than 100 messages on his work with the NDS alone. They showed how the contacts with the Taliban and the plan for the camp *had been directly approved by Karzai's own most senior officials*. 'This has all been authorized,' Cowper-Coles told the president, who looked taken aback. All his men had denied all knowledge.

But, however much he squirmed in his seat, the Afghan president was not about to back down, not even over his expulsion of Patterson, who had nothing to do with the camp plan or any contacts with the Taliban. As one diplomat put it, Patterson was just collateral damage in a 'perfidious strike' by Karzai.

Even before the Helmand governor rang Karzai talking of 'British plots', tension was already growing between the president and British diplomats. Much of it centred on a plan to appoint the former Royal Marine and Liberal Democrat leader Lord Ashdown as a new UN 'super envoy' to the country. Ashdown has a reputation for breaking china and for speaking bluntly. He had already declared the Afghanistan war as lost, saying success was 'now unlikely'. Everyone gave Karzai contradictory advice. Being plagued by 'mentors' was the story of his life. While President Bush was strongly backing Ashdown, some of his own advisers, including Zalmay Khalilzad, the influential Afghan-American US ambassador to the UN, were said to be warning Karzai that Ashdown would become a dominating 'viceroy'. Paradoxically, Ashdown had been a US idea, not a British one. In the end Karzai came to see the imposition of Ashdown as British power play, and Semple's ventures gave him the excuse he was looking for to vent some of his frustration.

In the weeks that followed the expulsions, what finally sealed Karzai's rejection of Ashdown was a leading article in *The Times* of London that described the president's 'precarious position' and how he had 'little say in security matters' and called him a 'lonely Pashtun in a government made up largely of Tajik veterans of the Northern Alliance'. A day later a *Times* news article suggested Lord Ashdown was the solution, quoting an Afghan businessman as saying, 'He is the last chance to save Afghanistan. I pray that it is him who will run our country, and not our useless president, who has so far managed to squander the best opportunity Afghanistan has had in 250 years.'[22]

Bill Wood, the US ambassador, pleaded with an incensed Karzai: 'You don't give your word to Bush and then go back on it just on the basis of a *Times* leader, which Ashdown had nothing to do with.'

Then, at the World Economic Forum in Davos on 24 January, Karzai blew another gasket – putting into the public sphere what he had been saying in private for a while: that the British and Americans were to blame for the violence in Helmand. The Musa Qala operation was correcting a problem that the British had made for themselves.

Briefing journalists, he said, 'It took us a year and a half to take back Musa Qala. This was not a failure but a mistake.' Then he repeated his old point about how the removal of the former governor, Sher Muhammad Akhundzada, had precipitated the violence. 'There was one part of the country where we suffered after the arrival of the British forces . . . Before that, we were fully in charge of Helmand.'

Karzai apologized immediately afterwards to Cowper-Coles, Gordon Brown and David Miliband, the foreign secretary, telling the British he never meant to insult their troops. But his calming words did not disguise the fact that relations had yet to recover – and that Karzai was now determined to reject Ashdown, who soon publicly withdrew.

In Helmand, Brigadier Mackay regarded the whole Semple debacle as a major lost opportunity. It undermined 'so much of the promise opened up by the capture of Musa Qala', he said. 'After that, reconciliation was dead in the water.'

There was at least one positive thing that emerged from the debacle. Mullah Omar's spokesman abruptly announced that he was expelling hardline commander Mansour Dadullah from the Taliban movement – soon after untrue press stories that Semple and Patterson had been talking to him. Dadullah had been treated almost as abruptly and unfairly by his bosses as the men from the EU and UN had been treated by Karzai.

Meeting the Taliban commander Mullah Sadiq at a safehouse, Qais, the journalist, still hoped he could somehow persuade him to stop fighting.

Sadiq was candid with him about his doubts. But, for all that, Qais knew that this man could be ruthless.

'This country needs blood. It is a war. I need to be martyred,' he would say.

'You have lots of children. And they are all young. They need you,' pleaded Qais. He could not help wanting to persuade Sadiq to end his brutal ways. But Sadiq said he wanted his eldest son to join the fight and be martyred too.

Sadiq had a role in the Taliban's counter-intelligence. He was a spy hunter. In Musa Qala he had identified two spies, who had been hanged. He had hanged two more in Sangin. 'I'm 100 per cent sure they were guilty!' he said, although it was in a tone of voice that made Qais think he had doubts. 'They had satellite phones, expensive equipment. They got rich all at once!'

Qais used to tell him bluntly, 'I think that's wrong. You don't know for sure.'

All this time Sadiq kept his home in Sangin and returned frequently to visit his wife and family. He did this right to the end – even with British troops back in the town and even as he rose up the ranks of Taliban commanders.

They began arguing about the taking of hostages. Some journalists had been killed by the Taliban, and Qais was furious. Some Koreans had been taken prisoner and released for cash. Sadiq said kidnapping for ransom was becoming an ugly business now. 'Now the Taliban will kidnap their mothers for money,' he confessed.

28. The Cost of It All

Outside Musa Qala, 20 January, 15.30

Lance-Bombardier Ian Wylie and the rest of A Troop panted their way up to the ridgeline after a patrol in the village beneath. There had been reports of enemy in the neighbourhood, but the patrol had passed without incident. It was mid-afternoon and finally getting warm after a freezing cold morning. The heat, as things turned out, was deadly.

At the top, they paused for breath and looked at the view. Before them was a dusty and dry rock-strewn slope down to the wide, flat expanse of the water-fed farmland of the Musa Qala wadi, with the town itself just over 2 miles in front to the left, and the Roshan mobile phone tower standing out on the sharp cliffs opposite. Behind was the undulating brown moonscape of a high desert plateau. Mount Musa Qala, what the soldiers called 'Mount Doom', stood towering to the north.

Wylie and the others reached the vehicles they had parked in a tight square in a dip just behind the ridge. C Troop's vehicles were elsewhere, providing cover on two positions on higher ground.

Wylie got into top cover position, manning the .50 cal machine gun on a WMIK. He had just got back to the Brigade Reconnaissance Force. After driving the WMIK that had struck the mine or explosive device that had killed Jack Sadler in the Musa Qala operation, he had been sent home with minor injuries. He had wanted to return, but, riding now in the position where Sadler had died, he was not comfortable, nervous of another mine going off.

The plan was to head off back into the desert that had long been the BRF's home. One of the vehicle commanders, Bombardier

Danny Kay, moved off. His driver, Trooper Adam Cox, turned his wheel right on full lock. As they circled across the sandy ground towards the edge of the ridge, the front wheel struck a mine. When the smoke cleared, Kay was still in his seat, but in agony. The front of the vehicle had twisted back on to him, shattering the bones in his legs and dislocating his toes. Cox had blast injuries to his legs. The top gunner, Troy Bayliss, was clutching his wrists.

Wylie stared in disbelief, fearing the same nightmare all over again. But Kay, a South African, broke the ice as they carried him out. He started swearing in Afrikaans and then even laughing. He was obviously in agony and needed treatment, but he had had a lucky escape. He was not going to die.

The BRF had lived in the desert around Musa Qala for more than two months, bar a three-day break just after the town was recaptured. But like most of 52 Brigade, they were still barely halfway through their tour.

Fighting had continued. A large British force was still in place, keeping the Taliban out while plans advanced for development in the town. The American paratroopers, 1 Fury, were only just leaving. They and the British had continued fighting in the villages up in the desert between Musa Qala and Kajaki, and in the hostile wadi south towards Sangin. A fortnight previously, 1 Fury's Sergeant David J. Drakulich, of Reno, Nevada, had been killed down there in an IED blast.

The constant moving and fighting and forever living from their vehicles was beginning to wear down the men of the BRF. After the deaths of Jack Sadler and Lee Johnson, they knew how vulnerable they and their vehicles were.

One of the biggest dangers was the so-called legacy mines left by the Soviets. The intelligence they had on threat maps they carried showed them practically everywhere. But the map was large-scale, 1:100,000. It gave you enough detail to keep you scared, but not enough detail to navigate round the danger. The map showed Soviet mines somewhere near this ridge top, but no real clue of where they were.

★

The battery sergeant major, Paul Hodgson, was organizing the rescue. The injured were brought on stretchers a couple of hundred yards along the ridge top to be treated by his vehicle, one of the four-wheel Pinzgauers.

It was obvious now there were mines about. But Hodgson and the stretcher-bearers stayed on the ridge top track, which they judged had effectively been cleared by their movements along it all day. 'It had been used by locals, which was clearly a good sign,' he recalled, 'but there were no recent tracks. No one had been here for a while.' The metal detectors were also brought out, and the soldiers were checking for other mines.

Hodgson himself walked further up the track and found a good helicopter landing site on flat ground. They had got word by radio of a Chinook that was already up in the Musa Qala area. It was not the Incident Response Team that carried medics but instead had on board a VIP, Major General Jacko Page.

Hodgson popped a green smoke grenade to guide the chopper in. As it came down Kay and the other injured were still being put on to his 'Pinz', about 400 yards back. Hodgson radioed back: 'If you don't get those casualties on there in the next sixty seconds then it's going to take off.'

The acting second-in-command, Captain Richard Waddell, was standing close to Hodgson's Pinz and got the message. He turned to the driver, a twenty-five-year-old corporal, Darryl 'Daz' Gardiner, and said, 'All right, you need to basically go.' He walked round the back to see the injured on board and then gave Gardiner the thumbs-up and shouted, 'They're on. You can go.'

Ever since the mine blast, Gardiner had been busy helping treat the injured. Now, Adam Cox was in his passenger seat, his legs on the dashboard. Cox said that after losing Jack Sadler and now this, 'I'm not sure how we're going to cope.' As he drove off, Gardiner replied: 'Don't be daft! You'll be on the chopper soon – and getting down a warm meal at Bastion!'

Hodgson remembered seeing Gardiner's vehicle go about 10 yards. Then there was a bang, and he saw Gardiner being thrown from his seat into the sky and landing about 20 yards away. His three tons of Pinzgauer was also flung into the air and spun round 180 degrees.

Hodgson turned towards the Chinook helicopter, the twin rotors of which were still thrashing the air. He made a cutting motion with his hand across his throat, meaning: 'Just go, leave.' The chopper roared off, and Hodgson went running back to the disaster. He saw the vehicle, which served as the ammunition resupply store, was now on fire. After what happened after the Sadler mine strike, his first priority would be to douse the flames quickly.

Waddell was so close to the blast that the flash burned the skin off his nose. His vehicle was parked right by. If Gardiner had not hit the mine, it might have been him. 'The strangest thing was how quickly that vehicle went from being a normal vehicle to being on its side, facing the wrong way and being on fire. You know, it was quicker than the blink of an eye.'

Further along the ridge, Sergeant Jonathan Walton was working his way down with a mine detector. 'No, this is – it's not happening!' he thought. A Fijian soldier was helping him. After seeing Gardiner being blown in the air, Walton asked the soldier, 'Who was that?'

'Oh, it's Daz . . . He's gone.'

'How do you know that? You don't know. He might be all right. Let's get up there and see if he's all right.'

But the deeply religious Fijian said he had seen an angel come out of Gardiner. Walton tried to calm him. He gave him the metal detector to keep him busy.

The three people injured in the first mine strike had now been through a second one. Miraculously, none seemed to have got more physical injuries. The casualties were triaged – a process of working out who needed the most help. Everyone seemed calm. Businesslike.

When one of the medics, Collin Vincent, first saw Gardiner, he found him unconscious but with a weak pulse. Working with Lance-Corporal Peter Langhelt, another medic, and Sergeant

Robert Leslie, who had good medical skills, they patched his wounds and tried desperately to get some fluids into his veins.

Those with metal detectors worked furiously meanwhile to clear a certain path to the landing site for when the medevac chopper came in. It was hardest for those, like most, who were told to stay put. No one wanted another blast to make things *even worse*. Wylie's face looked totally blank and shocked. He would remember that for almost an hour he just sat still, too choked to move one inch.

Eventually the medevac Chinook came in and took the injured away. Then it all sunk in. They were in fading light in the middle of the minefield, and no one knew whether Daz Gardiner was alive. He was close to them all. From Salisbury, Wiltshire, he was on attachment from the Royal Electrical and Mechanical Engineers as the BRF's armourer: fixing weapons. Everyone knew him. He had become one of them. A keen skydiver in his spare time, he always had something to say. He kept them all amused.

Vincent knew that Daz was not going to make it. So did Hodgson. He had seen the look of his eyes. But this was not the time to say anything. Everyone had such faith in the medevac choppers and the standard of care back at Camp Bastion. Some of the best surgeons in Britain were said to volunteer to work there.

It broke Vincent's heart. All he could do was mutter: 'He had a pulse when he left us. It is in their hands now.' It was depressing.

A little later the radio message came through. The men were called together and told, 'Daz didn't make it.'

It took the BRF another seven hours to clear their way off the ridgeline in the dark – down the slope and back into Musa Qala centre. Other mines and metal objects were found and marked. They were helped by 2 Yorks soldiers, who cleared up the hill from the town and met them halfway.

The next morning Wylie got on a helicopter for Camp Bastion and a week later returned to the UK. 'I didn't want to be involved in another similar incident. I didn't feel comfortable in a vehicle,' he recalled.

The rest of the BRF had been brought back to Bastion for a

rest too. But the day before Gardiner's repatriation ceremony – when his body was carried by pallbearers on to a plane for the flight home – most of them were flown back to Musa Qala, missing it all. The following day, Brigadier Mackay came out to see them. They were in a raw mood, almost rebellious. The soldiers asked the brigadier why they were out in the mine-strewn desert in the old design of WMIKs, while soldiers were driving round Camp Bastion in a newer version that had better mine protection.

The soldiers recalled Mackay telling them: 'You need to pick yourself up. You look like a unit that's down.' The BRF burned with resentment at that and reacted badly. It was not helped by the fact their OC, Tony Phillips, was away on his R&R.

Mackay, who was perhaps prouder of the BRF than any other unit, would harbour no resentment though. 'Tough soldiers speak their minds,' he said later, 'but there was a tough message I had to give them too.' The timing of his trip had been quite deliberate. He had heard the BRF's morale was plummeting. He remembered telling them that 'after all the success of your tour, this is not how you want to be remembered'.

Some used to think enviously of the BRF's desert mission as a kind of Mad Max fantastic adventure. Officers used to tell Phillips: 'It must have been brilliant!' But he used to say: 'No. It was unpleasant, dangerous. We were doing a job.'

The day of the mine strikes that killed Corporal Gardiner was also the day of the handover of Musa Qala from command of the 2 Yorks and Simon Downey to the Household Cavalry head-quarters under Ed Smyth-Osbourne, who had moved up from running Garmsir. By now, Mullah Salaam was officially the district governor, and, after his trips around the countryside talking to people at *shuras*, he was pressing to see when the promised aid would actually be delivered. The relationship between the British officers and Mullah Salaam was often comical. For one, they did not quite appreciate Mullah Salaam's personal hygiene – in particular waking up in the morning and walking out of their quarters, right next to Salaam's, only to see a turd steaming by their feet.

In February, Colonel Ed sent his C Squadron under Major Paul Bedford to launch a combined operation with the US Green Berets to attack the Taliban stronghold in the villages of Kariz de Baba, one of the main valleys in the desert east towards Kajaki. Among them was one rather special forward air controller, Second Lieutenant Harry Wales, and third in line to the throne. It was on 28 February, while Prince Harry was on this operation, and getting his first real experience of combat, that it was revealed (on an American website) that he had secretly been in Afghanistan since 13 December. Harry wanted to stay on regardless, but, back in London, the chief of the defence staff, Sir Jock Stirrup, ordered his immediate recall home. Captain Andy Dimmock, a fire support commander attached to the Household Cavalry, said the Prince had been 'treated like any equal'. Disguised by a radio call sign, he spoke to pilots as Widow 67. 'He wasn't Prince Harry. He was one of the many forward air controllers we had in theatre, and he was truly treated equally up until the point where he was taken out.' Interviewed on his return, Harry said he would 'love to go back out' to Afghanistan 'very, very soon'. 'Once you are back from operations everything is a bit of an anti-climax, you go back to your unit and there you are, day-in day-out, the same routine, nothing changes . . . In operations, you are kept on your toes the whole time. That's what guys join up for I guess, that adrenalin.'

By now Musa Qala was on the war tour of visiting VIPs to Afghanistan, an example of the way to capture a town with minimal destruction and arrive with a plan to win people's hearts. 'The eyes of the world will be on Musa Qala,' said the US ambassador, William Wood, when he visited the town.

When I returned in March 2008 the impact of development efforts could be seen. The mosque project was still being held up by bureaucracy, but a small road had been built, the market and the health clinic had reopened, a school was refurbished and teaching more than 800 pupils (though only boys), and a cash-for-work scheme was employing more than 300 people daily.

Salaam, however, remained unsatisfied with the pace of change.

★

I got a 'bluey', an army airmail letter, back home in London from Jake and his B Company, dated 29 February. He wrote with greetings from Sangin and an update:

Our time in Musa Qala after you left was broadly successful. There was still quite a lot of fighting as many of the Taliban moved back and we attempted to clear them. The lads were fantastic as ever and UK casualties were relatively light – sadly we had a couple of ANA killed in the last week.

Sangin is proving an interesting place. In many ways it is less developed than Musa Qala and certainly seems to be more heavily influenced by the Taliban. We've had a couple of quite cheeky fights, one in particular where we were outflanked and for a time I thought we would come off pretty badly. I think we were saved by accurate mortar fire and the good old Americans and their planes. I'm not sure how the lads keep doing it day after day but they do and in this particular fight there were some extraordinary acts of bravery for which I hope they are recognized. I think the death of Jonno more than anything else has made the Company very close and nobody wants to let anybody down.

The last three months of the 52 Brigade tour involved some fierce fights for many and a heavy toll of injury. The Danish battle group in charge of the central area of Helmand had tried hard to extend the zone of relative security around Gereshk. But in March the Taliban were creeping back in. A suicide bomber struck in the centre of Gereshk, killing two Danish soldiers, one Czech soldier and an interpreter. Then, at the end of March, two Danish soldiers were shot dead in the space of five days. Of all valiant acts I heard about from the soldiers, the story that stayed longest in my mind was of two Coldstream Guard mortar controllers who separately on successive days ran alone across open fields under fire to the Danish front line – amid scenes of utter confusion around. There was a moment when one of them, Sergeant Tony Bolton, sat in a besieged trench while comforting an injured Dane on his lap, firing his rifle with one hand and holding a radio handset with the other, calling in a mortar strike on a position just yards away. It seemed an odd business that neither got a share of the gallantry medals later handed out.

The biggest threat to life, time and again, proved not to be the stand-up fight, although there were plenty of those, but mines and IEDs. Throughout the winter, no British soldier died from a gunshot wound. All who died from hostile action were killed by blasts. It partly reflected smarter tactics by the Taliban but it was also just the season. When the vegetation stood tall in the irrigated fields, the Taliban could hide and ambush from close quarters. In the winter, bombs made more sense.

Towards the end of February, the 2 Yorks' C Company lost one of their team working with the Royal Marines in Kajaki. Corporal Stephen 'Damo' Lawrence, a twenty-five-year-old from Scarborough, was killed when he peered through a hole in a wall of a compound he was trying to clear and detonated a booby-trapped bomb. Some of the soldiers reckoned they heard him shout, 'Man down,' before he lost consciousness. That death shook the men hard. Private Gary McCabe, a twenty-year-old from Billingham, had grown close to Lawrence during their time in Kajaki, which for those soldiers who wanted to fight, he said, had been the place to be. 'It's sort of a mad feeling cos I never wanna go back again but I miss the place.' When Damo was blown up, in front of his eyes, he had had enough. That night, and for nights afterwards, he cried himself to sleep, 'and I'm not ashamed to say it,' he said. 'I never wanted to come home so bad after that.'

The pressure at Kajaki seemed relentless at times. When Royal Military Police investigators returned to check out the scene of Lawrence's death, two Royal Marines, Corporal Oliver Yates and Marine Ben McBean, were injured when another IED went off in a neighbouring compound. McBean, who lost an arm and a leg, ended up travelling home on the same flight as Prince Harry.

Then in the final days of the Royal Marines' time at Kajaki, a young officer, Lieutenant John Thornton, and a marine, David Marsh, were killed by a mine. They were driving the usual thin-skinned WMIK Land Rover. On a fire support mission, Thornton followed a path already cleared by soldiers with metal detectors. But, for some reason, they had missed the mine.

With photographer Nick Cornish I visited the marines of Alpha Company at Inkerman further down the Helmand River just the week before the two Kajaki deaths. The mood was already sombre there after the recent death of one of their number, Corporal Damian 'Dee' Mulvihill, who was also killed in a mine strike.

A camp like Inkerman was there as a soak for Taliban attacks so that fighting would stay out of Sangin district centre and reconstruction could finally begin there. Upriver from Inkerman to Kajaki – nineteen miles of green zone – it was still all enemy territory.

There seemed something ritualistic to Inkerman's defence line. Perched on the edge of the desert, the base overlooked the fertile land towards the river but could not hope to dominate it all. Slipping past to attack Sangin was a simple matter when the Taliban chose to do so. 'We are like a tethered goat,' said one marine presciently. 'We let them attack us here so they don't need to attack us in the town.'

South of Sangin, FOB Robinson performed the same function. Home to Task Force 32, the US Green Berets, it was garrisoned by what became 40 Commando's Echo Company. It was outside Robinson on Christmas Eve morning that Marine Mark Ormrod trod on a mine. He felt everything go numb like pins and needles. His first words to a medic were: 'No shit; I think my dancing days are over.' Ormrod lost both legs and an arm. It was a medical feat he stayed alive. When he woke up back in England he proposed to his girlfriend, and she accepted.

Ormrod's survival wasn't the last miracle near Robinson. On 9 February 40 Commando's Recce Platoon was out on night patrol when Lance-Corporal Matt Croucher hit a trip wire linked to a grenade. Before it exploded, Croucher, a reservist from Birmingham who in civilian life was a director of a security firm, dropped to the ground and covered the grenade with his rucksack. The batteries inside blew into the air like Roman candles and his body armour was peppered with shrapnel. But his only injury was a bloody nose. Croucher was later awarded the George Cross for his actions that night: the highest award for gallantry not in the presence of the enemy.

Further south from Robinson was a 10-mile stretch of hostile green zone including the village of Heyderabad, which was regularly attacked by Task Force 32. After one of the Green Berets was killed by an IED, another was charged with murdering a Heyderabad villager and then cutting of his ear as a trophy. But the soldier was acquitted later by a US military jury after testifying he shot the man in self defence, and that he was ordered by his commander to keep the ear.

There was worse. On 18 March a Task Force 32 strike operation using a Spectre gunship succeeded not only in targeting a Taliban council-of-war but in killing an estimated nineteen civilians, including a family of eleven that was entirely wiped out, except for a ten-year-old now made an orphan. 40 Commando's Delta Company learned of the tragedy when a truck with the victims pulled up outside their base. For some of the marines this was the last straw.

For all these troubles, there was a feeling in the brigade they were making some creeping progress, not only in the work of slowly building up Musa Qala, but in all the towns the British held.

In Sangin, the Bravo Company commander, Major Dan Cheesman, had his own special measure of success. In his entire six months, he never dropped a single bomb from an aircraft round the town. It was something he could tell the people at the *shuras*, a measure of how he was on their side and how things were changed. Holding back from using aircraft and heavy weapons demanded self-control. It was not always popular.

When 40 Commando returned from Afghanistan to their camp in Taunton, Somerset, the progress in Sangin, albeit in small measure, gave them a way of explaining to their families the reason for all the fighting. While there were exciting 'dits' (stories) of fighting to be swapped, killing a lot of Taliban did not seem like much of a measure that justifed the blood and sacrifice. Not to your family anyway.

Birrell's 40 Commando had lost three men on the tour, and twenty-six men got very serious wounds. When families asked, 'Was it worth it?' his response was: 'I can't tell you yet.' It was too early. 'In thirty years' time we'll know if it was worth it, if Afghanistan has changed.'

But they had at least made a difference in Sangin, he said. 'We built the new school, there was roads reconstruction, a bazaar that was thriving, and the fact that towards the end of the tour on Afghan Day there were thirty-three Afghan flags flying when we couldn't buy an Afghan flag when we first arrived.'

The boys had wanted a fight. 'They wanted to test themselves, to find out if they'd got what it took.' They found they had what it took, he said. They had their test. A month before Mulvihill was killed outside Inkerman, he said to Birrell: 'Right, sir, that's enough. I've had all the fighting I need to have now. If you could get it to stop, we'd much appreciate that.' It was just a joke. But his men understood that their combat was for the good of peace elsewhere.

Birrell kept a picture of girls getting taught inside a classroom in Sangin. 'And these little girls walk daily past the Afghan National Police, who threatened to rape them and slit their throats if they went into that school. But they still came because they trusted the British and they trusted the security environment we had given them.'

There were qualifications to that story. Rebuilding Sangin was going to require some serious investment and technical expertise. But it was painfully hard to get anyone up to even look at the place. Sangin only got a Foreign Office adviser towards the end of March, and health and safety rules that applied to civilians meant it was hard for such advisers to leave the base and visit any projects. Getting Afghan officials up to Sangin was equally difficult. The roads from Lashkar Gah were not safe.

And there was also the sobering reminder that much of the rebuilding work was work to repair things that NATO bombs had destroyed.

★

On 9 April 2008 Andrew Mackay handed over command of Task Force Helmand to a new brigadier, Mark Carleton-Smith, and his 16 Air Assault Brigade, the same airborne force that had first come to Helmand in the summer of 2006. This time, they had more than three times the strength and the new commander appeared to share Mackay's philosophy of avoiding needless combat. But the summer tour was hard. In the six months that followed a total of twenty-nine people were killed.

On the civilian side, fresh hope came with the appointment by Karzai of a new Helmand governor, Gulab Mangal, whom the British regarded as modern and competent. Efforts to boost development and improve government competence were strengthened by a greatly expanded Provincial Reconstruction Team in Lashkar Gah.

On the military front, the brigade was boosted by a battalion of US Marines, who, posted down to Garmsir, pushed the front line a few miles south, at last securing the town for the Afghan government. The operation had taken place at short notice. Foreign Office officials were aghast that the planning for what happened afterwards was nothing like it had been for taking Musa Qala. But a plan for 'stabilization' was soon taking shape.

The most concrete achievement of the summer was an operation involving 5,000 troops which finally delivered a 200-ton hydro-electric turbine for the dam at Kajaki, enough when working to supply 1.8 million homes. If the Kajaki dam could be finally repaired and electricity supplies improved then something positive for NATO's presence could finally be measured. But, as always in Helmand, success was not straightforward since electricity could only leave Kajaki if the Taliban chose not to destroy the power pylons. The Texan contractor in charge of the project, a chain-smoking Vietnam veteran known as 'Kajaki George', explained the Taliban charged people for using the power. He told Reuters news agency, 'They make money from the dam, they charge for the power . . . When there's more power, they could make more money.'

★

Interviewed in June, Carleton-Smith spoke of the continuing 'precise, surgical' strikes that had killed scores of insurgent leaders. Calling them 'target decapitation operations', the brigadier claimed they left the Taliban 'much weaker'. 'The tide is clearly ebbing not flowing for them. Their chain of command is disrupted, and they are short of weapons and ammunition.' Divisions were opening up among them. 'I can therefore judge the Taliban insurgency a failure at the moment,' he was quoted as saying. 'We have reached the tipping point.'[23]

Qais, the Al Jazeera journalist, got a call from the brother of the Taliban commander Mullah Sadiq soon after that interview. 'Your friend is no more!' The line went dead. Other family phoned to tell him as well. And that was the end of his story. He heard that they had moved Sadiq's wife and children away from Sangin to a place of safety.

On 29 June, the Ministry of Defence in London issued a statement announcing that a Taliban leader they called Sadiqullah had been killed by a Hellfire from a British helicopter the previous week. He was said to be the mastermind behind many roadside bombs and suicide attacks.

Lieutenant Colonel Robin Matthews, a British military spokesman, said, 'This was a deliberate and surgical strike against a man who facilitated a number of fatal attacks on British, NATO and Afghan forces and civilians. It strikes a blow at the heart of the Taliban leadership.'

Qais, however, was truly upset. 'You know I always believed that he was one of those guys who could have been brought over to the government side. When I first met him I couldn't imagine him killing anyone. But he did get more brutal as time went on and he got more success. Still, he was no extremist. The way he saw it, he was fighting for his country.'

While in Helmand there were some grounds for hope, the signs were that across Afghanistan the Taliban were broadly gaining in strength. They were creeping into provinces where they had rarely been seen before and returning to towns and villages that NATO troops had previously 'cleared'. Roads were becoming desperately insecure for ordinary Afghans with the constant threat of banditry, rebel roadblocks or intimidation by corrupt policemen.

So many Taliban leaders had been captured or killed by special forces raids or air strikes, yet it seemed to do nothing to stem revolt. It was as if rebellion was spreading, not from an organized leadership, but from the smouldering embers of discontent with Karzai's government.

Many chose to look across the Pakistan border for the centre of blame. It was true that the country's north-west frontier was becoming wilder than ever, and elements of Pakistan's intelligence service continued to provide succour to attacks in Afghanistan. The Pakistan Taliban were going from strength to strength, threatening the city of Peshawar and providing new bases for training and supplying their Afghan brethren. President Bush, in his last six months of office, authorized raids by US special forces across the border against these camps. Reports in the press suggested that British special forces were conducting covert missions there too. Pakistan vowed to defend itself. There were more reports of civilian casualties. Rather than lead to decisive action to neutralize the Taliban, the raids risked simply widening the war and further inflaming Muslim opinion across the world.

29. Cracking On

For many of the soldiers who fought in Afghanistan on the winter tour of 2007 and 2008, their return was but a brief respite before preparing for a new deployment.

The 2 Yorks (Green Howards) Battalion returned to their base at Weeton near Preston. Most of B Company were soon training again for a potential deployment in the winter of 2009. Many of their officers were moving on, though. Jake Little left B Company after completing his two years of command and went on to the directing staff of the army college at Shrivenham. He was awarded a Military Cross (MC) for his 'decisive, bold and skilful leadership' and gallantry. His second-in-command, Nick Mantell, decided to leave the army. He was not sure he wanted to do the same all over again.

Captain Andy Breach stayed on with the 2 Yorks, as commander of recce platoon. Jimmy Lynas stayed with B Company as a platoon sergeant. Both Lynas and his late friend Jonno got a 'mention in dispatches' gallantry award. Jonno's was for motivating the troops in the village outside Musa Qala. His citation read: 'Johnson, in an exemplary display of courage, drive, and leadership, energized an ANA company that had lost the will to fight and, notwithstanding the enemy threat or difficulties of language and culture, drove them forward.' Lawrence Fong passed a junior leaders' course that put him in line for promotion. Mike Scott, the sergeant-major in Sangin, was deployed to Iraq as a regimental sergeant-major attached to another unit. Dave McCarrick was working in the sergeants' mess at the 2 Yorks headquarters in Weeton. Mark Syron moved to Brecon in Wales to be a sniper instructor.

Of others in the 2 Yorks, the commanding officer, Simon Downey, received an OBE and was promoted to full colonel and left for a new appointment. From C Company, Onur Caglar got a mention in dispatches for his lone actions on the day that Captain McDermid died.

Among the Royal Marines, of the four injured on the patrol to Khevalabad from Kajaki on 4 November, all were making a slow but steady recovery. Matt Kingston, who was shot in the ankle, eventually opted to have his leg amputated after his wound failed to heal. But he was hoping he could in future return to front-line duty with the aid of a prosthetic limb. The men's troop commander, Captain Sim Jemmett, was himself seriously injured after that patrol. An RPG blast left him with burns to his eyes and throat and shrapnel to the neck. When he woke up back in Britain, he was all but completely blind. His sight has since recovered well, but he cannot drive or shoot. He was given a job as aide-de-camp to the Marines' commandant general. Also injured by the same blast were Corporal Jon Kersey and Marine Lee Stewart, both of whom have returned to duty. The Kajaki commander, Duncan Manning, received a mention in dispatches, as did Company Sergeant-Major David Layton for his quad-bike rescue on the Khevalabad patrol.

Marine Ogden, the medic in the Inkerman battle of 9/11, was also commended for his 'selfless actions and advanced medical skills' that 'undoubtedly saved lives' in dealing with nine casualties in a single incident. His OC, Major Morley, was awarded an MC for his 'magnificent leadership' at Inkerman.

Among the injured on 9/11, Paul Britton also won an MC for 'his outstanding display of professionalism, inspirational leadership and selflessness' during the 9/11 battle – a particular mention was made of his refusing morphine and evacuation so that he could continue to lead his team. Simon Greening, who was shot in the side, recovered from his injuries and returned to the Marines, promoted to sergeant. James Fletcher, who had blast injuries to both legs on the roof of the compound, and lost so much blood, is back running six miles in forty minutes. A reservist and painter and decorator by trade, he has been kept mobilized by the Marines until he makes a full recovery.

The Sangin commander, Dan Cheesman, got an MBE with a citation describing him as 'warrior and a diplomat in equal measure'. And 40 Commando's commanding officer, Stuart Birrell, got a DSO for 'his leadership, commitment and selfless service of the very highest order'. He moved to a job at the Ministry of Defence, as did the Household Cavalry commander, Ed Smyth-Osbourne, who got a mention in dispatches for his 'inspired leadership' and was promoted to full colonel.

Paul Pitchfork, who led the Gurkhas in their defence of Sangin on 10 December, was awarded an MC for demonstrating 'the very highest standards of leadership, courage and initiative under fire and in face of a most determined enemy threat'. Bhim Gurung's MC was awarded for his 'great courage' in crossing open ground that day, twice, under heavy fire and without cover.

James Fraser and James Manchip, the artillerymen, both received mentions in dispatches for their mission in Now Zad – Fraser for rescuing the truck containing British and American ammunition and supplies, and Manchip for the inspiration he offered his men.

Chris Bell, who led the Scots Guards in the desert, received an OBE and went on to become chief of staff at 20 Armoured Brigade, which was deployed to Iraq in November 2008. Tony Phillips, who led the BRF, received a mention in dispatches for displaying 'magnificent levels of bravery' and producing the same in his men. He remained to finish his command of his battery at Catterick, Yorkshire. The BRF's Simon Cooper, attached from the Royal Engineers, got a Queen's Commendation for Bravery for when he volunteered to clear the route out of the mine strike that killed Jack Sadler.

At headquarters, Andrew Mackay was awarded a CBE for his tour and was due to be promoted to become a two-star major general with command of a division. Mackay was not long in this role. In September 2009 he resigned from the Army. Although he did not speak out publicly, according to friends he had become increasingly disillusioned by being asked to implement a steady stream of spending cuts and by the failure of Whitehall to go beyond its 'muddling through' and demonstrate a real will to win in the conduct of the Afghanistan war. Mark Gidlow-Jackson received an MBE for his role as chief of staff and returned to his unit, 4 Rifles, as a company commander and deployed back to Afghanistan in the summer of 2009.

Major Nick Haston, the deputy chief of staff, decided to quit the army, in part in frustration at the Ministry of Defence's handling of equipment shortages and care.

Among the Chinook pilots, Nichol Benzie left the front line. He was awarded a Distinguished Flying Cross for his rescue in the 9/11 battle. The rest of the squadron was heading back to Afghanistan.

Among the Americans, the 1 Fury commander, Brian Mennes, was deployed to combat again within weeks of his return from Afghanistan, this time in command of a Rangers special forces battalion that deployed to Iraq in September 2008. Don Canterna, who had commanded Bravo Company, joined the 2nd Ranger Battalion, an elite combat unit, out of Fort Lewis in Washington State.

Sergeant First Class James Brasher was awarded the Silver Star, one of the highest American bravery awards, for his assault down from Roshan Tower on 8 December. The citation described how 'His quick decisions and aggressive stance against the enemy saved the lives of his men' and how, despite his serious arm injury, 'he continued to fight and give combat instructions. The medics had to force medical care on him.' Brasher told me his injured arm was 'not doing fantastic', but he was hopeful that an operation in the next few months would see him fit to return to combat. At Fort Bragg, I had also watched President Bush present Ronald Strickland, the man who led the first defence of Roshan Hill, with a Silver Star. This was for his actions in Kajaki in May 2007 when he led an assault to the site of a Chinook that had been shot down by Mullah Sadiq's fighters.

The Apache co-pilot injured in Musa Qala, Thomas Malone, was back in Arizona still recovering from his injury and as yet unable to fly.

Dan McNeill handed over command of ISAF on 3 June 2008 and, after forty years of service, returned to Fort Bragg and retired from the army a few weeks later.

Michael Semple was living in Islamabad, Pakistan, writing a contemporary history of Afghanistan.

Sherard Cowper-Coles was due to leave Kabul to take up a new post as special UK envoy to both Pakistan and Afghanistan.

President Hamid Karzai faced presidential elections in the summer of 2009. He wondered how much support he would get from Britain and America.

30. A Man with a Plan?

Mullah Salaam was in a gloomy mood when I met up with him in Kabul. 'I'm a marked man,' he told me. 'When you return to Musa Qala, I will most likely be dead.'

I had tracked down Salaam to a guesthouse in the capital where he was preparing to return home after a meeting with the president. I'd just heard word the Taliban were hoping to greet him back in Musa Qala with a suicide bomb.

As his comments were being translated, he fingered his black beard and kept producing a strange rasping noise. I thought at first it was something wrong with the tape recorder. Salaam's head was sinking steadily between his palms, as he contemplated the gap between promises of redeveloping Helmand and the grind of reality. Things were so bad, he told me, he was questioning his whole endeavour. 'I should never have changed sides. All this has been a big mistake. I should have stuck with the Taliban.'

This was all a bit ironic. The final twist in the Musa Qala tale was the allegation now circulating in intelligence circles that the man sitting before me, the one whose defection had caused such a stir, was in fact 'the wrong Mullah Salaam'. I had now been told that Mullah Salaam from the village of Shah Kariz outside Musa Qala had been initially confused with a man who, known as 'Gut Mullah Salaam', or Salaam the Lame, was also from northern Helmand. The latter was paralysed below the waist but was a former Taliban corps commander and was active in the rebellion with a large posse of armed followers.

'When there was all this talk of Mullah Salaam and all the fighters he was going to defect with, they thought they were talking about the other Mullah Salaam, the real fighter. In fact, the one who did defect was really a minor tribal elder,' said one source in the intelligence world. 'And when it became clear there were actually two of them, everyone just shut up and kept that quiet.'

For all that, right man or wrong man, the Salaam I was now meeting had proved useful to the coalition, diligently playing the part of a convert to the government side, and urging villagers across northern Helmand to turn their backs on the Taliban. But now, like many of his new allies, he was beginning to wonder if all the hopes he had raised would be dashed.

Salaam told me: 'I have promised the people so much, but we have delivered so little, and people will turn on me. Everything comes so slowly.' It wasn't foreigners like the British he blamed particularly. 'The whole government here; they are all criminals,' he said. 'They keep the money for themselves.'

Few western officials in Kabul would have offered much of a different view. While celebrating the laying of foundations for a mosque in Musa Qala, one diplomat casually mentioned that the mosque had actually been paid for by the British taxpayer twice before, but the money had disappeared.

Diplomats spoke to me about a *realpolitik* that defined British and American policy. Afghanistan was not for the squeamish. One intelligence officer characterized the policy of the British ambassador, Cowper-Coles, as a kind of 'reverse ethical foreign policy', based on the necessity of striking deals with bad people. 'I think he has come to realize that no one comes to any position of power in this country without having done something really awful. And yet you have to work with these people.'

The Afghan government's heroin-addicted policemen might stifle commerce with their illegal checkpoints to raise bribes. Its local officials might be in league with drug barons. But these people were still preferable to the Taliban. Better to educate and reform them than walk away in defeat.

None of this reflected cynicism. Oddly, most of these people *believed* in prosecuting this war. But it was a journey to the dark side, a vision of the real thoughts that apparently lay behind the public face of this war.

In Pakistan, the former EU official Michael Semple, now exiled from Afghanistan, affirmed his view that soldiers' lives were being put on the line to defend the opium interests of local political chiefs. For Semple, the whole Musa Qala operation had been not so much about restoring the power of the Afghan government in the valley, but about wresting back control of the opium trade into the hands of its restored police chief, Commander Koka.

Faced with a deeply negative view of the Afghan government and its officials, how should soldiers and their families judge a war the basic premise of which seemed to be a fight on behalf of that government?

As I interviewed soldiers who had fought and were fighting in Helmand, I found many who asked such searching questions. When briefed on the reality of government corruption, there were more than a few who found themselves wondering, if they had been a young man brought up in a valley in Helmand and confronted by foreign troops like the British, on which side would they now be fighting?

On a sweltering afternoon when I was at FOB Inkerman, a group of young corporals and medics from the Royal Marines sat around a makeshift table and started debating the war in Afghanistan. Expecting a round of incoming rockets from the Taliban before the sun went down, and having only recently lost a beloved comrade, the marines had more than an intellectual reason to ask why they had been sent to Helmand.

'It's all about oil. There must be oil here somewhere,' said one corporal. Another thought there was some deal, a secret one, with the Americans, perhaps the CIA. There was a rush for a pile of reference books to get the history straight.

In paying tribute to the dead and injured, politicians and generals have given many reasons for the war, talking of how poor Afghanistan was, of all the children now in schools in Afghanistan, or the numbers of health clinics built, or the threat of heroin arriving on Britain's shores, of the evils of the Taliban, or all the Al Qaeda terrorists that were being kept at bay.

On the ground that day, few were convinced the war was really about terrorism. 'If we wanted to destroy Al Qaeda, we would have to invade Pakistan. That's pretty obvious,' said one marine, reflecting a widespread consensus. Others thought it equally obvious that fighting a war amongst the Muslims in Afghanistan was as likely to stir up terrorist attacks on UK soil as it was to prevent them.

The war's defenders clutched at so many explanations to justify the conflict that they began to appear cynical and transparently half-hearted. I thought of a shocking statement I had read of a French colonel back in the 1950s during his country's Indochina war. Puffing on a Gauloise over lunch in Hanoi, he declared of his soldiers, 'If they knew they were dying uselessly here, it would be like shooting them in the belly and kicking them in the behind at the same time. And when my aide eventually fries in his tank, I want him to believe that he's frying for the good of the country. That's the least thing I can do for him.'[24] Nothing I heard in Afghanistan was *that* cynical. But you did get the sense of people clutching at straws to justify a war that many in high command and across government would say in private was a ghastly mistake.

According to Lieutenant General Nick Houghton, the commander of joint operations, this kind of ambivalence about the Afghan mission that 'still infects national, international and NATO thinking' was dangerous. If the Afghan war was regarded as a sort of pick-and-choose venture then the 'absolute fact' of the casualties in any military operation became harder to justify or explain. 'That is why I say, for Christ's sake, you know, give us political conviction, moral conviction about what we're doing in Afghanistan!'

In his view, some of the 'woollier agendas' for justifying the war – like for example arguing it would help prevent heroin reach the streets of Britain – only distracted from the much clearer 'hard security' message that Afghanistan needed to be made secure to prevent it becoming again a lawless safe haven, the sort of place from which another attack like 9/11 could be staged.

As a strategic goal, Houghton's seemed the most defensible. But it was also a high-stakes game, depending for success not just on what his soldiers achieved but on the success of the wider US-led military campaign across the country, as well as political factors, both of which Britain would struggle to influence. And his argument still did not solve the conundrum of whether this campaign was 'discretionary'. After all, there were plenty of other places in the world that could serve as Al Qaeda bases or were security threats. Why Helmand?

Personally I was more persuaded by a view in the army articulated to me by a lance-bombardier from the Royal Artillery. 'We're here simply to pick up the pieces. We made a mess of this place and we have a responsibility to sort this out, to get things straight.' It seemed a less lofty goal, but also an honourable one.

In its Special Edition declaring the end of the Malaya Emergency in July 1960, the *Straits Times* newspaper commented: 'Perhaps there is no great point in recalling all the tragic and idiotic blunders, all the false optimism, all the unrealism of the first phases of the war, but it is not possible to appreciate fully the heroism of the Security Forces unless the stupidities of some of those in command are remembered.'[25] Applied to Afghanistan that might seem a little too harsh. At the time of writing, the war in Helmand was barely two years old, and few wars start without their share of ghastly mistakes.

Returning from Helmand, I was given unequalled access to all of Britain's most senior military commanders as well as to Whitehall officials. As I toured the corridors of power, I heard much talk about the 'long term'. Wars against guerrilla armies like the Taliban take years to win (or lose), I was told. Yet frequently it all seemed like a smoke screen for admitting to what had been going wrong.

While success might take decades, short-term failure contributes nothing but bitter lessons. As General David Petraeus used to tell his aides when US commander in Iraq, 'Without the short term, there is no long term!' Dannatt, the head of the army, seemed to share that concern. 'Some people are comfortable for this to take quite some time to resolve itself. But time for us is invariably measured not so much in hours and days and months, but actually in terms of lives lost and lives shattered on our side, and to an extent amongst the local population as well.'

Dannatt seemed candid about what had been going wrong. He argued the initial deployment to Helmand was under-strength and under-resourced, mainly because of a judgement by Tony Blair that 'we'd be substantially out of Iraq' by the time they were deployed to Helmand. 'We would never have knowingly engaged on two major operations to run simultaneously with an army organized to do one,' he said. At the same time, there was far too much wishful thinking that the population in southern Afghanistan would welcome NATO troops with open arms 'and would quickly see us as beneficial'. Instead the reaction was 'rather similar to prodding the lion who was otherwise kipping in the corner, minding his own business'.

Troops became too engaged in fighting an enemy they called the Taliban but whose soldiers were often just local men.

David Richards, who was due to replace Dannatt as head of the army in August 2009, was even more critical of early British actions in Helmand, particularly in the period in 2006 when he was NATO commander in Kabul but was yet to be given charge over British troops deployed in the south.

According to Richards, the first British deployment had spread itself far too thinly for a combination of reasons including 'over-optimism, over-confidence and a misunderstanding of the intelligence picture', as well as pressure from the then Helmand governor. The result was that the British became stuck in small platoon houses, besieged by the Taliban. 'They were achieving little civil effect and were starting to alienate everybody from Karzai downwards.'

It was this absence of 'civil effect' – the failure to go beyond the fighting and do something concrete for the Afghan people – that continued to be the anvil of a great divide in opinions.

Time and again, front-line soldiers lamented the absence of engineers or development experts alongside them to repair the war damage and deliver aid to an impoverished country. The lead for such work lay with the Foreign Office and the Department for International Development (DfID). But security concerns and health and safety rules, according to the soldiers, had kept their officials and experts far from the front lines.

'I find it frustrating,' said Richards, 'that in the army for example we've got people who could do a lot of this but we're prevented from doing it because it's considered a civilian's job.'

At the Foreign Office officials smarted at this kind of criticism. A senior official pointed to an 'absence of serious planning' that had bedevilled the Helmand deployment. He said, 'Development experts aren't formed up like an army battalion. They can't just be flown out at the drop of a hat. And it's no good complaining the civilians aren't there with you if they haven't been involved from the outset.' In Helmand, many soldiers envied the American approach, where ground-level military commanders had access to not only a powerful corps of engineers but also a large pot of money to spend rapidly on quick-start projects like building bridges or health clinics.

The British approach was different, focused on mentoring the Afghan government to deliver the aid and organize the reconstruction themselves. While American aid emphasized that it was delivered 'from the American people', British aid tended to be more covert, funding local contractors and charities, for example, who could disguise their involvement with the coalition.

For Air Chief Marshal Sir Jock Stirrup, the chief of the defence staff, the British approach of 'exercising Afghan muscles' made sense. 'Let's face it, most of these muscles, where they exist, are pretty atrophied at the moment. So, there's only a limited amount they can do. But you do have to work them, you have to exercise them, you have to build them up. If you don't do that, then you don't have any long-term sustainable solution.'

In Kabul, Cowper-Coles was forthright in his condemnation of quick-fix reconstruction. The view that 'hearts and minds' could be won over by development spending was naive.

'Our military could bring in legions of engineers and experts and do all the reconstruction ourselves but that would be akin to military colonization – it's like putting a patient in an intensive care unit and on an adrenalin drip: it does produce an improvement in the vital signs, but it's not sustainable. Curiously, our rather more muddled British way may actually produce the more sustainable effect.

'There is a mindset among some that if you sink a well or rebuild a school you somehow win consent of the population.' Cowper-Coles described visiting a school and hospital that had been rebuilt with US money in 2004 and then 'taken and trashed by the Taliban' two years later. 'Westerners are impatient, they want to get on with things. They want to show they've made a difference. But you could tar all the roads you want in Musa Qala, build all kinds of things but . . . that is not what will make the population resist the Taliban from coming back in. What will make the population resist the Taliban is the sense that the Afghan government is in charge and that the Afghan government is there to stay, with our support as necessary.

'This country is littered with shiny things built by the Russians, but, as the Russians learned to their cost, they don't actually win the sustainable consent of the population.'

Brigadier Andrew Mackay, though, would describe such talk of long-term thinking as a cover for an inexcusable delay in helping the population. Time and again, he said, he spoke to civilian experts prevented from reaching and helping a town in Helmand not because of sound development arguments but because of 'duty of care' rules imposed by the Foreign Office and DfID.

Although military operations were supposed to be there to support agencies like the Foreign Office and DfID, in practice 'the military were doing the vast majority of the delivery', he said, and there was not initially 'a plan worthy of its name'.

Money spent on helping ordinary people was as powerful a weapon in this war as any high-powered bomb, and yet, while British soldiers were hardly trusted to use it, no one else came forward to deploy it either. 'One of the central tenets of counter-insurgency doctrine is failing,' Mackay warned.

★

Returning from the front line, many soldiers wondered if what they had achieved really fitted into a wider design.

'I have the impression of a series of tactical successes but no real strategy or plan that gives them meaning,' said Lieutenant Colonel Ed Smyth-Osbourne, of the Household Cavalry.

His widely shared doubts had major consequences. If capturing a hill or a town had little ultimate value in a bigger plan, then what happened if someone died – civilian or soldier – in the process? How would a commander explain to his men why their comrade had been killed?

'That is the nature of what we call mission command,' said Major Tony Phillips. 'I had a basic mission to "disrupt the enemy" around Musa Qala. But it was entirely my decision when, where and how to patrol. It's the same for every company commander; you continue to confront the enemy but when a soldier is killed you also know it was your decision that put them there. And you can't help asking – what *really* was the point of that fight?'

Under Mackay and his successor, Carleton-Smith, the army seemed to be drawing together the elements of a reasonable road map for the war in Helmand, based around the classic counter-insurgency doctrines of minimizing the use of force, building local security forces that could garner local respect and aiming to design each and every operation with an eye to influencing and assisting the local population.

But for all this talk of counter-insurgency thinking, many spoke of an army that was still a long way from adapting to these goals. Few soldiers spoke the Afghan languages let alone understood the culture. A six-month 'tour' of Helmand was barely long enough to learn the problems of an area, let alone to think up some innovative solutions. While half a year was long enough for infantry soldiers in daily combat, Mackay described it as 'nonsensical' for senior figures or those whose jobs involved intelligence or working closely with the population to have such short tours.

Major Steve Hart, who was operations officer of 40 Commando, said that, while the direction from commanders to minimize force had been clear, the military was fundamentally not configured to go much beyond the 'kinetic solution'. A soldier's rules of engagement, for example, made it simple to fire a Javelin missile, which at around £70,000-a-go was as valuable as a Porsche. 'We use them as a sniper rifle, for people-sized targets,' he said. But filling in the paperwork to authorize $100 to give an Afghan farmer to dig a ditch could take weeks. 'We are pennies-wise and pounds-stupid,' according to Hart.

Others said that, while the mission was to maintain security until the Afghan government stepped up to the task, it was far from clear if the Afghan army or government would be ready in time.

'We're still covering too much territory too far, too fast,' said one senior officer. 'You capture some village or town and you raise hopes. But we'll be long gone before any of those hopes can be delivered.'

As Major Jake Little said in the letter that he wrote to me from Sangin: 'I firmly believe there is still a long way to go and I'm not sure the Afghan public support will go before we are close to succeeding.'

After his return, Mackay reflected that one of the problems lay in its approach of working from the grassroots in a country where even the choice of a town mayor like Mullah Salaam was a matter for the country's president. 'We have been reliant for good reason on a bottom-up approach,' he said, but that only bought breathing space for action at a national level to strengthen government, tackle corruption and the drugs trade and advance reconstruction. Yet the two approaches were not in tandem because action on these broader strategic fronts 'has not occurred in any substantive or effective manner'.

In the military campaign, Taliban fighters were being killed in the hundreds – but still they kept on coming back in wave after wave.

This war was about more than killing, reflected Task Force 1 Fury's commander, Brian Mennes, who became tired of operations across the country that seemed to have little purpose. There needed to be the follow-up. There had to be the development.

And there had to be – above all else – a commitment to provide a stable future, to secure an area and keep it secure. Only then would the population dare to reject the Taliban.

Yet, speaking to me in Whitehall, Sir Jock Stirrup said the arguments against clearances could be exaggerated. In the successful Dhofar campaign in Oman in the 1970s, for example, where Stirrup served as an RAF pilot, the campaign was ultimately successful 'when they ran out of anybody to fight'. Improving government, progressing development, addressing grievances and reconciliation were all important, but so was the basic military work of hunting down and eliminating the enemy. 'Not all military operations are about seizing and holding ground,' he said. 'In a complex operation like this it is important to be able to defeat the enemy militarily whenever they manifest themselves. Because in the long term the Afghan population will tend to go with those who they think are winners rather than losers.'

This, though, seemed like the old canard, repeated endlessly by those trying to find meaning in ultimately pointless fighting. Built in was the cultural assumption once expressed by General Paul Harkins, a US commander in Vietnam, when he spoke of 'the common man of the Orient', ever respectful of the strong.

In their war with the Afghans, the Soviets had rarely lost a battle, but they found little respect. Why? Because their war like this war was not a contest of gladiators with the population as an audience watching safely from the cheap seats. War in the green zones destroyed their homes and endangered their lives. Afghans told me they would far more respect a man who protected their families, homes and fields than a strongman who had proved his prowess.

Month after month, the biggest story that emerged from Afghanistan was the latest incident of a raid by special forces that ended up killing ordinary Afghans.

In one of the worst, on 22 August 2008, at least thirty-three civilians were killed during a raid by a Spectre gunship in the province of Herat according to a Pentagon inquiry ordered after the US military at first said only five or six civilians died. According to the Afghan parliament, another air strike in July also hit a wedding party and killed forty-seven people including the bride. These were just the biggest incidents.

After Barack Obama was elected president, rather than sending his congratulations, President Karzai appealed for action to stop these raids. 'The fight against terrorism cannot be won by bombardment of our villages,' Mr Karzai said. 'My first demand from the US president, when he takes office, would be to end civilian casualties in Afghanistan and take the war to places where there are terrorist nests and training centres.'

The facts as always were murky, but what many continued to question was the very strategy of the 'take down' of senior Taliban commanders. After two years in which a cross had been put through the name of almost every identified senior Taliban leader in Helmand, there was precious little evidence of any effect.

Stirrup said while killing Taliban foot soldiers might be 'absolutely necessary' when you were confronted by them, strategically it did not take you forward. Key leaders, such as those who organized suicide bombers, for example, were people 'you need to target in terms of your offensive operations'. He believed that those who replaced the dead leaders were likely to be less effective than their predecessors. But others feared they were killing those who ultimately could deliver a peace settlement – and helping instead to spawn a new generation of extremists.

Most of the raids that killed civilians were led by US special forces, who operated under rules of engagement which allowed them to judge the prize of a high-value target as worth the risk of some civilian deaths. British special forces, under NATO command, operated under different rules which, as senior generals explained, boiled down to less tolerance of civilian casualties.

Yet it was wrong to see British special force raids as immune from killing civilians. When I last visited Helmand, there was local outrage over a Special Boat Service raid on an alleged drugs smuggler in the Nad Ali district in which a villager and his six-year-old son were killed. A soldier thought the man was reaching for a gun, although he proved to be unarmed. A ricocheting bullet struck the boy. Speaking at a *shura*, Colonel Neil Hutton, then deputy commander of British forces in Helmand, said some military operations involved 'forces coming from other areas' and 'very often they don't tell us' in advance. 'It only takes one incident to undermine everything we are doing here.' Hutton had the courage to visit the family involved to apologize and pay compensation. But even as this case was being dealt with, reports came in of a patrol by British special forces in southern Helmand which had called in an air strike during a fire fight with the Taliban. The bombs killed two women and two children who had been 'hiding in the rocks with the insurgents', according to commanders.

When I returned to the UK, I asked General Richards whether 'take down' operations really served a purpose. He accepted that 'constantly going for names and putting crosses through them means that you're probably further alienating a lot of people, and anyway they'll be replaced'.

But the real problem, he felt, was that the balance was 'probably wrong' because there simply were not enough troops around to adopt the classic tactics of counter-guerrilla warfare – namely dominating the ground and training powerful indigenous forces.

Across Afghanistan, the steady encroachment of the Taliban and a widening sense of growing corruption were prompting political demands in the United States for the kind of 'surge' of thousands more troops that, it was argued, had worked successfully in Iraq.

Incoming US President Obama argued that the war in Afghanistan was far more vital to America than the conflict in Iraq. As I write, he was drawing up plans to send as many as 15,000 to 30,000 extra troops to the country. Among them, military commanders suggested, could be an entire extra brigade for Helmand, with accompanying firepower far exceeding Britain's contribution.

In an interview just before he ended his tour as NATO commander, General McNeill told me the combination of foreign forces and Afghan police and army added up to 'little better than 100,000 men' – barely a quarter of what US counter-insurgency doctrine said was needed to control such a large country. 'Most people don't realize that this place is one and half times the size of Iraq, and with a bigger population.' Allied forces were short of both infantry troops that could be moved around the country without restrictions, in helicopters and planes, and of intelligence and surveillance systems. 'This theatre is under-resourced, and NATO has to step up to it,' he said.

But was it worth bringing in extra troops without a credible strategy in place?

Although a whole new generation of American soldiers and commanders spoke the language of counter-insurgency, it was proving as hard for the US army to go beyond mere sloganeering as it was for the British.

Still infected by the language of the 'war on terror', which labelled all those who supported the Taliban as terrorists worthy of punishment or death, too many from the old school seemed to find it impossible to understand just why so many Afghans wanted to fight both the foreigners and Karzai's government. Just like in the Vietnam war there were still those who believed that, if only the war was prosecuted harder, if only the base camps across the border could be attacked without those annoying 'political restrictions', then somehow this revolt could be quelled.

One senior official spoke starkly of platoons of US soldiers in eastern Afghanistan who were 'lost in a private war, filled with the preaching of evangelical padres who viewed Afghanistan as a kind of American jihad against Godless heathens'.

Major Guy Jones, the operations officer of 1 Fury, described a gulf in attitudes between different US units that explained why, in some parts, too many innocents got killed. In the Korgal valley in eastern Afghanistan, more Americans had been killed than any-where else. They were hated there because the fighting had destroyed the only local source of income, timber logging. 'It is a vendetta fight on both sides now. After you lose so many people, things change, and it takes a very strong commander at every level to resist that'. After that, it doesn't matter what happens, it's always going to be, "I'm going to kill whoever is out there." And they could be as guilty as sin, but it doesn't necessarily mean the best choice is to kill them.'

There were places like Korgal, said Jones, 'all over the place' across Afghanistan where the vendetta fight meant, for example, that if an improvised bomb struck a patrol then 'anybody that is seen in that area is killed – guilty or innocent, doesn't matter'. A hard-to-reverse mentality took hold that put self-protection above all else, rather than pausing and verifying who was good or bad.

The lesson his battalion had learned in all their months in Afghanistan, ending with the battle of Musa Qala, was to give the Afghans they met, even hostile ones, the benefit of the doubt. 'Some people have weapons, and some of them don't, but unless they're actually firing at you, nine times out of ten, they're not all bad.'

'The current situation is bad, the security situation is getting worse, so is corruption, and the government has lost all trust,' said Cowper-Coles, according to a leaked version of a conversation with the deputy French ambassador in Kabul.

The British ambassador was quoted in the French diplomatic cable dispatched on 2 September as arguing that NATO troops exacerbated the conflict by propping up an unpopular regime, postponing its inevitable downfall. 'The presence of the coalition, in particular its military presence, is part of the problem, not part of its solution . . . Foreign forces are the lifeline of a regime that would rapidly collapse without them. As such, they slow down and complicate a possible emergence from the crisis.'

Reacting to the leak, a Foreign Office spokesman said the words attributed to Cowper-Coles were a 'parody' of his views and did not represent British government policy. Others suggested they were more a reflection of the French diplomat's own views. But – whether they were the British ambassador's position or not – some of the quoted remarks had resonance.

Cowper-Coles allegedly told the French diplomat that the US should be dissuaded from getting 'further bogged down in Afghanistan'. A reinforcement of troops would 'have perverse effects: it would identify us even more strongly as an occupation force and would multiply the targets for the insurgents'. There was no option but to back the United States, but the current US strategy was 'destined to fail'.

In an interview with the *Sunday Times* as he prepared to leave Helmand, Brigadier Mark Carleton-Smith said the public should expect no decisive victory against the Taliban. Two months after his optimistic talk of reaching a 'tipping point' in suppressing the Taliban, he now declared: 'We're not going to win this war. It's about reducing it to a manageable level of insurgency that's not a strategic threat and can be managed by the Afghan army.' The brigadier thought that the war could be resolved only through political settlement.

'We want to change the nature of the debate from one where disputes are settled through the barrel of the gun to one where it is done through negotiations,' Carleton-Smith said. 'If the Taliban were prepared to sit on the other side of the table and talk about a political settlement, then that's precisely the sort of progress that concludes insurgencies like this. That shouldn't make people uncomfortable.'[26]

As he spoke, secret talks were beginning, some brokered by the Saudi government, which aimed to begin a dialogue with senior Taliban. Intermediaries were sent to talk to the Taliban leadership in Quetta, Pakistan, and a list of demands was received.

What frustrated many western officials, however, as it had before, was uncertainty over President Karzai's attitude. In public, Karzai talked the talk of reconciliation and tribal solutions. But in private he was accused of undermining such efforts. A deal with the Taliban would, many realized, ultimately be Karzai's surrender. And reaching out to the many tribes in armed revolt against his rule would mean breaking ranks with all his supporters and friends across the country who sustained the president in power – and extracted favours in return.

The envoys of the powers at war in Afghanistan seemed at least united on one point: peace in Afghanistan needed not only a deal with the enemy. It would also require a new Afghan government.

Yet the fact remained that regardless of who was president there was also a lack of clear strategy, leadership and strength from the western powers who backed the Afghans.

Not only did Karzai face the almost impossible task of holding together a country bitterly divided by faction, tribe, culture and language, he was also confronted by western nations who could not agree among themselves. 'I think the west is hugely guilty of expecting far too much from him,' said David Richards, 'because we ourselves don't know what we want; we're all singing off a different song sheet to a greater or lesser extent. Is there any surprise that he's being accused of indecision?'

If the war failed in Afghanistan, there was no one British or American, commander or diplomat, whose career would be over, who knew they owned this struggle, who felt ultimately accountable. This was perhaps the biggest flaw of them all.

Field Marshal Montgomery's note over Malaya to Britain's then colonial secretary, Oliver Lyttelton, was as relevant in Afghanistan in the twenty-first century as it had been in December 1951.

Dear Lyttelton,
Malaya
We must have a plan.
Secondly we must have a man.
When we have a man and a plan, we shall succeed: not otherwise.
Yours Sincerely,
Montgomery (F.M.)[27]

For all the willingness of statesmen to praise the sacrifice of soldiers and to mourn the death of civilians, none of their well-meant kind wishes absolved those men and women of the obligation to forge a strategy that could even conceivably make some good of all this horror and strain. The failure of departments to end their sniping and work together, to go beyond the endless 'muddling through', was to my mind inexcusable.

I could not think of better words than those that end the combat in Spielberg's *Saving Private Ryan*. As the fictional Captain John

H. Miller lay dying, he looked up to Private James Ryan and said: 'James . . . earn this. Earn it.'

Those who have died or suffered in this war look down today on those in command, and indeed on all of us. They demand that we earn their sacrifice.

It was Armistice Day, 11 November 2008, when I took the train up to Stockton-on-Tees to see Lee 'Jonno' Johnson's parents, Alan and Sandra. It was Alan's birthday. 'I grew up with hearing the Last Post on my birthday,' he said.

On the wall in the living room is a large framed photograph of Lee and his brother and two sisters all in their judo outfits. They were all champions. They have about 800 judo trophies in the loft, they say. But taking the kids round the country had been expensive. For a while Alan had been unemployed. He used to buy turkeys and fatten them up and kill them and pluck their feathers to sell them to make a bit extra. Lee and the kids used to be out on street corners selling whelks and vegetables from the allotment garden – all of that to pay for the judo.

The phone rings. It's their other son, Don, who has phoned from Warminster, where the 2 Yorks have sent him on a course. He wants to wish his dad happy birthday. They have a brief chat and then, as it always is, the phone is passed from father to mother. Sandra goes off to the kitchen to take the call.

'I'm not very good on the phone. I never have been. I don't even want to answer it,' said Alan.

This reminds us of Lee's phone calls home from Afghanistan.

The first was to say he had decided to marry Lisa, the mother of his then two-year-old girl, Lilly. The last time, a few days before he died, was to say he might not live. 'They're things happening here I can't tell you about,' he said. He wanted them to know he was doing what he loved and to make sure they told everyone that, if he died. Lee thought the Afghan soldiers he was training were great too. 'They'll follow you anywhere!' he enthused.

Don had called from Kajaki shortly after Lee's last call and told them of the mine explosion that killed his interpreter, the blast that should have killed Don if he hadn't kneeled down for some reason.

'Lee says he loves it out there.'

'He wouldn't say that if he had been through what I've just been through.'

Alan's father was in the Parachute Regiment in the Second World War. He was dropped in the ill-fated Arnhem venture – the 'bridge too far' – and was taken prisoner by the Germans. He was never the same man afterwards. He would never talk about it. He would walk out the room if the subject even came up.

Alan works in Stockton Foundries, dodging the sparks that fly as he melts scrap metal in a 1,500-degree furnace and then casts it. His work begins at 6 a.m. each day, but since Jonno died they never wake after 4 a.m. Often it's a lot earlier. Alan does not like his breaks at work any more. He hardly likes talking to anyone though, as he admits, 'Once I start, there is no stopping me.

'The strange thing is that, when he was alive, I hardly used to think about Lee. Now I think about him all the time.'

There was talk of burying his son in a military cemetery alongside all the world war victims, but he is glad Lee is laid to rest in Stockton's Durham Road, where many of his family are buried and where Alan and Sandra have booked their plot next to his. Alan often drops by on the way home from work and before his tea.

He still kicks himself a little that he was always hard on his son. He can't remember ever praising him. 'He came back and said he was made sergeant. I told him I would have made general!'

Lee seemed strangely lonely in the last few months. 'He had so many friends, and I'm not sure any of them would realize.' He used to come back home frequently, but his mind was far away, like he was trying to sort things out in his head. 'I only wish he could have just come back and sat down for an hour and told us what he wanted to make of his life.'

Strange things happened after Lee died. A kettle started boiling for no reason. A living-room ornament they thought was silent started to play a tune. They asked the heavens for a sign that Lee was up there. The sky was dull with clouds. Then just one small patch in the clouds opened up, and a star shone through.

We talk about coping with his death. I mention a great-grandfather of mine who died with the Durham Light Infantry in the First World War. In those days, you just got a telegram to say your son or husband was dead. But then the nation as a whole could share your grief. These days no one really knows about this conflict. As General Dannatt put it to me, 'I think the army is at war; the nation is not at war.'

People say the strangest things to the Johnson family. They don't mean to be rude, probably. They just don't know how to react. Alan and Sandra were at a military museum and told the curator they had lost their son in the war. 'He just said, "How interesting!" and walked off back to his work.'

When I see Lisa, with little Lilly sitting near by watching the television, we talk about the same thing. 'No one really understands the army or squaddies,' she says. 'They don't know what they are doing or the brave things they are doing. And the sad thing is they have to die before you find out!' She works at Tesco, and managers there 'who just stack shelves' are paid more than most soldiers.

I find it hard to keep my eyes dry as I speak to Lisa. Lilly has abandoned the television and is starting to leaf through an album of photographs of her dad. She told Lilly what happened soon after he died. She had to explain why everyone was crying. 'She knew he was a soldier, and I told her the truth. I explained that Daddy got killed and that, when she sees the stars twinkling in the heaven, that is Daddy watching her.'

I was thinking of all the other people I had met and all those horrific tales and of those who would be heading back to Afghanistan soon, even if their kit was not quite what they wanted.

But I mention to Lisa a message left on my website by an anonymous friend of Jonno's. 'My heart goes out to Lee's family but hope that everyone also will remember he will be up there having a drink and having a laugh at everyone for being so sad,' it said.

'Yeah, that will be him,' said Lisa, 'laughing at us for being so gloomy.'

Epilogue: The End of the Beginning

There are going to be more long nights, more cold mornings,
more memorial services, more frustrations, more questions,
more answered questions and more Afghans with a chance.

General Stanley McChrystal, NATO commander

Musa Qala, 7 November 2009

I had heard the growl of the circling planes all day, and seen them
as black specks beneath the grey clouds above. Now, without
warning, an aircraft appeared above the wall like a ghostly appar-
ition – close, massive and terrifying. It made a croaking sound,
unleashing a hail of cannon-fire towards a compound behind me
where the Taliban were sheltered.

There was quiet for just a moment, and then the whistle above
the wall of more incoming bullets, and a clang on metal of some
ricochets. I crouched down again. The British and Afghan
machine guns opened up with a deep bass roar. The battle was
far from over.

With the photographer Nick Cornish, I was back again in
Musa Qala, back with B Company, 2 Yorks, nearly two years
after I'd joined this band of warriors in the capture of the town.
Just two miles from the district centre, today's clash was over what
had since become a fairly fixed front line. I was, of course, as
frightened as ever.

This time I was with a team from B Company led by Lieutenant Colin Lunn, the officer who had 'Jonno' as his first platoon
sergeant in 2007. They had cut their teeth in combat together
over at the Kajaki Dam. I headed to Lunn's base, an Afghan Army
post north of Musa Qala, in a Vector, the same kind of armoured

vehicle in which Jonno had died. I had mistakenly believed that the Ministry of Defence had by now phased these lethal trucks out of the combat zone. Instead, I found out that a soldier from the RAF Regiment, Senior Aircraftman Marcin Wojtak, had recently been killed in a Vector, in just the same way as 'Jonno' had.

Up in their base in Musa Qala, Colin Lunn's team of eight were living, mentoring and fighting with an Afghan Army that was now better armed, better trained and more able to lead its own operations. But, after three years of constant fighting in Helmand without relief, many were also exhausted. Nearly 200 of their soldiers had died. Brigadier Mohaydin, the man who raised the flag in Musa Qala, was still Helmand's army chief. He had watched British units come and go. 'If I learned a hundred things from each of my mentors, that makes eight hundred different lessons,' he said.

Returning for the second 2 Yorks (Green Howards) tour of Helmand, the faces were different. Most officers had moved on with their careers, and many soldiers had switched between companies. But I was still among friends. Among those up front today was Alex Temple, now an acting corporal, one of those who had led the charge into the village with B Company on the first day of the Musa Qala battle.

No one was finding it easy being back. Striding forward despite a load on his back of a machine gun, a 66 mm rocket tube and a light mortar, Temple appeared to be in his element. But, like many, he warned that this time the combat was getting tougher. 'It's changed,' he said. 'The fighting is harder. The Taliban can shoot more accurately and they don't give up so easily.' I watched as the Taliban were pounded with bullets, grenades, shells, missiles and air strikes – and still they came back for more.

It was not long since I had last been in Helmand – just eighteen months. In that period, though, more than 140 British servicemen had died. That was the bitter harvest of two summers and another winter of heavy fighting, and of a Taliban that had learned to plant ever bigger and more sophisticated improvised explosives capable of destroying even the heaviest armoured vehicles. Soldiers returning for a second tour said the scores of these booby-trapped bombs laced around their bases meant it was harder than ever to operate. 'It means we can't dominate the ground as we used to,' said one corporal.

Much had also changed for the better. This was a British military campaign that had finally embraced the ideas and experiments first promoted by Andrew Mackay and his 52 Brigade. Soldiers really did seem to be trying to put the population first. Alongside fighting units were 'influence teams' that aimed to consider the effect of any operation on the Afghan families who lived in the neighbourhood. As James Cowan, the new brigade commander, put it: 'You are not here to beat the enemy. You are here to win the people. Therefore, it is a much more complex mission than just a force-on-force activity in which one side seeks to defeat the other. Because the enemy will always be able to regenerate. What you have to be able to do is to give people the security they crave.' Remarkably, Cowan also said he was not seeking to make his mark as a brigade commander in his (what seemed to me still an absurdly short) six-month tour, but rather he was 'determined to fit within a campaign plan with a long-term objective'.

At a strategic level, a sea change had also come with the sacking of one US NATO commander in Afghanistan and his replacement in June 2009 by General Stanley McChrystal, a 55-year-old former Special Forces commander in Iraq. McChrystal brought with him a strength of purpose that allowed him to acknowledge publicly that a worsening security situation 'will likely result in failure' unless bold action was taken. Even so, he told President Obama: 'While the situation is serious, success is still achievable.' One of his clearest demands was to require US and other NATO troops to go to almost any length, and be prepared to risk their own lives, in an effort to avoid killing innocents. He also signalled, at last, an end to the long progression of 'mowing the lawn' operations. If NATO captured a town or village from the Taliban, the object now was to stay put.

Switching tack from constant manoeuvre to the implementation of the US doctrine of 'clear, hold, then build' was made possible by an initial decision of the new US President, Barack Obama, to send more than 17,000 extra troops to the country. After considering his options, McChrystal said this still was not enough – and he asked Obama for 40,000 more.

But quelling the Taliban rebellion required more than foreign soldiers, he knew. It meant establishing faith in the Afghan government. That was not helped by a presidential election, held in August, with a low turnout. It re-elected Hamid Karzai, with around half of the 4.8 million votes cast nationally. But this final outcome was only declared after three months of wrangling over what almost all independent observers agreed was widespread stuffing of ballot boxes with votes for Karzai. Almost none of the key players emerged stronger from the election. Those western governments who secretly hoped that a new, less corrupt and more competent president might have been elected were bitterly disappointed – and more than a few were forced to eat their words.

In Helmand, the cancer of rebellion, far from being contained, had been spreading – engulfing the once-calm central parts of the province in conflict. Over the summer of 2008, intelligence had already been emerging of a growing Taliban strength around Lashkar Gah, and on 12 October 2008 came the shock – an audacious Taliban raid against the Helmand capital. Rockets landed near the governor's compound.

In response, Brigadier Gordon Messenger, the commander of 3 Commando Brigade, launched a Christmas offensive in the poppy-rich district of Nad Ali, west of Lashkar Gah, which had become a Taliban stronghold. That was followed in the summer of 2009 by a further British offensive, known as Operation Panther's Claw, in the neighbouring districts of Malgir and Babaji.

All of this meant a rebalancing of the campaign, as attention and resources were taken from the north of Helmand – the focus of the first three years of fighting – and were redirected to the 'enemy at the gates' of Lashkar Gah. As they fought an ever more expanding campaign, with only marginally greater numbers, British forces were stretched more than ever to their limits – squeezed between the ambitious plans of generals and the manpower caps of politicians. They paid the price of their under-resourced campaign in blood. Forty men died in July and August alone.

By the summer of 2009, British, Danish and Estonian forces in Helmand had been reinforced by a huge influx of US Marines, part of President Obama's first troop increase. Comprising more than 10,000 servicemen, and with an integral force of helicopters and strike planes, the arrival of Task Force Leatherneck at a base adjoining the British Camp Bastion had brought at least the possibility of dramatically altering the balance of military advantage in Helmand. But rather than reinforcing UK and Danish positions in the north of Helmand, the US Marines launched their own Strike of the Sword operation in July and fanned across the south of the province, taking control of the central district of Nawa, pushing south from Garmsir, and taking the town of Khan Neshin in the far south.

When I joined the Marines in Khan Neshin for a fortnight in October, I found that after only four months in place they had moved rapidly from the fighting phase to a different focus of delivering benefits to the Afghan population: rebuilding canals, creating jobs, facilitating microloans, opening a school and providing medical facilities. By arriving with great firepower, and showing their ability to use it during the first few weeks of fighting, the Marines believed they had persuaded the Taliban to melt away and avoid a battle they would lose. Instead, the Taliban hoped to move back in, infiltrate and undermine the new regime. Christopher Conner, a company commander, told me: 'The Taliban rationale was if they stood and fought they would all die; so they chose a strategy to sit and wait.' But the work being done to win the population in Khan Neshin was 'pushing the Taliban away'.

One striking fact was the lack of any kind of Afghan force in any numbers to work alongside the American presence. A few dozen border policemen were living alongside the Marines. Khan

Neshin in total had fewer than a dozen local police. And there were no Afghan Army soldiers at all.

Even with the combat strength of the US Marines, they still only had the manpower to control a stretch of the Helmand green zone. Whole swathes of the population remained under Taliban control, notably in the poppy fields of Marja to the south-west of Lashkar Gah, in the stretch of river between Garmsir and Khan Neshin, and in the smuggler towns on the border with Pakistan. As they waited for news of further hoped-for reinforcements, the Marines were laying plans to take these towns back. Yet, realistically, the Marines knew they would only be there for so long. No long-term security was conceivable, they argued, without the establishment of a credible Afghan force to take over from them.

As I write, President Obama has just announced plans to deploy another 32,000 troops to Afghanistan, going most of the way towards meeting General McChrystal's plan to secure populated areas, most notably in central Helmand and around the former Taliban capital city of Kandahar. President Obama has promised the troops will start withdrawing in 2011.

I met McChrystal on my trip and was impressed. He exuded an infectious belief that this war could be won. He promised to concentrate his forces, and to avoid the kind of pointless 'clearance' that Helmand had seen too often. He was sharp, and he grasped the complexity of the Taliban revolt – knowing full well that most of those who fought NATO troops had nothing to do with any terrorist grouping. He had correctly identified to President Obama that his NATO command was 'poorly configured' for counter-insurgency and was 'inexperienced in local languages and culture'. He knew that only Afghans themselves could bring about a solution to this conflict, even as all the widespread abuse of power and corruption and NATO's own errors 'have given Afghans little reason to support their government', and he knew that political and military action needed to be synchronized. He seemed, in many ways, just the kind of 'man with a plan' that NATO soldiers had cried out for.

There were plenty of those in high places I spoke to who still had reservations, and I sympathized with their doubts. First and foremost, the military strategy left the political question unresolved: namely, how to help make the Afghan government effective. I wondered too if this great surge of troops was coming too early, coming before anyone had really developed the tactics required to win, or before the military and its approach had been sufficiently transformed. Too often I had seen how the arrival of more foreign troops led to things getting worse, not better.

My instinct said that what was required was a wholesale change of the way we did business. It seemed to me that what was needed was not huge bases or vast new legions but men of the old school who could speak the language, who understood the culture, and who, above all, had the competence to use those skills to live and breathe this beautiful country and to understand and persuade, barter and cajole its people into finally making peace and rejecting extremism. These were some of the gifts required of the old 'political officers' of the North-West Frontier – what a friend calls the 'expert tea drinkers'. We had them in the days of the Empire, but these are scarce people now. They should, in my view, be in command – and yet I doubt they ever will be.

Was the military prepared to transform itself to acquire those skills? Did it have the patience to get to know intimately the tribal and social landscape of Helmand – or, indeed, wherever else we were deployed? Would it promote to positions of authority the kind of brainy eccentrics who actually cared and knew about the place? It would require great resources. It would require too a will to win. And still now – despite the passionate speeches of those who declared this war was important – I looked in vain in high places to see such real commitment to making those changes. In that light, all those military plans seemed so short term, so ephemeral in nature, and the commanders so unwilling to grasp the lessons of decades of foreign intervention in this country.

For all that, I am no soldier or general, and still less a sharp hand at prediction. But for all my darker thoughts, I could think of no worse thing than to give up and fail in this campaign – to leave this great country to fall into chaos and into a far, far worse civil war. McChrystal had the look of a man who might, if anyone, win a war, and he deserved his chance. And, judging by the rate of Taliban advances, some bold generalship was needed to arrest their progress. If nothing else, the arrival of all these new forces would give the NATO campaign an important boost in morale and psychological advantage.

Quoting Winston Churchill, as Americans like to do, McChrystal told his troops after President Obama's speech: 'Now this is not the end. It is not even the beginning of the end. But it is, perhaps, the end of the beginning.' Whatever followed, I shared his feeling that the next phase of this long war would be very different, and that the stalemate I had witnessed would be broken.

We set off just after dawn, in the direction of the looming Musa Qala mountain. Tomorrow will be Remembrance Sunday and, as the fields turn golden in the rising sun, I look up at the ridge-line above and remember it as the place where Darryl Gardiner died. I think about his brave family. A Mastiff struck another mine up there more recently. 'We think they're picking up the old mines and moving them around,' says Colin Lunn.

We are passing through the village of Towghi Keli, a stretch of high-walled compounds in the desert just to the west of the vegetated 'green zone' of the main Musa Qala wadi. Walking to the front line, it is easy to get some awful premonition of death. But the soldiers have taught me now that everyone gets these feelings occasionally.

We pass by shady alleyways between compounds that, so far, are occupied – a sign the front line is still some way off. Children stand warily at doorways to watch. Farmers are working small patches of vegetables, ignoring us. On our left flank, to the east, a company of Royal Anglians is edging up in parallel through the green zone. A handful of Mastiffs run by the Household Cavalry is also lurking in reserve in the wadi. Our movement is being covered by a British-manned observation post and artillery up on the Roshan Tower.

It is the Royal Anglians who are ambushed first. We hear the sound of machine-gun fire on the flank. The Taliban's radio announces: 'Get ready for the big thing.' Lunn and Temple go ahead with a group of Afghan soldiers to clear some buildings. Suddenly, a crowd moves past to our rear – men on motorbikes or pushbikes, some with women in blue burkhas sitting behind. Farmers walk past with pitchforks. It's a sign of imminent 'contact'.

Firing is getting more intense in the green zone. The Taliban are firing rocket-propelled grenades (RPGs) to airburst over the Household Cavalry. Then, at 9.15 a.m., as the Afghan Army takes up position on the roofs, our battle begins. 'Keep down; watch out for the ricochets,' I hear. I hug the wall.

A deafening roar of the machine guns starting off; pings, whizzes, cracks of the bullets going out and in. There's a boom and a puff of smoke through an archway. I wonder if a rocket has struck – but it's just the afterblast of an outgoing RPG.

There is shouting as an Afghan soldier prepares to fire again. He's aiming too low, at the dome of the roof on which he's sitting. He raises his arm – there's another bang and a cloud of smoke, and a whoosh as it rushes away – then a distant thud. The Taliban are in buildings about 100 yards to the north. They manoeuvre in alleyways behind the building, unfazed by the torrent of lead pouring from the Afghan Army lines.

Time passes. There are long bursts of deafening firing and then lulls, punctuated by single gun potshots from either side. An Afghan sniper proudly makes a slitting gesture across his throat: he has killed two Taliban. In the wadi, the Anglians have found a suspected factory for improvised explosive devices – IEDs. It will take hours to check it out and destroy it.

Air cover is now overhead. An American A10 tank-buster is thundering around beneath low cloud. It doesn't stop the enemy. A strike is called on one big concentration of Taliban. The plane's engines seem to rise in pitch as it dives and fires a missile. There is a whoosh and a boom, and I feel the shock wave.

Artillery now comes in support from Roshan Tower. They're firing rockets and using a 105 mm field gun. Even then, the target compound is not silenced. Temple opens up his plastic box and fires his missile at the same target. There is finally silence, for now.

I move up the alleyway. Most of the men are in front across a small field. They pop up, shoot and then crouch down into cover behind a small wall. Temple is up on the right; Corporal Andrew 'War Pig' Wardle mans a machine gun on the far left. 'It's getting to be like a pattern; me on my own,' he shouts.

Incidents start to blur. More firing comes in from other compounds. 'They're manoevring,' says Lunn. Tall and fearless, Lunn quips, 'I could do this every day.' He inspires confidence. 'Get some rounds downrange, lads,' he yells. Temple is using his light mortar – eating up the 'bombs' that weigh down his men's backpacks. It is an earblast of bangs, roars and cracks. Then, for a while, total silence – the sound only of a boot on a pebble, and birds tweeting. The flies make an angry buzz.

There's still no sign that the Taliban want out. 'We're looking for a way to break contact,' says Scott 'Georgie' Halliday, the platoon sergeant. Today the mission is only to hold this line. Maybe another day they will strike forward. 'The Afghans would like to clear out all of this village. But holding more ground would take more troops,' says Lunn, later.

A plane has swooped down; it suddenly appears right before me, no longer a speck in the clouds but full-sized and terrifying. There's a croak as it lets loose a burst of cannon fire on to the Taliban behind me. More strikes come in and, during a brief lull, it's decided that now is the time to slip away. It's 3.45 p.m. – six and a half hours since the start of the battle. We go back in single file, marching through the alleyways. The villagers stand at the doorways to stare at dusty men. Behind us, there are more volleys of firing but no one flinches. Bullets up here are the ambient noise.

Returning to the Musa Qala centre that night, I hear things have moved on slowly. When we entered the town two years ago, one of the first promises made by soldiers was to rebuild the mosque that had been destroyed by a NATO bomb in 2006. All these months later, building work has still not even started.

Mullah Abdul Salaam appeared, as ever, overwhelmed with gloom when I saw him. He blamed the Afghan government for failing to deliver on 'all those promises of improvement that I have made to the people here'. Salaam was at war with his police chief, the notorious Haji Koka.

Amid the recriminations, the British take comfort that up to 20,000 people are now secured in the 'bubble of security' behind the front lines. The town centre is safer than ever and the central bazaar is thriving. The Household Cavalry Regiment, back in command here, say their mission is not to expand but to 'bite and hold'. Captain Roly Spiller, an intelligence officer, said the aim was for a deeper effect 'to show the tangible benefits of good government'. The security of the bubble is attracting families to move from Taliban territory. And the Taliban themselves are looking increasingly fractured.

There is talk in high circles of pulling out of Musa Qala, that it's a town too far, too remote, too surrounded by Taliban and too absorbing of resources. But twenty British soldiers alone have died in taking or defending this place. Pulling out would be controversial and painful, and I've heard the anger of some over talk of a 'retreat' from this town. For me, such emotion misses the point. We will all leave, sooner or later. Musa Qala, the Fort of Moses, has been the place of experimentation with ideas that both worked and failed. It has been a battle laboratory of reconciliation with the Taliban, of truces and 'tribal solutions', of putting an 'Afghan face' on a military operation, of Special Forces 'decapitation' strikes, of courageous joint battles by British, American and Afghan troops, and of an intention to put the interests of the population first.

Hold it or lose it, the town will remain the stuff of legend.

Appendix: Killed in Action in Helmand Province, 17 September 2007–31 March 2008

Corporal Ivano Violino, 36 Engineer Regiment, 17 September 2007 (hostile explosion).

Private Thorbjørn O. Reese, The Royal Life Guards (Denmark), 26 September 2007 (hostile fire).

Private Mikkel K. Sørensen, The Royal Life Guards (Denmark), 26 September 2007 (hostile fire).

Major Alexis Roberts, The Royal Gurkha Rifles, 4 October 2007 (IED).

Major Anders J. S. Storrud, The Royal Life Guards (Denmark), 16 October 2007 (hostile fire).

Major Jeffrey R. Calero, 20th Special Forces Group (USA), 29 October 2007 (IED).

Lance-Corporal Jake Alderton, 36 Engineer Regiment, 9 November 2007 (vehicle accident).

Captain John McDermid, The Royal Highland Fusiliers, 14 November 2007 (IED).

Private Casper A. Cramer, Guard Hussar Regiment (Denmark), 29 November 2007 (hostile fire).

Private Mark Visholm, Guard Hussar Regiment (Denmark), 29 November 2007 (hostile fire).

Trooper Jack Sadler, The Honourable Artillery Company, 4 December 2007 (mine strike).

Sergeant Lee Johnson, 2nd Battalion, The Yorkshire Regiment, 8 December 2007 (mine strike).

Corporal Tanner O'Leary, 1–508 Parachute Infantry Regiment (USA), 9 December 2007 (IED).

Sergeant David J. Drakulich, 1–508 Parachute Infantry Regiment (USA), 9 January 2008 (mine strike).

Corporal Darryl Gardiner, Royal Electrical and Mechanical Engineers, 20 January 2008 (mine strike).

Staff Sergeant Donald T. Tabb, 6th Military Police Detachment (USA), 5 February 2008 (IED).

Corporal Damian S. Lawrence, 2nd Battalion, The Yorkshire Regiment, 17 February 2008 (IED).

Corporal Damian Mulvihill, 40 Commando Royal Marines, 20 February 2008 (IED).

Private Morten K. Jensen, The Royal Life Guards (Denmark), 24 February 2008 (accidental shooting).

Senior Sergeant Sonny K. Jakobsen, Guard Hussar Regiment (Denmark), 17 March 2008 (suicide bomber).

WO2 Milan Sterba, Czech Special Operations Group, 17 March 2008 (suicide bomber).

Captain Christian Damholt, Home Guard (Denmark), 17 March 2008 (suicide bomber).

Private Anders B. Storgaard, The Royal Life Guards (Denmark), 26 March 2008 (hostile fire).

Lieutenant John Thornton, 40 Commando Royal Marines, 30 March 2008 (mine strike).

Marine David Marsh, 40 Commando Royal Marines, 30 March 2008 (mine strike).

Lance-Corporal Christian Raaschou, The Royal Life Guards (Denmark), 31 March 2008 (hostile fire).

Acknowledgements

In publishing this story, I owe a great debt to the many authors of books and publications on counter-insurgency. I was most influenced by John A. Nagl (principally his book *Learning to Eat Soup with a Knife*), Colonel Thomas X. Hammes (*The Sling and the Stone*), Ian Gardiner (*In the Service of the Sultan*, on the Oman war), Bernard Fall (*Street without Joy*, on Indochina), and articles by David Kilcullen. On Afghanistan, I drew from, among others, James Fergusson's *A Million Bullets*, Sarah Chayes' *The Punishment of Virtue*, David Loyn's *Butcher & Bolt*, and the series of books on the Soviet-Afghan war edited by Lester W. Grau and whom I would like to thank for his additional advice.

In the main, however, this was the result of more than 230 interviews conducted throughout 2008 in the UK, USA, Afghanistan and Pakistan with members of the British and US armies, a variety of officials and diplomats in the British, American, and Afghan governments, as well as many other experts. In order to tell a coherent story, I have been able to mention only a limited number of individuals and incidents, although there are many others that deserve the telling. As I trimmed down what became a vast manuscript there was a painful process of cutting out mention of many people, units and incidents. But I would like to thank *all* those who spared the time to help me, all of whom made a difference – whether their experiences are recounted here or not – in shattering at least some of my prejudices and helping to educate this account of some of the complexities of this war. It has been an honour to meet all of you choosing to serve your country in such a harsh environment. Due to the sensitivities of their position, I cannot name many of those in the various corridors of power who assisted me, but, while the mistakes remain my own, I would like to particularly thank the following for their time:

Air Chief Marshal Sir Jock Stirrup, chief of the defence staff, and from the British Army general staff: Gen. Sir Richard Dannatt, Gen. Sir David Richards, Lt. Gen. Sir Nick Houghton, Lt. Gen. Peter Wall and Maj. Gen. Paul Newton.

From 52 Infantry Brigade staff: Brig. Andrew Mackay, Col. Stuart Skeates, Col. Neil Hutton (16 Air Assault), Lt. Col. Simon Millar, Lt. Col. Richard Wardlaw, Maj. Mark Gidlow-Jackson, Maj. Nick Haston, Maj. Geoff Minton, Sqn Ldr Simon Tatters, Maj. Sarah Henderson-Lea, Maj. Dai Bevan, Maj. Mark Haywood RLC, Maj. Jo McCord, Padre Neil Allison, Maj. John Cook, Maj. Andrea Magowan, Capt. Stuart Beattie, Capt. (Tfc) Clint Barker, Capt. Jim Reid, Flt. Lt. Rob Quaife, Capt. Mark Davis, Capt. Rob Hedderwick, Capt. Lenny Gill, Capt. Gavin Darke, WO1 Tim Bellis, Sgt. Graeme Scott, Cpl. Stacey Adamson.

From 40 Commando and others in the Royal Marines: Lt. Col. Stuart Birrell, Maj. Dan Cheesman, Maj. Alex Murray, Maj. Duncan Manning, Maj. Steve Hart, Maj. Tony Chattin, Maj. Neil Wraith, Maj. Adrian Morley, Maj. Jez Stemp, Capt. Mark Elliott, Capt. Ian Preece PWRR, Capt. Sim Jemmett, Capt. Iain Sutherland, Capt. James Glancy, Capt. Dan Venables, Capt. Ben Baldwinson, Lt. Paul Newall RN, 2nd Lt. Jonathan Lasker, 2nd Lt. Rich Hughes, 2nd Lt. Ed Middleton, WO1 Neil Warrington, WO2 (CSM) Andy Brownrigg, Sgt. Pete Leahy, Sgt. Dave Young, Sgt. James Liepa, Sgt. Jim Wright, Sgt. Trevor Bennett, Cpl. Jon Kersey, Cpl. Danny Spencer, Cpl. Wayne Jones, Cpl. Ian Hulling, Cpl. Nick Martin Jones, Cpl. Gaz Ahearn, Cpl. Mark Mounfield, Cpl. David Flett, Cpl. Ali Inglis, Cpl. Nick Bushby, Cpl. Simon Greening, Cpl. James Fletcher, Cpl. Chris Harding, Cpl. Gordon McCrae, Cpl. George Alford, Cpl. Adam Lesley, LCpl. Dave Andrews, LCpl. Matt Croucher, LCpl. Phil Barber, LCpl. Nick Atkinson, LCpl. Paul Cook, LCpl. Guy Conti, LCpl. Matt Kingston, LCpl. Gareth Patterson, LCpl. Simon Stroud, Mne Mkhuseli Jones, Mne Kieron Yeoman, Mne Tom Elliott, Mne O'Dell, Mne Gary Ogden, Mne Doug Badcock, Mne Matthew Fenwick, Mne Josh Riches, Mne Mark White, and Capt. Andy Terrell USMC.

From the Right Flank, 1st Battalion Scots Guards: Maj. Chris Bell and Capt. Matthew Jamieson.

From the Household Cavalry Regiment: Col. Edward Smyth-Osbourne LG, Capt. Tom Armitage LG, Maj. Paul Bedford RHG/D, and his squadron, including Capt. Lorian McCallum RHG/D, CoH Victor Stevenson LG, Cpl. Maj. Jason Lochrane RHG/D, Tpr. Gautan Tamang RHG/D, Tpr. Jesse Morris RHG/D and Tpr. Mark Hall RHG/D, who met me on a difficult day.

From 4 Royal Artillery: Lt. Col. Greg Cole, Maj. Paddy Sherrard, Maj. Andy Dimmock, Capt. Ben Baldwinson, Capt. Chris O'Halloran, Capt. Kirstie Main, Capt. James Manchip, Capt. Paul Britton, Capt. David Ferguson, Capt. Stuart Deakin, WO2 James Fraser, WO2 Digger Barnes, SSgt. John Knight, Sgt. Dean Barnes, Sgt. David Baxter, Sgt. Scott Henshaw, Sgt. David Powell, Sgt. Mark Wilde, Sgt. David Elstob, Bdr. Sheldon MacAulay, Bdr. Simon Snape, Sgt. Craig Douglas, LBdr. Adam Lusby, Gnr. Burton Valentine, Gnr. Michael Barnard.

From the 1st Battalion Coldstream Guards: Lt. Col. George Waters, Maj. Guy Bartle-Jones, Maj. Jon Brinn, Maj. Tom Charles, Maj. Wayne Hennessy-Barnet, Maj. James Colby, Capt. Tom Radcliffe, Capt. Rob Sugden, Capt. Dominic Clive, Capt. Jamie Russell, Capt. Tom Bailey, Lt. Dan McMahon, Lt. Storm Green, WO2 (CSM) Michael Murphy, CSgt. Dean Markham, Sgt. Tony Bolton, Sgt. Alan Hanger, Cpl. James Southall, LCpl. Ozzy Read, Gdsm. Paul Dunn, Gdsm. Nathan Whybrow.

From 4/73 Special Observation Post Battery and others in the Brigade Reconnaissance Force: Maj. Tony Phillips, Capt. James Ashworth, Capt. Richard Waddell, WO2 (BSM) Paul Hodgson, WO2 Anthony Richards, SSgt. Tim Godfrey, Sgt. Matty Cockburn, Sgt. Jonathan Walton, Cpl. Darren Clark, Cpl. Nicky Cooper, Bdr. Simon Annan, Bdr. Danny Kay, LCpl. Collin Vincent, LCpl. James Clark, LBdr. Ian Wylie.

From the 2nd Battalion, Yorkshire Regiment battlegroup: Col. Simon Downey, Maj. Paul Holder RLC, Maj. Jake Little, Maj. Matt Adams, Maj. Barrie Terry, Maj. Gary Wolfenden, Maj. James

Bryden, Capt. Andy Breach, Capt. Tim Exton, Capt. Nick Stone, Capt. Nick Mantell, 2nd Lt. Colin Lunn, WO2 (CSM) Daniel Benson, WO2 Mike Scott, CSgt. Mark Syron, Sgt. Jimmy Lynas, Sgt. Dave McCarrick, Sgt. Michael McConnell, Cpl. Don Johnson, Cpl. Carl Peterson, Cpl. Gregory 'Cagey' Roberts RLC, LCpl. John Dickens RE, LCpl. Terry McDonald, LCpl. Onur Caglar, Kgn. Lee Bellingham, Pte. Andy Allsop, Pte. Matt Anderson, Pte. Lawrence Fong, Pte. Kevin Woodall, Pte. Luke Ibbotson, Pte. Gary McCabe, Pte. Geoff Nicholson, Pte. Andy Allsop, Pte. Daniel English.

From 1st Battalion The Royal Gurkha Rifles: Maj. Mark Milford, Maj. Paul Pitchfork, Capt. Chandra, Lt. Peter Houlton-Hart, 2nd Lt. Lou Connolly, WO2 (CSM) Shuresh Thapa, Sgt. Bahadur Budha-Magar, Sgt. Punn, Sgt. Naresh, Cpl. Khobindra Gurung, LCpl. Dhruba, LCpl. Rajesh Gurung, Rfn. Sojit.

Of the pilots and crew from 18(B) Squadron RAF: Sqn Ldr Paul Curnow, Capt. Tristan Jackman, Flt. Lt. Nichol Benzie RN, Flt. Lt. Al Sparks, Flt. Sgt. Sam Murray, Sgt. Scott Todd, and other members of the MRT teams.

From the King's Royal Hussars: Maj. Richard Slack, Lt. Tom Perrott, Lt. David Warwick, SSgt. Kevin Taylor, SSgt. Rob Sinclair, Sgt. Mark Budd, Cpl. James Young, Cpl. Andrew Martin, Cpl. John Bradley, LCpl. Adam Mossop.

From Signal Squadron (258), the Royal Corps of Signals: Maj. Tom Crapper, Sgt. Matthew Lane, Cpl. Lee Wilbor, Cpl. Nicola Thompson, Cpl. Tony Talbot, LCpl. Jennifer Blackburn, LCpl. Michael Singer, LCpl. Richard Ward, Sig. Matt Hughes.

From the 1–508th Parachute Infantry Regiment (Task Force 1 Fury) and others in the 82nd Airborne Division: Lt. Col. Brian Mennes, Maj. Guy Jones, Capt. Don Canterna, Capt. Will Eberle, Capt. John Pelikan, Capt. Jerwin Ruazol, Capt. Brian Schneider, Capt. Adam Wehrle, 1Lt. Anthony Fera, 1Lt. Joe McGovern, 1Lt. John Wall, 1Lt. John Robie, 1Lt. Abraham Anderson, Lt. Chris Copolla, Sfc. Matthew Hatfield, Sfc. Ronald Strickland, Sfc. James Brasher, Sfc. Shane Summers, Sfc. John Nesmith, Sfc. Joseph Kumagai, Sfc. James Knops, Sfc. Brian Reese, SSgt. Otilio Vasquez,

SSgt. Nelson Gil, SSgt. Stephen Brown, SSgt. Johann Herzog, SSgt. Josh Lawrence, Sgt. Tyler Clas, Sgt. Billy Lee, Sgt. Harry Jauert, Sgt. Jason Murray, Sgt. Bryce Hamilton, Sgt. Nicholas Thompson, Sgt. Vincent Corona, Sgt. Lance Bell, Sgt. Chris Donaldson, Spc. Dustin Jones, Spc. Jules Dyman, Spc. Javier Molina, Spc. William Cochran, Spc. Robert Spafford, Spc. Robert Wallace Spc. David Goth, Spc. Levi Kull; and Sfc. Fitzgerald Mann of Fort Bragg for follow-up information; and from the Arizona National Guard, Maj. Paul Aguirre and CW2 Thomas Malone.

From the UK Ministry of Defence: Col. Ben Bathurst, Col. Andrew Jackson, Lt. Col. Kevin Stratford-Wright, Maj. Keith Scott, Paula Edwards, and Tim David for helping arrange interviews among the military and for advice on some changes to protect the security of ongoing operations.

In Kabul and Helmand: former Helmand governors Sher Mohamed Akhundzada and Asadullah Wafa; Musa Qala governor Mullah Abdul Salaam; police chiefs Haji Koka and Muhammad Andiwal; the army chief Bismullah Khan; the minister of counter narcotics, Khodaidad Khodaidad; the spokesman for President Karzai, Humayun Hamidzada; journalists Aziz Mohamed Shafi, Ekrem Shinwari, Akbar Shinwari, Qais Azimy and James Bayes; Jean Mackenzie of the IWPR; at the British Embassy, Sir Sherard Cowper-Coles, Col. Simon Newton, Daniel Sherry, Michael Howes; at NATO headquarters, Gen. Dan McNeill, Maj. Gen. Bernard Champoux, Air Cdre Sean Bell and Mark Laity; and from the shadowlands, 'Paul' and 'Vince'. At the Provincial Reconstruction Team in Helmand: Michael Ryder and many additional others interviewed on background.

Also Michael Semple, Najibullah Razaq, Chiade O'Shea in Pakistan, Alan and Sandra Johnson and Lisa McIntosh, Paul Gardiner and his family, Ian Sadler, Gill McDermid, Dr Farid Popal at the Afghan embassy in London; Dr John W. Whitney of the US Geological Survey for help with the introduction to Helmand, Dr Tony Heathcote for help on historical sources, Rupert Grey for some legal advice, Cathrin, Adrian, Adam and Peter for reading the drafts. And for backing my trips in Afghanistan: Sean Ryan,

John Witherow, Rhonda Schwartz, Brian Ross, Peter Barron and Jasmin Buttar. And to Jonathan Heffer, with Joseph Zeitlyn and Damandeep Singh for additional research help.

None of this would have happened without all the support and inspiration of Christina Czapiewska, my amazing researcher, Tony Lacey and Jon Elek and the team at Penguin, and agents Emma Parry and Christy Fletcher.

Thanks finally to Ian Moores for his brilliant maps and to all who allowed me to use their stunning photographs in the book, most particularly to Alex Gardner, who was on the Roshan hill, Nick Cornish, the photographer with whom I travelled to Helmand, and to Phil Coburn, who was there too with us in the battle of Musa Qala.

Glossary

.50 cal: a Browning heavy machine gun that fires half-inch diameter (.50 calibre) bullets; pronounced 'fifty cal'.

105 mm field gun: also known as a light gun, an artillery weapon firing 105 mm calibre shells with a range of about 10 miles.

240 or M240: a US machine gun.

2 Yorks: 2nd Battalion of the Yorkshire Regiment.

A-10: an American single-seat plane providing close air support to ground forces, also known as a 'tank buster'.

AK-47: a Soviet-designed assault rifle used by both the Afghan army and the Taliban.

ANA: Afghan National Army.

Apache: the AH-64 attack helicopter.

AWACS: or airborne warning and control system, an aircraft used for surveillance, tracking targets and providing air traffic control for other aircraft.

B-1B bomber: a US long-range bomber aircraft carrying a large payload of both guided and unguided weapons.

Black Hawk: the Sikorsky UH-60 Black Hawk is a medium-lift transport or assault helicopter.

BRF: Brigade Reconnaissance (Recce) Force.

burqa: an enveloping outer garment worn by women in some Islamic traditions.

C-130: or Hercules, a military transport aircraft with four propeller engines.

C2: Command and Control.

CAS: close air support.

Chinook: the Boeing CH-47 Chinook is a twin-rotor heavy-lift helicopter used to transport troops and supplies.

CIA: Central Intelligence Agency.

COMISAF: the commander of NATO (ISAF) forces in Afghanistan.

contact: an engagement with hostile forces.

Dushka: a nickname for the DShK 1938 heavy machine gun used since the Second World War by Soviet forces, and used by the Afghan army and the Taliban.

EW: electronic warfare.

F-15 / F-16 / F-18: US fighter aircraft.

FOB: Forward Operating Base.

forward air controller: an individual who directs the action of combat aircraft engaged in close air support and other offensive air operations.

green zone: the fertile, irrigated land along the river and tributaries of the Helmand River.

Harrier: the Harrier GR7/7A is an RAF offensive aircraft.

HCR: Household Cavalry Regiment.

Hellfire missile: the AGM-114 Hellfire missile is a laser-guided, air-to-surface missile.

H-Hour: the hour, either secret or as yet undecided, when an attack or operation begins.

HIDACZ: a high-density airspace control zone, a declared 'box' of airspace into which no one may enter without permission.

HQ: headquarters.

Humvee: a nickname for a US armoured car, the High Mobility Multipurpose Wheeled Vehicle (HMMWV).

IED: an improvised explosive device, a bomb constructed from improvised materials.

ISAF: International Security Assistance Force, the NATO force in Afghanistan.

JDAM: or Joint Direct Attack Munition, a bomb fitted with a satellite guidance kit for precision targeting.

JSTARS: or Joint Surveillance and Target Attack Radar System, a large US aircraft that tracks movements on the ground.

kandak: Afghan word for battalion.

kinetic operation: an operation involving combat.

KRH: King's Royal Hussars.

landing zone: a landing site for helicopters or a parachute drop.

leaguer: overnight temporary camp.

M4: an American assault rifle favoured by airborne and special forces.

Mastiff: a heavily armoured 6 x 6 wheel-drive patrol vehicle.

medevac: medical evacuation.

NATO: North Atlantic Treaty Organization.

NCO: non-commissioned officer.

OC: officer commanding.

Pinzgauer or 'Pinz': a four-wheeled off-road vehicle with light armour.

PKM: a Soviet-designed light machine gun.

Predator: a pilotless plane used for military surveillance and offensive operations which can be armed with *Hellfire missiles*.

R&R: rest and recuperation, a period of leave.

RAF: Royal Air Force.

Reaper: a newer version of the *Predator* that can carry both missiles and bombs.

RPG: rocket-propelled grenade.

sangar: guard post or watchtower.

SAS: Special Air Service.

SBS: Special Boat Service.

SF: special forces.

shemagh: also known as a *keffiyyh*, an Arab headdress worn by soldiers in the desert.

shura: an Afghan word for a meeting or gathering, typically of tribal elders.

Spectre: a slow-flying gunship aircraft operated for night-time surveillance and assaults by US special forces; it is an adaptation of the Hercules *C-130* transport plane.

UAV: unmanned aerial vehicle, also known as a drone; a pilotless plane.

Vector: a fast, lightweight six-wheeled off-road vehicle, it is the more heavily armoured version of the *Pinzgauer*.

Viking: an armoured amphibious tracked vehicle used by the Royal Marines.

Warrior: a British tracked armoured infantry fighting vehicle.

WMIK: a desert-modified open-top Land Rover with a weapons mounted installation kit that can be used to fit a heavy machine gun or grenade launcher.

Notes

1 Quoted in Michael Herr, *Dispatches* (New York: Vintage International, 1991), p.38. Stone was believed killed in 1971 by the Khmer Rouge in Cambodia.

2 Obituary to Colonel Harry G. Summers, Jr, by David T. Zabecki, available at: www.clausewitz.com/CWZHOME/SummersObit Text.htm.

3 Stephen Tanner, *Afghanistan, a Military History from Alexander the Great to the Fall of the Taliban* (Cambridge, Mass.: Da Capo Press, 2002), pp. 37, 102.

4 Bost was razed by the Ghorid dynasty in 1150 and completely destroyed by Genghis Khan in 1225. After its irrigation systems were destroyed by Tamerlane in 1383, it never rose up again. Sources: Carol Miller, 'Bost or Qala-i-Bist', http://ejournal.thing.at/LitPrim/ bost.html; and Ludwig W. Adamec, *Historical Dictionary of Afghanistan*, 2nd edn (London: Scarecrow Press, 1997), p. 200.

5 Adamec, *Historical Dictionary*, p. 144.

6 Arthur Bonner, 'Afghan Rebels' Victory Garden: Opium', *The New York Times*, 18 June 1986.

7 'If Hilmand were a country, it would once again be the world's biggest producer of illicit drugs,' said the Executive Director of UNODC, Antonio Maria Costa, in a press release reporting that opium production had decreased across the country, except in Helmand, where it had increased. See UN Office on Drugs and Crime (UNODC), 'Opium Cultivation Down by a Fifth in Afghanistan', press release, 26 August 2008, and 'Afghanistan Opium Survey 2008', www.unodc.org/unodc/en/press/releases/2008-08-26.html, p. vii.

8 UNODC, 'Afghanistan Opium Survey 2008', p. 15.

9 See James Risen, 'Poppy Fields Are Now a Front Line in Afghan War', *The New York Times*, 16 May 2007, www.nytimes.com/

2007/05/16/world/asia/16drugs.htm, and US Drug Enforcement Administration Congressional Testimony by Karen P. Tandy, Administrator, DEA, before the Committee on Armed Services, US House of Representatives, 28 June 2006, www.usdoj.gov/dea/pubs/cngrtest/ct062806.html.

10 See, for example, details in James Risen, 'Reports Link Karzai's Brother to Afghanistan Heroin Trade', *The New York Times*, 4 October 2008.

11 The dam was opened in April 1953. A turbine for producing power was added in 1975. The dam is '300 feet high and 887 feet long, with a 32 mile reservoir and a capacity of 1,495,000 acre-feet of water,' Louis Dupree, *Afghanistan* (Princeton: Princeton University Press, 1973), p. 484.

12 This was McNeill's view, but while Americans like him regarded the Musa Qala truce as a mistake, British commanders were convinced it was both a tactical necessity and an important early experiment in trying to separate the local Taliban confronting the British with the most extremist and irreconcilable Taliban leadership based in Pakistan. 'The tribal elders in Musa Qala were absolutely shell-shocked and bombed to bits,' remembered the then NATO commander General David Richards. 'They were fed up with both the Taliban and the British.' The British believed the deal that followed had actually worked. It could not be said publicly at the time but, according to several sources, they had continued monitoring the town intensively – with all their panoply of spy planes and interceptions. Key Taliban leaders were followed constantly and the Afghan security service kept a network of agents in the town who reported back. Richards believed the local elders had kept their part of the deal. 'They basically preserved a situation in which there was no fighting,' he recalled. Ultimately, within the British camp, there was a widespread suspicion that provocative action by some US agencies had deliberately undermined a deal they opposed.

13 Quoted by journalist Harry Miller in John A. Nagl, *Learning to Eat Soup with a Knife* (Chicago: Chicago University Press, 2005), p. 74.

14 As described by John Cloake, in Nagl, *Learning to Eat Soup with a Knife*, p. 90

15 Quoted in Colonel Thomas X. Hammes, USMC, *The Sling and the Stone: On War in the 21st Century* (Grand Rapids: Zenith Press, 2006), p. 46.

16 Major Waller Ashe, ed., *Personal Records of the Kandahar Campaign: by Officers Engaged Therein*, Elibron Classics facsimile replica of the 1881 edition published by David Bogue (BookSurge Publishing, 2005), p. 98.

17 Matiullah Minapal and Aziz Ahmad Tassal, 'Foreign Troops Accused in Helmand Raid Massacre', Afghan Recovery Report No. 277, 11 December 2007, Institute for War and Peace Reporting, www.iwpr.net/?p=arr&s=f&o=341341&apcstate=henparr.

18 Task Force 373 identified publicly in a US Air Force photo release, along with a photograph of its commander, Brigadier General Raymond Palumbo, at: www.militaryphotos.net/forums/showthread.php?t=139629&page=3. TF 373 was identified as a 'takedown' unit by William Arkin, 'Elite Terrorist Hunters in Iraq', *The Washington Post* online, 28 March 2007.

19 Aziz Ahmad Tassal, 'Musa Qala: The Shape of Things to Come?' Afghan Recovery Report No. 275, IWPR, 27 November 2007. Available at: http://iwpr.net/?p=arr&s=f&o=340961&apcstate= henparr.

20 Michael Evans, 'Brigadier Strides into Battle against Taleban', *The Times*, 17 December 2007.

21 Sam Coates and Michael Evans, 'Forces May Be Locked into Afghan Conflict for Decade, Brown's Trip to Front Line Reveals', *The Times*, 11 December 2007.

22 Nick Meo and Richard Beeston, 'Lord Ashdown Called in to Overhaul Reconstruction of Afghanistan', *The Times*, 17 January 2008.

23 Thomas Harding, 'Afghan Insurgents "on Brink of Defeat" ', *Daily Telegraph*, 2 June 2008.

24 Bernard Fall, *Street without Joy* (Barnsley: Pen and Sword Books, 2005; first published 1961).

25 Quoted in Nagl, *Learning to Eat Soup with a Knife*, p. 103.

26 Christina Lamb, 'War on Taliban Cannot Be Won, Says Army Chief', *Sunday Times*, 5 October 2008.

27 Quoted in Nagl, p. 87.